Associative Engines

Associative Engines

Connectionism, Concepts, and
Representational Change

Andy Clark

A Bradford Book
The MIT Press
Cambridge, Massachusetts
London, England

Printed and bound in the United States of America.

Library of Congress Cataloging-in-Publication Data

Clark, Andy.
  Associative engines : connectionism, concepts, and representational change / Andy Clark.
    p. cm.
  "A Bradford book."
  Includes bibliographical references and index.
  ISBN 0-262-03210-4
  1. Artificial intelligence. 2. Connectionism. 3. Cognition. I. Title.
  Q335.C58 1993
  006.3—dc20   93-18722
                                                                                  CIP

for Pepa

Contents

Preface: Confessions of a Neural Romantic

Things move apace. In the space of about a decade, connectionist approaches to learning, retrieval, and representation have transformed the practice of cognitive science. For better or for worse, neural nets are now strung across just about every problem domain you once could shake a LISP atom at. But, for all that (or perhaps because of all that), it is becoming harder and harder to keep track of whatever fundamental advances in the understanding of cognition all this activity expresses. As a philosopher and a cognitive scientist long interested in the connectionist program, I remain convinced that the change is indeed a deep and important one. This conviction makes me, I suppose, a neural romantic. Connectionism (a.k.a. neural nets or parallel distributed processing) promises to be not just one new tool in the cognitive scientist's toolkit but, rather, the catalyst for a more fruitful conception of the whole project of cognitive science. My main purpose in this book is to make this conception as explicit as I can and to illustrate it in action.

At the center of these events is, I claim, a fundamental shift from a static (code-oriented) conception of the subject matter of cognitive science to a much more deeply developmental (ability- and process-oriented) view. This shift makes itself felt in two main ways. First, what might for now be called structured representations are seen as the products of temporally extended cognitive activity and not as the representational bedrock (an innate "language of thought"—see, e.g., Fodor 1975, 1987) upon which learning is based. Second, the relation between thoughts (taken to be contentful mental states as characterized by folk psychology) and inner computational states is loosened by a superpositional and distributed model of concepts. Here a code-based image of concepts as stable inner representational states is replaced by a much more fluid and ability-based view, according to which the folk-psychological notion of a concept, at best, names a roughly demarcated region of a high-dimensional space. Such spaces are not, it is argued, loci of symbol systems in any familiar sense; they must be conceived in fundamentally different terms.

The course of even neural romance does not, however, always run smooth. There remain cognitive capacities which seem at times to cry out for us to posit some more stable, text-like, and easily manipulable inner code. Thus, it is not my aim to renege on the cautious ecumenism of my previous treatments (e.g. Clark 1989a, 1991b). I hope, nonetheless, to cast these problems in a slightly new light, and to show that—even if some fraction of our mature representational repertoire is much as more classical approaches have painted it—a great advance lies in beginning to address the question of origins. Where do such representations come from? What are the conditions of their emergence? How do they develop over time?

Connectionism invites cognitive science to treat seriously the issues of conceptual change and the transitions between what I shall be calling Significant Virtual Machines. Its gift is to loosen the grip of the image of stored knowledge as text and of reasoning as a kind of internal word processing. Instead, we are confronted with the pervasive interpenetration of knowledge and processing and with our best chance yet to place the modeling of change and process at the heart of cognitive science. Whoever said romance is dead?

Acknowledgments

My intellectual debts are embarassingly numerous, but the following authors and friends deserve special mention: Daniel Dennett, whose influence is apparent throughout; Paul and Patricia Churchland; Annette Karmiloff-Smith; Tim van Gelder; Martin Davies; Michael Morris; Chris Thornton; Kim Plunkett. Local support and discussion from faculty, students, and visitors in the School of Cognitive and Computing Sciences at Sussex University has also been an invaluable source of ideas and criticisms. Special thanks to Margaret Boden, who read an early draft and made many useful comments, and to Tim van Gelder and Dan Lloyd, whose comments on the same draft resulted in several changes and reorganizations. Tim van Gelder, in particular, convinced me to finally bite the bullet and stop insisting that beliefs must be straightforward causes of behavior. Special thanks also to Annette Karmiloff-Smith for her careful reading of the final draft, which resulted in numerous improvements.

Three visiting positions contributed enormously to the final product: a visiting fellowship at the Research School of the Australian National University (thanks specially to Frank Jackson and Neil Tennant for making my stay there so fruitful), a brief stay with the philosophy and psychology faculty at the University of Iceland (thanks especially to Mikael Karlsson for organizing the visit), and a visiting position in the Institute for Advanced Studies at the University of São Paulo (organized by Marcos Balbeiro de Oliveira). Thanks again to all concerned.

Thanks also to the participants at the 1991 Joint Session of Mind and the Aristotelian Society, the 1991 annual meeting of the British Psychological Society's developmental section, and the Perspectives on Mind Conference at Washington University in St. Louis. Feedback from talks presented at these events helped me avoid several painful errors. Thanks also to the University of Sussex, which granted me a research leave in the summer of 1990 during which several of the ideas developed here began to take shape, and to the McDonnell-Pew Foundation, whose summer school in developmental connectionist modeling (led by Kim Plunkett) was a rich source of experience and ideas.

Parts of chapters 3, 4, 6, and 10 have appeared in the following papers:

"Connectionist minds," *Proceedings of the Aristotelian Society* 90# (1989–1990), pp. 83–102

"Connectionism, competence, and explanation," *British Journal for the Philosophy of Science* 41 (1990), pp. 195–222

"In defense of explicit rules," in *Philosophy and Connectionist Theory*, ed. W. Ramsey, S. Stich, and D. Rumelhart (Erlbaum, 1991)

"The presence of a symbol," *Connection Science* 4, no. 3–4 (1992), pp. 193–205

Some of the ideas floated in chapters 6 and 7 were originally developed during my collaboration with Annette Karmiloff-Smith on "The cognizer's innards: A philosophical and psychological perspective on the development of thought," a version of which is to appear in the journal *Mind and Language*.

Figures 2.1, 3.3, and 3.4 are from J. Elman, "Distributed representations, simple recurrent networks and grammatical structure," *Machine Learning* 7 (1991), pp. 195–225. Figures 7.1 and 7.2 are from J. Elman, "Incremental Learning, or The Importance of Starting Small," technical report 9101, CRL, University of California, San Diego. Thanks to Jeff Elman for permission to use these. Figure 3.2 and tables 3.1–3.3 are from D. Sanger, "Contribution analysis: A technique for assigning responsibilities to hidden units in connectionist networks," *Connection Science* 1, no. 2 (1989), pp. 115–138. Thanks to Dennis Sanger and to CARFAX for permission to reprint these. Figure 3.1 is from P. M. Churchland, *A Neurocomputational Perspective* (MIT Press, 1989). Thanks to Paul and to The MIT Press for allowing me to use it. Figures 4.1–4.4 are from A. Karmiloff-Smith, *Beyond Modularity: A Developmental Perspective on Cognitive Science* (MIT Press, 1992). Thanks to Annette, to The MIT Press, and to Elsevier Science Publishers for permission to use this material. Figure 4.5 is from F. Allard and F. Starkes, "Motor skill experts in sports and other domains," in *Towards a General Theory of Expertise*, ed. K. Ericsson and J. Smith (Cambridge University Press, 1991). Thanks to the authors and to Cambridge University Press for allowing the use of this material here. Figure 5.1 is from K. Plunkett and C. Sinha, "Connectionism and developmental theory," *British Journal of Developmental Psychology* 10 (1992), pp. 209–254. Thanks to the authors and to the British Psychological Society. Figure 9.1 is from S. Nolfi and D. Paresi, "Auto-Teaching: Networks That Develop Their Own Teaching Inputs," technical report PCIA91-03, Institute of Psychology, C.N.R., Rome. Thanks to the authors for allowing me to reproduce it here. Figure 9.2 is from Y. le Cun et al., "Back propagation applied to handwritten zip code recognition," *Neural Computation* 1, no. 4 (1989), pp. 541–551. Thanks to Yann le Cun for permission to use it here.

The endless revision and reorganization of the various versions of the manuscript were only made possible by the grace of Berry Harper and James Clark. Special thanks to both. A large vote of thanks also to Teri Mendelsohn and Paul Bethge (of The MIT Press), whose skills and encouragement contributed enormously to the final product.

Lastly, and most importantly, thanks to my parents, James and Christine Clark, and to my wife, Josefa Toribio. Their love and support was of the essence.

"Bullshit. Can you read my mind, Finn?"
"Minds aren't read. *See, you've still got the paradigms print gave* *you. . . ."*
William Gibson, *Neuromancer* (Ace, 1984), p. 204

"you dealin' wi' th' darkness, mon."
"Only game in town, it looks like."
ibid., p. 217

PART I

Melting the Inner Code

Chapter 1

Computational Models, Syntax, and the Folk Solids

A Three-Point Turn

Concepts, propositions, beliefs, desires, hopes, fears, and the medley of psychological states: these are the things that folk psychology is made of. But what is the relation between this descriptive vocabulary and the internal machine which cognitive science seeks to understand? The answer I shall canvass is that the relation is more distant, and the inner machine correlatively more exciting, than a familiar tradition has led us to expect. The familiar tradition has three main characteristics:

> It is anti-developmental.
> It is text based.
> It is oriented toward folk psychology.

The contrasting picture, which it is the purpose of this book to describe, is opposed on all three counts:

> It is genuinely developmental.
> It is process based.
> It is independent of folk psychology.

In this introductory chapter, I shall try to make this contrast intelligible.

The Many Faces of Folk Psychology

Folk psychology is characterized by its commitment to explaining actions by citing *contents* of various kinds. These contents are typically structured items, such as "Pepa went to the fridge because she wanted a cream soda and she believed that the cream soda was in the fridge." The mental contents ascribed to Pepa and used as explanatory of her action are structures of concepts and relations ('cream soda', 'in', 'fridge') embedded in propositions governed by attitude verbs (believing and wanting). What is the significance of these solids (concepts, propositions, and attitudes) for cognitive science? The literature of cognitive science generally countenances three possible and not mutually exclusive answers.

First Answer

The folk solids (concepts, propositions, and attitudes) provide a vocabulary with which to specify some of the *targets* of the cognitive scientific endeavor. Part of what makes cognitive science truly cognitive is presumably that it sets out to explain the mechanisms implicated in events which are recognizably psychological in nature, such as reasoning, planning, and object recognition. Specific examples of such tasks must, in the first instance, be specified by means of the folk solids. The system must judge that an arch is above a pillar, or it must amend its plan in the light of new beliefs about the time available, or it must reason about the rate of flow of a river, and so on. The folk vocabulary is heavily implicated at the specification stage of any such project. Insofar as it specifies targets, folk psychology is surely here to stay (though not all the targets of cognitive science need be so described—consider work in low-level vision). This role for the folk solids is defended on pages 52–54 of Clark 1989a.

Second Answer

The basic framework of human language (the medium in which folk-psychological explanations are couched) is suggestive of the organization of a system of internal representations. The idea here is that a linguiform inference-supporting symbol system is our best model of the nature of the underlying computational economy. The key attraction here is the way such familiar symbol systems exploit logical form and combinatorial structure. We can construct completely novel sentences because a finite stock of words is available for combination and recombination according to a set of rules. Moreover, the successes of proof theory show that generative symbol systems of basically this type (though slightly more regimented) can be manipulated so that transitions between well-formed symbolic expressions (ones built up by the proper application of the rules of combination) can be guaranteed to preserve truth. We thus have a simultaneous demonstration of how to achieve *productivity* (the ability to generate an open-ended set of new structures) and what I shall term *semantic good behavior*. A little expansion on the last term is in order.

It is the lot of some parts of the physical world to be *semantically well behaved*. A pocket calculator (to give a mundane example) is semantically well behaved with respect to the arithmetic domain; its physical state transformations, when subjected to a specific and static kind of interpretation, turn out to track semantically sound (i.e. correct) arithmetical derivations. A tax-calculating program, run on a standard PC, produces a physical system that is semantically well behaved with respect to some particular tax system. Normal, adult human beings are the most extraordinarily semantically well-behaved physical systems, producing sensible behavior and inferences with respect to domains as disparate as trout breeding and subatomic physics. The big question, then, is this: By what magic does a physical device limn the contours of the distal, the abstract (numbers), and even the nonexistent (unicorns)?

One immediate response is that all this semantic good behavior must somehow be the result of careful organization (by design or by evolution) of physical states in a system sensitive only to physical parameters. Who could disagree?

A slightly more detailed answer is that semantic good behavior is to be explained by viewing the brain as a *syntax/semantics device*[1] of a particular kind. A syntax/semantics device is a physical system in which semantic good behavior is made possible by the system's manipulation of symbols, where a symbol is just a physical state which can be both nonsemantically individuated (i.e., recognized by its weight, its shape, its location, or any other property which can be specified without mentioning the content of the state) and reliably interpreted (i.e., assigned a meaning).

Syntax/semantics devices are *automatic symbol crunchers* (see the discussion in Haugeland 1981) in which canny design by humans (for the pocket calculator) or by evolution (for the humans) ensures that, for example, the physical state designated as meaning P gives way, under set conditions, to a state meaning Q just so long as (under those conditions) Q is a proper thing to do or believe given P. Symbols, by having one foot in the physical (they can be picked out by the system by entirely nonsemantic means) and one foot in the mental (they can be treated as contentful items), bridge the divide between syntax and semantics.

The rule-governed combinatorial structure of familiar linguistic and logical systems and their exploitation of symbols is thus put forward as a model of at least the form of our inner computational life (Block 1990; Fodor and Pylyshyn 1988). However, in positing a linguiform inner symbol system we leave open the question of the contents carried by the inner symbols. The claim about contents (which brings folk psychology back into central focus) is the distinguishing mark of our third and final answer.

Third Answer
The folk framework provides both a model of our computational organization and a set of contents (the folk solids) which have reasonably close analogues in the inner economy. According to this answer, the folk framework tells us something about both inner *vehicles* (they are symbols organized into a quasi-linguistic code) and their *contents* (there are computationally significant vehicles for the individual contents—concepts and propositions—mentioned in good folk-psychological explanations).[2] This is, clearly, the strongest position to take concerning the role of the folk framework in cognitive science. I shall label it the Syntactic Image. According to the Syntactic Image we are not just syntax/semantics devices; rather, we are syntax/semantic devices in which

> strings of inner symbols can stand in sufficiently close relation to the contents cited in ordinary mentalistic discourse for us to speak of such contents' being *tokened* in the string and having causal powers in virtue of the causal powers of the string

and

> the symbol strings are structured entities which participate in a compositional computational economy.

A word about each of these two points. First, the idea of inner strings' standing in "sufficiently close" relation to ordinary contents needs some further pinning down. Fodor, at least, is reasonably specific. The folk taxonomy of propositional attitudes (the belief that so and so, the hope that such and such, and so on) will, he expects, be vindicated by a science of the mind to the same extent as was the "intuitive taxonomy of middle-sized objects into liquids and solids" (Fodor 1987, p. 26)—that is, the taxonomy will be largely respected, but will be amended in some small ways (think of glass' counting as a liquid). Moreover (and here the first point phases into the second), the items in the inner code which carry such contents will be "morphosyntactically indistinguishable from English" (Fodor 1991, p. 316). This means that, where the content-ascribing sentence contains semantically evaluable subformulas as constituents, the inner representation will likewise contain (as literal constituents) well-formed substrings which bear the constituent contents. Such substrings will be *tokens* of general computational *types*, and the meanings of larger strings will be built up, in regular ways, out of the concatenation of such tokens. Thus, to take Fodor's own example (1987, p. 137), if I should raise my left foot because of an *intention* so to do, inspection of the inner code would reveal that "the subexpression that denotes 'foot' in 'I raise my left foot' is a token of the same type as the sub-expression that denotes 'foot' in 'I raise my right foot'. (Similarly, mutatis mutandis, the 'P' that expresses the proposition P in the formula 'P' is a token of the same type as the 'P' that expresses the proposition P in the formula 'P and Q'.)"

Thus, well-formed elements (not necessarily atomic ones, of course) of the inner code correspond to familiar constituents of thoughts. Such constituents are *transportable* in the sense that they reappear, in different thoughts, as syntactically identical tokens. This type/token story, in which familiar semantic constituents are constantly coded for by syntactically identical fragments of the inner language ("mentalese"), is one of the major claims to be considered (and rejected) in this book.

One way to understand the role which the third answer assigns to folk psychology is in terms of a *suggestive competence theory* for the domain of intentional action. A competence theory (see chapter 3) is a specification of the knowledge required to negotiate a given domain. Thus, the competence theory for naive physics (our everyday grasp of the behaviors of liquids, solids, etc.) would specify heuristics and rules which would (ideally) describe and predict our daily judgments and actions in the domain. A *suggestive* competence theory is then one which is taken as not just a specification of our behaviors (recall the first answer above) but also a clue to the nature of the algorithms which yield the behaviors (the second answer above) and the specific symbolic structures to which they apply to (the third answer above). Just as Hayes (1979, 1985) sees a finished naive physics as a suggestive competence theory for the domain of everyday physical reasoning, so Fodor (I claim) sees folk psychology as a suggestive competence theory for the domain of *intentional action*. The difference is that the competence theory for naive physics must still be made explicit, whereas we are fortunate enough to have already done much of the necessary work in the case of folk psychology—its fruits are there for all to see in the rich and predictive repertoire of daily mentalistic explanation (see Fodor 1987, chapter 1 and epilogue).

The Syntactic Image and Super-Fodorian Realism

Having fixed a space of options for the relation between the folk framework and a computational one, I can now canvass the question of the philosophical significance of such a relation. What bearing, if any, does the choice among the three answers have for the philosophical study of mind? The view that I shall be defending (extending the basic position outlined in Clark 1989a) is quite radical. I shall argue that the legitimacy and the value of the folk solids are independent of the truth of the Syntactic Image as an empirical model of mind. This position accords surprisingly well with the view of Fodor, who is at pains to insist that the Syntactic Image, in its familiar guise as the Language of Thought Hypothesis (Fodor 1975, 1987), is an empirical hypothesis which is supposed to explain certain observed facts (including the efficacy of the folk framework; see Fodor 1987, chapter 2) and the productivity and systematicity of thought. (See Fodor and Pylyshyn 1988.) But no conceptual impossibility attaches to the idea of beings who are properly described as intentional agents yet whose computational innards are of some radically different kind.

Fodor's separation of the two questions is, however, challenged by various accounts in the recent literature. Ramsey, Stich, and Garon (1991) argue that unless our computational innards fit the Syntactic Image in certain crucial respects, some of the central tenets of the folk framework will be contravened. The result (said to follow from, e.g., the discovery that certain kinds of connectionist model describe the inner economy) would be the elimination of the folk framework. In a similar vein, Davies (1991) has suggested that the picture of human thought as involving grasp of concepts makes a tacit commitment to a specific kind of inner organization (again, one which models cast in the Syntactic Image exhibit but which certain kinds of connectionist model seem to lack). Both Davies and Ramsey et al. thus insist that, unless something like Fodor's empirical vision turns out to be true, the folk framework is in jeopardy. I shall label such positions (for obvious reasons) Super-Fodorian Realism. I view them (without malice—they are often illuminating and brilliantly argued) as a kind of philosophical rot which should be kept out of the cognitive scientific woodwork. A secondary objective of the present text is to stop the rot. The primary objective, however, is to sketch the lines of a developing alternative to the Syntactic Image. Hence the next and final stop on our introductory tour.

Mind as Text versus Mind as Process[3]

Both the beauty and the ultimate poverty of the Syntactic Image are rooted (I shall argue) in its commitment to a profoundly text-based understanding of mind. The cornerstone of the Syntactic Image is a stock of inner items which are context-independent content bearers and which figure as the bedrock upon which computational operations (in particular, combination, decomposition, and processing according to logical form) are defined. The model upon which such an image is based is directly grounded, as Fodor and Pylyshyn (1988, p.

44) admit, in the way linguistic symbols carry rather fixed contents and are combined and recombined to yield new structures. This kind of compositionality (in which identical physical tokens occur across contexts and bear relatively fixed semantic contents) is labeled by Fodor and Pylyshyn (1988, p. 46) the "compositional principle of context-invariance." Were it not for such invariance (the stability of the meaning of a symbol across contexts of occurrence), it would not be easy (and it might not even be possible) to set up such symbol systems so as to achieve truth-preserving inferences. As Fodor and Pylyshyn (1988, p. 46) point out, a sequence of inferential steps which is clearly valid if the symbols retain their meanings independent of local context becomes problematic if their semantic import is allowed to vary across contexts. If P means something different in (P → S) than in (P and R), then it will be problematic (to say the least) to decide what follows from the conjunction of the two premises. Here, then, lies one deep respect in which the Syntactic Image relies on a text-based (and, more generally, language-based) view: It builds in a commitment to a stock of stable syntactic atoms which are relatively context-independent content bearers. Another respect, already covered above, is that the kinds of content which we imagined to have such syntactic vehicles include the daily items picked out by folk psychology. Yet another respect concerns the static and "given" nature of the set of basic symbols. Just as an individual confronts a ready-made system of symbols (her native language) and must use this as her combinatorial base of linguistic operations, so we are supposed to inherit a fixed set of inner symbols (an innate language of thought) which likewise sets the fixed combinatorial base of our potential thoughts. There is no interesting sense (that is, none which goes beyond recombination) in which new inner symbols are developed by the thinker (more on this below). And finally, the image of action as sometimes mediated by inner text is invoked, within the Syntactic Image, to distinguish intentional action from mere reflex. As a result, the computational organization underlying thought is conceived as involving (on key occasions) the generation of *explicit symbolic structures* which are both causally potent states in the computational nexus and the vehicles of structured contents as identified by folk psychology. (As we shall see at various points in the forthcoming chapters, the very ideas of explicitness and structure upon which the Syntactic Image trades are deeply and misleadingly inspired by reflection on textual vehicles.)

The point about intentional action bears expansion. To get the full flavor of the proposal, we need to fill in a few more details concerning Fodor's famous unpacking of the Syntactic Image.

Fodor asked two key questions: What kind of state is a mental state such that it can be a cause of behavior? How can its causal powers march in step with its content? These questions are the immediate legacy of taking folk psychology seriously. A very neat answer, which once claimed the dubious virtue of being the only game in town, is embodied in the aforementioned Language of Thought Hypothesis, which in turn is best understood as an ingredient of a particular explanation of the semantic good behavior characteristic of human mental life. This explanation, which goes by the name of Representational Theory of Mind (Fodor 1987, chapter 1), has three essential ingredients:

> Propositional attitudes are conceived as involving computational relations to *mental representations.*
> The mental representations form a *symbol system.*
> Mental processes are *causal* processes involving the explicit tokening of symbols from the symbol system.

The idea that propositional attitudes are computational relations to mental representations goes back a long way (Fodor 1975). A currently fashionable way of expressing the claim is to introduce the idea of a belief box, a hope box, a desire box, etc. The box talk just indicates a kind of role in a complex functional economy. To be in a particular propositional-attitude state is then to have a representation of the content of the proposition tokened in a functional role appropriate to that attitude. Thus, writes Fodor (1987, p. 17), "to believe that such and such is to have a mental symbol that means that such and such.tokened in your head in a certain way; it's to have such a token 'in your belief box,' as I'll sometimes say."

To hope that P is thus to token, in a suitable functional role, a mental symbol that means P. The same symbol, tokened in a different functional role, might cause effects appropriate to the fear that P, or the longing that P, and so on. (Recall the foot-raising example.)

So far, then, we have a requirement that there be mental symbols (viz., items which can be nonsemantically individuated but which are consistently the vehicles of a certain kind of content) and a requirement that the recurrence of such symbols in different functional roles explain the content commonalities among various attitudes toward a single proposition. As it stands, however, these mental symbols could be unique and unstructured. That is, there might be one symbol for each and every proposition. This has seemed empirically unattractive, since we seem capable of an infinite (or at least very large) number of distinct thoughts. Hence the second feature touched on above: Such representations form a symbol system.

A symbol system is a collection of symbols which is provided with a syntax which allows for *semantic compositionality*. In such a system we will find atomic symbols and *molecular* representations. A molecular representation is just a string of symbols such that the content of the string is a direct function of the meanings of its atomic parts and of the syntactic rules of combination. Thus a very simple symbol system might consist of the atomic symbols A, B, and C and a rule of concatenation such that the content 'A and B' is tokened as 'AB', the content 'A and B and C' as 'ABC', the content 'C and B' as 'CB', and so on. Such symbol structures are supposed to "correspond to real physical structures in the brain," and their syntactic (combinatorial) properties are supposed to correspond to real "structural relations" (Fodor and Pylyshyn 1988, p. 13). For example, just as the symbol A is literally part of the complex molecule AB, so the brain state which means that A could be literally part of the brain state which means that AB. (See Fodor and Pylyshyn 1988, p. 13.) The advantages of deploying a symbol system include the ease with which we can specify that certain operations can be applied to *any* string of a given syntactic form; e.g., for any string, you may derive any member from the string. Thus, AB implies A, ABC implies A, CAB implies A, and so on. (See Fodor and Pylyshyn 1988, p. 13.) Another advantage is the ease with which such systems yield a *systematic mental life*. A being deploying the simple symbol system described above who can think (that is, token) AB can *ipso facto* think (token) BA. This systematicity is echoed, so Fodor and Pylyshyn claim, in a distinctive feature of human mental life: that (for example) humans who can think that Mary loves John can also think that John loves Mary. This *a posteriori* argument for a language of thought is the mainstay of Fodor and Pylyshyn (1988). Note that, for the argument to have any force, the symbols which feature in the public language ascriptions of thoughts must have recombinable, context-free correlates in the internal code. They need not constitute atomic items in such a code, but the code must support recombinable content-bearing structures whose syntactic combinatorics match the semantic combinatorics highlighted by Fodor and Pylyshyn.

Now I can address mental causation. The content-faithful causal powers of our mental states, according to Fodor, are nothing but the causal powers of the physical tokens in the inner symbol system. Consider the two characteristic kinds of effect (according to folk psychology) of a mental state of believing that P. One kind of effect consists in the belief's bringing about some action. Another consists in its bringing about further mental states. In both cases, Fodor's motto is "No Intentional Causation without Explicit Representation" (1987,

p. 25). The idea is that a particular propositional attitude that P can act as a cause only when there occurs a token of the syntactic kind that means that P and when that token causes an appropriate action, a further thought content, or both. By understanding the way a symbol's syntactic properties (in the context of a particular functional economy and symbol system) determine its causal powers, we can see one way in which content and physical work can march in step. The Fodorian vision is thus sold as "a vindication of intuitive belief/desire psychology [insofar as it] shows how intentional states could have causal powers; precisely the aspect of commonsense intentional realism that seemed most perplexing from a metaphysical point of view" (Fodor 1987, p. 26).

Fodor continues the account with a few subtleties meant to take the sting out of familiar objections. Consider emergent rule following, a classic case of which is Dennett's (1981b, p. 107) example of a chess-playing program which is described as "wanting to get its queen out early" even though "for all the many levels of explicit representation to be found in that program, nowhere is anything roughly synonymous with 'I should get my queen out early' explicitly tokened." Fodor's response to this worry is to introduce the idea of *core cases*. The vindication of commonsense psychology by cognitive science requires, he suggests, only that "tokenings of attitudes *must* correspond to tokenings of mental representations when they—the attitude tokenings—are episodes in mental processes" (Fodor 1987, p. 25).

The core cases, it seems, are cases in which a given content (such as the belief that it is raining) is supposed to figure in a mental process or to constitute an "episode in a mental life." In such cases (and only in such cases) there must, according to Fodor, be an explicit representation of the content which is at once a syntactic item (hence a bearer of causal powers) and an item which gets a recognizably folk-psychological interpretation (e.g., as the belief about rain). The chess-program "counterexample" is thus said to be defused, since (Fodor insists) "entertaining the thought 'Better get the queen out early' never constitutes an episode in the mental life of the machine" (1987, p. 25). By contrast, Fodor (ibid.) claims, "the representations of the board—of actual or possible states of play—over which the machine's computations are defined *must* be explicit, precisely *because* the machine's computations *are* defined over them. These computations constitute the machine's 'mental processes,' so either there are causal sequences of explicit representations or the representational theory of chess-playing is simply false of the machine."

The claim, then, is just that, *if* the Representational Theory of Mind (RTM) is to vindicate commonsense psychology, then the *contents* of our thoughts must be tokened in an explicit inner code. But the "laws of thought"—the rules which determine how one content yields another, or yields an action—need not be explicitly represented. In the familiar form of words, "programs . . . may be explicitly represented, but 'data structures' . . . *have to be*" (Fodor 1987, p. 25). This may seem a little confusing since in his 1975 book (p. 74, n. 15) Fodor wrote that "what distinguishes what organisms do . . . is that a representation of the rules they follow constitutes one of the causal determinants of their behavior." Despite appearances, this is consistent with the current claim. The idea must be that in any case where the *consideration* of a rule is meant causally to explain a judgment or an action, *then* the rule must be explicitly tokened; otherwise not. Thus, a novice chess player whose action involved a train of thought in which a rule was recalled would have had (according to the RTM) to token the rule in an inner code (distinct from her public language—see Fodor 1975).

What Fodor has offered is, I believe, a conceptually coherent and physically implementable account of how thoughts can be causes. He does not explicitly claim, however, that it is conceptually *necessary* that every intentional agent conform to the story. (That is the province of the Super-Fodorian Realists, although the talk of "vindicating" folk psychology is somewhat worrying in this regard.) But, elegant though it is, the story is (as we shall see) in all likelihood false, even as a model of human thought. It is false because there *is* no pervasive text-like inner code, and it is false because (*a fortiori*) the folk solids do not have inner vehicles in the form of context-free syntactic items in such a code.

The story is also false in another way—one which brings us, at last, face to face with the issue of code versus process. A major failing of the Syntactic Image (at least in its worked-out, Fodorian version) lies, I suggest, in its failure to locate representational change and development as a key feature of mind and a central target for the cognitive scientific endeavor. In at least some quarters of cognitive science (see Bates and Elman 1992; Plunkett and Sinha 1991; Marchman 1992), the idea that human cognition involves kinds of representational change undreamt of in the Syntactic Image is gaining support. Where that image depicts learning as essentially weak (see below) and as often effectively environment independent, the new image casts it as strong (see below) and highly environment dependent. Moreover, the deep distinction (central to the Syntactic Image) between the representations and the processes defined over those representations is itself cast into doubt. Representation and process develop in inextricable intimacy, and both undergo genuine developmental change. Putting flesh on this picture is the major goal of this book.

The text-based image of mind depicts cognition as involving the manipulation of context-free inner content bearers (symbols). What model of learning fits that image? The standard answer (see especially Fodor 1981) is that learning consists in the systematic construction of complex structures of inner symbols to express new concepts and thoughts. Thus, there must be an innate *representational base* (a repertoire of semantic atoms) which is not learned (although aspects of it may need to be triggered by some minimal stimulus). And aside from such episodes of triggering, all[4] conceptual change and development is to be understood in terms of a process of generating and testing hypotheses—a process in which items from the representational base are conjoined or otherwise brought into construction with one another in an attempt to express novel contents and concepts. This kind of learning is weak insofar as it does not allow for the expansion, as a result of learning, of the representational capacities of the system. In ways that will be explored and exemplified at some length in subsequent chapters, the emerging connectionist approach to cognitive modeling allows us to begin to make sense of much stronger kinds of cognitive change—partly because such systems do not depend on (though they may exploit) initially given ("innate") sets of semantic atoms and partly because learning in such systems is not well pictured as the generating and testing of hypotheses within a fixed representational environment. The lack of a firm data/process separation (see chapter 2) means that representations and processing strategies coevolve in ways which can radically change the processing dynamics of the system. As Bates and Elman (1992, pp. 14–15) put it, learning in these systems involves *structural change* of a kind which can at times result in a "qualitative shift" in the overall nature of the processing the system engages in. Such shifts have generally been linked, in more classical approaches, to genetically predetermined structural change (see note 4). A key feature of the new approach is its ability to locate the origins of some such shifts (e.g., from rote to rule-based production of classes of linguistic items) in the environmental inputs to the system. Breaking down the code/processing divide thus encourages us to shift some of the burden once borne by the innate structure of the processor to the input corpus and the way it is presented (see chapters 7–9).

The exciting prospect is that, by using connectionist ideas to help us transcend a text-based Syntactic Image, we may begin to address genuine (strong) representational change. Instead of taking context-invariant symbols for granted as a representational baseline, we can ask how increasingly sophisticated representational structures emerge in systems in which code and processing are deeply intertwined. To temper the excitement, we can already locate some potentially serious problems. How can such systems achieve systematic, structure-sensitive processing? How, if we abandon the image of an inner text faithful to the folk solids, are we to make sense of intentional causation? We may have to rethink the nature of folk explanation, and we shall certainly have to revise our understanding of structure, syntax, and explicit representation. These are interesting times.

Chapter 2

Connectionism, Code, and Context

The USP Uncovered

In the world of marketing, the USP is all. A USP is a *unique selling point*—a feature or a number of features strongly associated with your product and distinct from those associated with its retail rivals. The modest goal of the present chapter is to display what I see as the USP of a certain breed of connectionist model.[1] This breed is distinguished by three features, each of which will be crucial to my subsequent development of a more process-oriented conception of the study of thought: superpositional storage, intrinsic context sensitivity, and strong representational change.

Superposition—a Key Feature

The key determinant of the class of interesting connectionist models lies, I believe, in their use of superpositional representations. Here we locate the source of their genuine divergence from so-called classical approaches and the source of the features (representation-process intermingling, generalization, prototype extraction, context sensitivity, and the use of a "semantic metric"—more on all of which below) which make the models psychologically suggestive.

The basic idea of superposition is straightforward. Two representations are fully superposed if the resources used to represent item 1 are coextensive with those used to represent item 2. Thus, if a network learns to represent item 1 by developing a particular pattern of weights, it will be said to have superposed its representations of items 1 and 2 if it then goes on to encode the information about item 2 by amending the set of original weightings in a way which preserves the functionality (some desired input-output pattern) required to represent item 1 while simultaneously exhibiting the functionality required to represent item 2. A simple case would be an autoassociative network which reproduced its input at the output layer after channeling it through some intervening bottleneck (such as a small hidden-unit layer). Such a net might need to find a single set of weights which do multiple duty, enabling the net to reproduce any one of a whole set of inputs at the output layer. If all the weights turned out to be playing a role in each such transition, the representation of the various items would be said to be *fully* superposed. (In most real connectionist networks, the totality of stored representations turns out to be only partially superposed.)

This general notion of superposition has been rendered precise in an extended treatment by van Gelder (1991). Van Gelder terms a representation R of an item C *conservative* just in case the resources used to represent C (for example, a set of units and weights in a connectionist network) are equal to R—that is, just in case all of R is involved in representing C. It is then possible to define fully superpositional representation as follows:

> A representation R of a series of items C_i is superposed just in case R is a conservative representation of each C_i. (van Gelder 1991, p. 43)

As van Gelder notes, this definition, though quite general, can be seen to apply directly to familiar cases of connectionist superposition. These range from the partial superposition found in so-called coarse coding schemes (in which individual units process overlapping inputs) to the total superposition created by tensor product approaches (Smolensky 1991) in which the representation of a structured item is achieved by addition (or sometimes multiplication) of the vectors coding for the constituents. The most basic case of connectionist superposition, however, is the standard information-storage technique of multi-layer feedforward networks using distributed representations. The details of learning and representation in these systems are by now boringly familiar to many readers, and I shall not attempt to reproduce the necessary detail here.[2] The fundamental features responsible for the superposition are, however, worth spelling out. These features are the use of distributed representations and the use of a learning rule which imposes a *semantic metric* on the acquired representations.

Consider a network of units and weights. A representation may be said to be *local* in such a network if it names the content associated with the activity of a single unit (e.g., if it specifies that a single unit represents grandmothers). It will be said to be *distributed* if it names a content associated with the joint activity of several units. This standard sketch of the distinction is, however, potentially misleading. As van Gelder (1991) points out, distribution, conceived as the mere *extendedness* of a representational vehicle, is not distinctive of connectionist models, and is not the source of their attraction. Instead, what counts is the use of *internally structured* extended representations. A representation can be said to have internal structure if it is in some sense a *nonarbitrary construction*. An example will help.

One way to represent the letter A in a connectionist network would be to have a single unit stand for that letter. In such a system, different units could stand for B, for C, and so on. This is clearly a localist representational scheme. Now consider a second scheme in which the letters are represented as *patterns* of activity across 78 units and the encoding scheme is as follows: The joint activity of units 1, 2, and 3 is the representation of A, the joint activity of units 4, 5, and 6 is the representation of B, and so on. Clearly, despite the intuitive extendedness of the representations of each letter, the scheme is still effectively localist, because the representations, although spread out, do not exploit that extendedness in any semantically significant way. Finally, consider a scheme in which individual units (or groups of units) stand for features of letterforms in a given font, such as |, -, and _. The system's representation of the letter A can then be just the joint activity of the various features which distinguish it, and likewise, for B, C, etc. Here, at last, we are dealing with distributed representation in an interesting sense. Notice that in such a scheme the fact that the letterform E shares more features with F than it does with C will be reflected in the system's use of resources to code for the letters. The E representation will involve the activation of many of the same units involved in the F representation, whereas it may be almost (or even completely) orthogonal to the pattern associated with the letter C. This is what is meant by speaking of such a system as imposing a *semantic metric*. The semantic (broadly understood) similarity between representational *contents* is echoed as a similarity between representational *vehicles*. Within such a scheme, the representation of individual items is *nonarbitrary*. A new letterform (say Z) would *have* to be represented by a vehicle (a pattern of activity across the set of units) which reflected its position in the relevant similarity space. The upshot is that "the particular pattern used to represent an item is determined by the nature of that item, and so similarities and differences among the items to be represented will be directly reflected in similarities and differences among the representations themselves" (van Gelder 1991, p. 41). The great achievement of connectionism is to have discovered learning rules which cause networks to *impose* such a semantic metric as the natural effect of the process of learning (see note 2). This effect is visible in NETtalk's discovery and encoding of phonetic features, and it is the prime source of the attraction of such approaches as a means of modeling knowledge of concepts. The tendency of such networks to represent semantically similar cases by means of overlapping inner resources (that is, to use superpositional storage techniques) is also the root of the important properties of prototype extraction and generalization.

Connectionist models are usefully seen as deploying *prototype-style* knowledge representations. The idea of a prototype is just the familiar idea of an especially typical example of an item which falls under a given category or concept. A robin may count as an especially typical bird whereas a penguin does not. A major advantage of organizing knowledge around prototypes is the easy explanation of *typicality judgments*. We judge that a robin is a more typical bird than a penguin because the robin shares more features with the prototypical bird than does the penguin. The limiting case of such feature sharing is the case where the instance is identical to the prototype, though we need not suppose that the prototype always corresponds to any concrete exemplar of the category. A related advantage is that we can judge deviant cases to fall under the category just so long as they exhibit enough of the prototypical features to raise them above some threshold.

How, then, do connectionist models come to embody prototype-style knowledge representations? The basic idea is that, as a result of the distributed, superposed encoding of a set of exemplars, the features common to the exemplars become strongly associated (i.e., form powerful mutually excitatory links). The natural mechanisms of connectionist learning and superpositional storage immediately yield a system which will extract the *statistical central tendency* of the exemplars. That means, it will uncover which sets of features are most commonly present in the learning set. It will also learn commonly occurring groupings of features. To see how superpositional storage can figure in this, consider that a network using superpositional storage techniques must amend existing resources if it is to encode new information which overlaps (in respect of, say, some subset of semantic features) with information already stored. Connectionist learning techniques do precisely this. As a result, semantic features which are statistically frequent in a body of input exemplars come to be both highly marked and mutually associated. By "highly marked" I mean that the connection weights constituting the net's long-term stored knowledge about such common features tend to be quite strong, since the training regime has repeatedly pushed them to accommodate this pattern (although it is equally true that beyond a certain point such "overtraining" will not result in any further increase in the relevant weights—see, e.g., French 1991). By "mutually associated" I mean that where such features co-occur, they will tend to become encoded in such a way that activation of the resources encoding one such feature will promote activation of the other. The joint effect of these two tendencies is a process of *automatic prototype extraction:* the network extracts the statistical central tendency of the various feature complexes and thus comes to encode information not just about specific exemplars but also about the stereotypical feature-set displayed in the training data. The organization of knowledge around such stereotypical feature sets is an important theme in recent psychological literature. The description of connectionism as crucially involving the organization of knowledge around representations of prototypes has recently been pursued in detail by Paul Churchland (see, e.g., Churchland 1989, especially chapters 6 and 10), who also depicts *explanatory understanding* as a process of assimilation (of some input pattern) to a stored prototype.

Prototype extraction, thus conceived, is of a piece with *generalization.* A net is said to generalize if it can treat *novel* cases sensibly, courtesy of its past training. Any net which responds to a barrage of training exemplars by extracting a prototype will be well placed to succeed in future, novel cases. As long as such cases display some of the central themes (such as subcomplexes of features) extracted from the training corpus, the network's response will be sensible. For example, a novel instance of a dog (say, one with three legs) will still be expected to bark just so long as it shares enough of the doggy central tendencies to activate the knowledge about prototypical dogs. Such a "dog-recognition network" is detailed in chapter 17 of McClelland, Rumelhart, and PDP Research Group 1986. We can use it to introduce one last property of connectionist-style knowledge of prototypes: its *flexibility.*

The dog-recognition network (see also Clark 1989a, chapter 5) is trained on a variety of cases in which descriptions of correlated sets of dog features (supposed to correspond to individual dogs) are fed to the network. These descriptions are obtained by selecting one set of features and stipulating that these describe the prototypical dog. The training cases are then derived by creating a series of deformed version of this description (that is, by changing individual features). The network is then trained only on these deformed instances; it never "sees" the "prototypical" dog. Nonetheless, it is able (courtesy of the learning rule) to act as a statistical "signal averager" and hence to extract the general pattern exemplified in the overall set of deformed instances. The result is that not only can it recognize the deformed cases as cases of dogs, but it can *also* reproduce the pattern of activation for the prototypical dog (to which it was never exposed) if it is fed a portion of that pattern as an input cue. It can also generalize (that is, categorize new but deformed exemplars on the basis of similarity to the prototype). In short, the net has come to encode a multi-dimensional feature space organized around a central point (the signal average, prototype, hot spot, or harmony maximum—call it what you will). In addition, such a network can find assignments of weights which enable it to store knowledge about *several* categories in a single set of weights. As a result, the network "does not fall into the trap of needing to decide which category to put a pattern into before knowing which prototype to average it with" (McClelland and Rumelhart 1986, p. 185). That is, distributed connectionist encoding provides for a high degree of flexibility in the system's use of the correlated-feature information it stores. It is not forced to "decide," in advance, on a particular set of prototypes. Instead, it can settle into "blended responses" which, in effect, mix up elements (or sets of elements) from two (or more) prototypes. Thus, the dog-recognition network, if it also encoded information about cats, could (in response to ambiguous inputs) produce a response blending elements of both (McClelland and Rumelhart 1986, p. 188). Likewise, a network which encodes featural information which amounts to knowledge of proto-typical room contents (e.g. the contents of a normal kitchen or bedroom) can, if the context-fixing input is sufficiently peculiar (in-cluding, say, a *bed* feature and a *sofa* feature), complete to a pattern of activation which departs from both the typical bedroom and the typical living room and instead fills in features appropriate to a "large fancy bedroom" (Rumelhart et al. 1986, p. 34). This ability depends on the network's encoding only *local* information about correlations and inhibitions between groups of features. It has not decided in ad-vance just how this local information should be used to carve up the world. Instead, such decisions can be made according to the con-text of use (see chapter 5) and are thus maximally sensitive to input information.

The three central features of the connectionist exploitation of prototype-style encoding are, therefore, the following:

(1) The prototyping is a natural effect of the way in which such systems store information.

(2) The prototype need not correspond to any concrete instance to which the system has been exposed. Instead it is the statistical central tendency of the various feature dimensions of the exemplars.

(3) The prototype knowledge can be flexibly deployed in a way that is sensitive to local context (as in the "blended response" cases detailed above).

To sum up: The most fundamental feature of the class of connectionist systems I shall be discussing is their use of superpositional storage techniques. Such techniques, when combined with the use of distributed representations, yield

> non-arbitrary representations,
> a semantic metric among representations,
> automatic prototype extraction,
> generalization,

and

> flexible deployment of prototypes.

And so the USP begins to emerge. We next coax it further into view by considering a powerful consequence of the organization of non-arbitrary representations into a semantic metric: the deep context sensitivity of such connectionist representations.

Intrinsic Context Sensitivity

Suppose we concentrate, for now, on *activation patterns* as the locus of representational activity in a network. (The idea of weights on connections as representations will be addressed later in this section.) We can then observe that the representation of a specific item will involve a distributed pattern of activity which contains subpatterns appropriate to the feature set involved. Such a network will be able to represent several instances of such an item, which may differ in respect of one or more features. Such "near neighbors" will be represented by similar internal representational structures—that is, the vehicles of the several representations (activation patterns) will be similar to one another in ways which echo the semantic similarity of the cases (this is the semantic metric in operation). One upshot is that such a network can learn to treat several inputs, which result in subtly different representational states (defined across the hidden units), as prompting outputs which have much in common; for example, they could all activate a common label, such as 'dog'. The property of context sensitivity, as I understand it, relies on essentially this kind of process, but taken in reverse. Thus, a net exposed to a label like 'dog' will need to fix on one of the several inner states which are associated with the label. To do so, the net relies on contextual information. Thus (to adapt the kind of example given in McClelland and Kawamoto 1986), the representation of 'dog' in the context of 'wore a woolly jacket' might be driven to a position in the overall representational space appropriate to a poodle feature complex, whereas in the context 'mauled the burglar' it might activate a Rottweiler feature complex. This variability in the inner vehicles and in the detailed content represented is what leads Smolensky (1988, p. 17) to claim that "in the symbolic paradigm the context of a symbol is manifest *around* it and consists of *other* symbols; in the subsymbolic paradigm the context of a symbol is manifest *inside* it, and consists of subsymbols." The idea of a *subsymbol*, as the word is used in the above quote, is a potential source of misunderstanding. Properly understood, it reflects a deep fact about the *status* of symbolic descriptions of content in these approaches. But it is all too easy to trivialize it as the claim that the symbols involved (that is, the patterns of activity strongly associated with specific features) are simply *smaller* than, e.g., 'dog', being instead items like 'has-legs' and 'barks'. We are not quite in a position to remedy this yet, but we will do so before the close of the current section. Patience.

The standard example of the kind of context sensitivity just described is the infamous 'coffee' case, in which Smolensky (1991) describes a connectionist representation of 'coffee' which is distributed across units or groups of units which code for various features of coffee-involving scenarios. Consider now the distributed representation of 'cup with coffee', and suppose (for simplicity's sake) that the set (or vector) of active hidden units is just that set comprising the units coding for the microfeatures 'upright container', 'burnt odor', and 'brown liquid contacting porcelain'. What, then, constitutes the network's representation of the conceptual constituent 'coffee'? One suggestion (due originally to Zenon Pylyshyn) is that to isolate the representation of coffee one just takes the representation for 'cup with coffee' and subtracts the cup parts. But subtracting the cup microfeatures (e.g. 'upright container') leaves us with a set of microfeatures which includes a number of *contextually biased* items, such as 'brown liquid contacting porcelain'. Now imagine that instead of starting with 'cup with coffee' we started with 'can with coffee'. In that case—as Smolensky (1991, pp. 207–212) points out—the representation of coffee would include a contextual bias for the can scenario (e.g. 'granules contacting tin'). The upshot is that there need be no context-independent, core representation of coffee. Instead, there could be a variety of states linked merely by a relation of family resemblance.[3] The unit-level activation profile which characterizes the system will thus not map neatly and accurately onto a conceptual level specification. A single, recurrent conceptual-level item will have a panoply of so-called subconceptual realizations, and which realization is actually present will make a difference to future processing. This feature (multiple, context-sensitive subconceptual realizations) makes for the vaunted fluidity of connectionist systems and introduces one sense in which such systems merely approximate their more classical cousins. Fodor-style classicists were seen to picture the mind as manipulating context-free symbolic structures in a straightforwardly compositional manner. Connectionists, not having context-free analogues to conceptual-level items available to them, have to make do with a much more slippery and hard-to-control kind of "compositionality" which consists in the mixing together of context-dependent representations. Smolensky (1991, p. 208) writes of the coffee example that "the compositional structure is there, but it's there in an *approximate* sense. It's *not* equivalent to taking a context-independent representation of coffee and a context-independent representation of cup—and certainly not equivalent to taking a context-independent representation of the relationship in or with—and sticking them all together in a symbolic structure concatenating them together to form syntactic compositional structures like 'with (cup, coffee)'."

The most radical description of this rampant context sensitivity would be that (these) connectionist systems *do not involve computations defined over symbols.* Instead, any accurate (i.e., fully predictive) picture of the system's processing will have to be given at the numerical level of units, weights, and activation-evolution equations, while more familiar symbol-manipulating computational descriptions will at most provide a rough guide to the main trends in the global behavior of the system. The proposal, then, is just that there are no syntactically identifiable elements which both have a symbolic interpretation and can figure in a full explanation of the totality of the system's semantic good behavior—that is, "there is no account of the architecture in which the same elements carry both the syntax and the semantics" (Smolensky 1991, p. 204). This is what is meant by Smolensky's description of connectionism as a two-level architecture: "Mental representations and mental processes are *not* supported by the same formal entities—there are not 'symbols' that can do both jobs. The new cognitive architecture is fundamentally two-level; formal, algorithmic specification of processing mechanisms on the one hand, and semantic interpretation on the other, must be done at two different levels of description." (ibid., p. 203)

Mental processes, according to Smolensky, are best understood by reference to the numerical-level descriptions of units, weights, and activation-evolution equations. The elements at this level defy semantic interpretation. Whereas the larger-scale activity of such systems *allows* interpretation but the patterns thus fixed on are not capable of figuring in accurate descriptions of the actual course of processing.

(See Smolensky 1991, p. 204.) This is because the *interpreted* patterns (for example, the groups of vectors associated with a single conceptual-level item like 'coffee') paper over those more microscopic differences, which nonetheless make a difference to the future course of processing.

Since the coffee example is now stale, it may help to introduce a slightly more complex case. We can then get down to the real question raised by all this: In what sense, if any, does the idea of a subsymbol or a subconceptual constituent amount to anything more interesting than the idea of *smaller symbols*? Here, then, is a second example case.

Elman (1991b,c) describes a net which aimed to categorize words according to lexical category (verb, noun, etc.). The goal was to learn, by exposures to sequences of linguistic input, something about the classes and categories of the words presented. The simple recurrent architecture consisted of a standard three-layer feedforward network and an additional set of *context units* connected to the hidden-unit layer. The context units were set up to copy the activation at the hidden-unit layer and, on the next time step, to feed that information back to the hidden-unit layer, which thus simultaneously received the external input (from the first layer of the standard three-layer net) and the "temporal context" information (i.e., the copy of its own previous state). This approach was closely related to that of Jordan (1986), except that Jordan's network copied back the state of the output units rather than the hidden ones. Figure 2.1 illustrates Elman's simple recurrent architecture.

The task of Elman's network was to take a succession of input words and predict (by output-layer activation) the next word in the sequence. A lexicon of 29 nouns and verbs was used, and these were composed into a training corpus of 10,000 two- and three-word sentences. Structurally, these sentences reflected properties of subclasses of the lexical items; for example, "only animate nouns occurred as the subject of the verb eat, and this verb was only followed by edible substances" (Elman 1991c, p. 348). Naturally, there is no unique answer to the question "What word should come next?" in this task. Nonetheless, there are certainly words which should not come next, and the network's performance was evaluated on that basis—that is, on whether or not it identified a valid succession-*class* word.

Elman's network proved fairly successful at the task, and a subsequent analysis (see chapter 3 below) of the internal representations at the hidden-unit layer revealed that it was indeed partitioning the space into recognizable lexical categories. For example, it displayed very similar hidden-unit activation for mouse, cat, and dog, thus war-

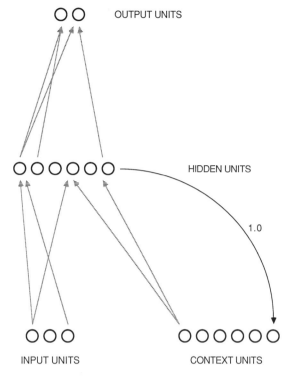

Figure 2.1
A three-layer recurrent network. The context units are activated, one by one, by the corresponding hidden units. For simplicity, not all the activation is shown. (After Elman 1991b, with permission.)

ranting a cluster label of 'animal', and at a coarser grain it displayed a similarity in its treatment of all nouns in the lexicon, and a similarity in its treatment of all verbs. In a sense, then, it "discovered" the categories 'noun' and 'verb'. Mid-range sensitivities indicated groupings for animate and inanimate objects, foods, and breakable objects.

Two of Elman's observations are especially pertinent to the present discussion. First, the categories are "soft"—there can be genuine borderline cases, and membership is always "more or less" rather than "all or none." Second: "In this simulation the context makes up an important part of the internal representation of a word. Indeed, it is somewhat misleading to speak of the hidden unit representations as word representations in the conventional sense, since these patterns also reflect the prior context. As a result it is literally the case that every occurrence of a lexical item has a separate internal representation." (Elman 1991c, p. 353)

Imagine that Elman's network is dealing with information concerning an individual, John. Elman (1991c, p. 353) insists that "we cannot point to a canonical representation for John; instead there are representations for $John_1$, $John_2$ . . . $John_n$. These are the tokens of John, and the fact that they are different is the way the system marks what may be subtle but important meaning differences associated with the specific token." The various tokens of John will be grouped together insofar as they involve very similar patterns of hidden-unit activity. However, the subtle differences between them will *make* a difference; they will build in information concerning the current context of occurrence of the word.

Thus, Elman's model is deeply *dynamic*. Against a classical picture in which a language master stores context-free representations of lexical items, which are retrieved when the word is heard and which "exist in some canonical form which is constant across all occurrences" (Elman 1991c, p. 377), Elman urges (p. 378) a fluid picture in which "there is no separate stage of lexical retrieval. There are no representations of words in isolation. The representations of words (the internal states following input of a word) always reflect the input taken together with the prior state. . . . The representations are not propositional and their information content changes constantly over time in accord with the demands of the current task. Words serve as guideposts which help establish mental states that support (desired) behavior; representations are snapshots of those mental states." (See also Elman 1991b.)

The hard question to which I have gently been leading up can now be formulated: How far can such context sensitivity go, and mustn't 'it "bottom out" in some set of context-free representations which (*pacé* Smolensky; see his claim quoted above) really do deserve the title of symbols? The question is best taken in two parts:

> Could all of the system's *word-level* knowledge be thus context sensitive?
> Even if that makes sense, mustn't there still be some context-free content bearers which, although they are not identical in meaning to any public-language *words*, still deserve the title of 'symbols' (e.g., the *real* microfeatures out of which so-called hokey ones like 'burnt odor' are built up)?

I shall argue that the answer to each of these questions is No, and that there is indeed a clear sense in which the whole idea of context-free inner symbols ("building blocks" of thought) is inapplicable to connectionist systems. The apparently paradoxical air of supposing that a system's representations can be context sensitive "all the way down" is caused by our persistent tendency to think in terms of static, "classical" symbols which persist as unaltered, stored syntactic items and which are *retrieved* (rather than constructed) in the course of processing. In the next section an alternative model is developed.

Why Context Sensitivity Does Not Have to "Bottom Out"

In a February 1992 posting to the global newsgroup "Connectionists-request" I raised the problem of context sensitivity as follows:

> Current wisdom in philosophical circles depicts a major subclass of connectionist representations as context sensitive. Standard examples include Smolensky's (in)famous coffee story (in "Connectionism, Constituency and the Language of Thought," in Loewer and Rey (eds.), *Meaning in Mind: Fodor and His Critics,* pp. 207–209) in which the occurrent state which represents coffee is composed of a set of microfeatures which vary according to the overall context. Thus in a 'spilt' context, the distributed pattern for coffee might include a 'contacting tablecloth' feature. Whereas in a 'cup' context it includes e.g. a 'contacting porcelain' feature.
>
> Now things, clearly, can't stop there. For we need to ask about e.g. the feature 'contacting tablecloth' itself. Presumably it too is context-sensitive and is coded as a bag of microfeatures whose exact make-up varies according to context (e.g. it includes 'paper' in a 'transport cafe' context, cloth in a 'Hilton hotel' context).
>
> My question, then, is this: must this process bottom out somewhere in a set of microfeatures which are genuinely SEMANTIC (genuinely contentful) but which are NOT prone to contextual infection? If the process DOES bottom out, don't we have a kind of language of thought scenario all over again—at least insofar as we have systems which systematically BUILD new (context-dependent) representations out of a basic stock of context-free atoms?
>
> But if it is supposed instead that the process does NOT bottom out, isn't there a puzzle about how the system builds appropriate representations AT ALL? Context-sensitivity seems intelligible if it involves combining BASIC representational resources as some input probe suggests. But without any such basic resources it seems like the ex-nihilo creation of complex representations. (Such creation seems to occur in a learning phase proceeding from random weights to encoded knowledge. But contextual

shading of occurrent representations does not involve learning as such.)

I raise this question because it seems unclear which (if either) of the following two claims best characterizes the highly distributed 'sub-symbolic' connectionist vision, viz:

1. Really Radical Connectionism (RRC)
   Representation is context sensitive all the way down.
2. Radical Connectionism (RC)
   The representation of all daily CONCEPTUAL LEVEL items ('folk' objects, states, and properties) is context sensitive BUT this sensitivity consists in the systematic combination of unfamiliar (but genuinely contentful) micro-representations which are context-free content bearers.

Finally, it is of course true that representation itself must stop at some point. My question is not "Is there a NON-representational level?" but rather "Is there a level of CONTEXT-FREE REPRESENTATION?"

The response was enormous, and enormously divided. Many working connectionists opted for the semi-classical vision (RC), in which context sensitivity is conceived as the combination of context-free representational primitives; however, just as many (including, notably, Jeff Elman) opted for context sensitivity all the way down (RRC). I now believe (see below) that the root of the trouble lay in my phrasing the apparently exhaustive and exclusive options in the vocabulary of symbols and combination. I was in fact offering only a Hobson's choice or a no-win situation. Once the problem is conceived in such terms, the "context sensitivity all the way" option is indeed nearly unintelligible. But we do not have to think in those terms. Before I expand on this, it is worth reviewing the two most important issues raised by various respondents. These concern the context-free element contributed by sensory transduction and the position of context-free contents in a developmental progression.

Regarding sensory transduction, several people pointed out that any system must terminate, at the sensorimotor surfaces, in some set of sensors which respond in a context-free way to the environment—for example, cells which respond to light of a certain intensity.[4] Nonetheless, context sensitivity may cut in very rapidly after that; for example, what information thus received is carried over and used to guide further computational activity may depend heavily on current goals and beliefs (Chalmers et al. 1991)[5]. These dimensions of context-free receptivity and context-dependent filtering, though interesting and important, remain largely orthogonal to the question of how we should think of representation *within* a distributed superpositional network of the kind described above.

Closer to the real issues, I believe, is the idea (raised in somewhat different forms by Jeff Elman, Elizabeth Bates, and Michael Dyer) that the connectionist, insofar as she acknowledges context-free representations at all, will locate them toward the end of a learning trajectory and not (as the theorist of an innate Language of Thought does) at the beginning. Thus, Elman commented that during learning a system might be forced to learn abstractions which encompass more and more of the various context-infected representations. Such a process might culminate in some representations which are "close to context free" in the sense that they represent a variety of different situations as being the same in some crucial respect and in that they do so by virtue of the same inner representational vehicle being evoked by all these various cases. In the same vein, Bates raised the possibility of systems' learning multiple context-bound feature maps but also needing to harmonize the maps in ways which allow the joint activity of sets of such maps to act as detectors of much less context-bound features (e.g., of the same object, both seen and touched).

The most suggestive comments, however, were those which questioned the vocabulary in which my initial question was posed.[6] Consider the very idea of a 'context-free atom'. What can it be? One reasonably clear definition is this:

> Something is a 'context-free atom' if (a) it is a syntactic item (i.e., one that can be individuated purely by its nonsemantic properties) and (b) it plays a fixed representational role in a symbol system.

An inner state which makes the same semantic contribution to each of the larger states in which it figures thus counts as a 'context-free atom'. (Fodor's innate Language of Thought posits a set of innate representational atoms in just this sense.) Correlatively, consider the very idea of a microfeature. This can, it seems, be nothing but the idea of a context-free atom of the kind just described. What else could it be? At this point, nothing except the conservative, semi-classical vision of a symbolic economy (albeit one involving "smaller" symbols) seems to make sense.

The difficulty of seeing how the connectionist approach could avoid such context-free atoms is compounded by the fact that systems in which activity in single units is associated with specific and combinable features will fit the above definition pretty well. But, as is so often the case, concentrating on localist microfeatural nets is a mistake. The more interesting connectionist systems will, as we saw, code for *many* features by means of nonarbitrary *patterns* of activation. Such patterns will be affected by current context (that is, they will be slightly varied in ways dictated by other current activity in the system). Where, in such systems, do we look for the context-free representational atoms? The obvious answer is "in the individual units, or subpatterns of units." But these may easily resist interpretation while still figuring in a number of nonarbitrary (because systematically interrelated) distributed patterns. (See, e.g., van Gelder 1991, p. 39; McClelland, Rumelhart, and Hinton 1986, p. 33.)

Why, then, do we seem to find it so hard to imagine bottomless context sensitivity? The reason, as hinted above, is that the vocabulary in which the question is posed is itself deeply classical, and leads us to make the crucial error of trying to understand an essentially dynamic approach in essentially static terms. This becomes clear if we recall the definition of 'context free' given above and ask what is the 'it' which is supposed to either make or fail to make the same semantic contribution to any larger representational state of which it is a part? In familiar classical approaches, the answer is clear: It is a syntactically defined item taken as the persisting vehicle of some single content. In such approaches, these items may be brought together in several ways which reflect any contextual nuances. (See the discussion of concatenative compositionality in van Gelder 1990 and in chapter 6 below.) But the items themselves are not affected by this bringing together, and they contribute what they do largely independently of their current "neighbors." In connectionist approaches of the kind detailed above, however, such items simply do not exist. Symbols, insofar as we can use such talk at all, exist in these systems only as a present *response* to an input of endogenous or exogenous origin. And *these* transient constructs internally reflect the local context in their very structure. To justify the claim that there are context-free atoms acting as the representational baseline of such systems, we would need to discover syntactic structures which *persist* unaltered and carry a fixed content. The only contenders for such persistent content bearers are the weights which moderate the various context-sensitive activity patterns. But a given weight, or set of weights, cannot be identified with any fixed content in these superpositional systems, for each weight contributes to *multiple* representational abilities. It makes no sense to ask what this or that weight *means*; it is only relative to some specific inputs that the weights give rise to activation patterns which can be seen as expressing this or that (context-involving) content.

The mistake, then, is to suppose that connectionist systems use symbols *in the familiar sense* and then to ask whether some of them are then best seen as a baseline of atomic representations. Context sensitivity does not have to bottom out in context-free symbolic primitives; there are no *symbols* here at all, taken *independent* of some context. Symbols, in short, do not *exist* in these systems except as context-sensitive responses to inputs. No wonder it is context sensitivity all the way!

One possible source of confusion here is the common and laudable use of techniques such as cluster analysis (see chapter 3) to generate a static symbolic description of a network's knowledge. Such analyses effectively *transform* a body of episodes of actual context-reflecting processing into a static (context-transcending) symbolic description. Such analysis is indeed crucial, but we should not be misled into thinking that the symbols thus discerned somehow exist as long-term syntactic items *in* the network. They do not.

To sum up: It is indeed possible to view superpositional distributed connectionist systems as context sensitive all the way down, for the fixed resources out of which the various representations (activity patterns) are nonarbitrarily constructed are just the weights which encode *multiple* items and types of knowledge and which do so in a way which yields, on any given occasion, only a highly context-reflecting occurrent representation. When Smolensky claims (see above) that in his approach there are no symbols which figure both in mental processes and in mental representations, he may thus be taken as meaning that the idea of a symbol as both a bearer of some fixed content and a persistent inner item over which computational processes can be defined is not applicable to these models. Now we know why.

Strong Representational Change

Several of the themes I have been developing come together to yield the final property to be examined: the potential of connectionist approaches to model what I shall call Strong Representational Change. The notion of Strong Representational Change is best understood by contrast with (did you guess?) one of Weak Representational Change. An example of Weak Representational Change is found in Fodor's (1975, 1981) discussions of nativism and concept learning. Fodor suggests that concept learning is best understood as a rational process involving the generation and testing of hypotheses. 'Rational' here is contrasted with other ways in which our conceptual repertoire might be affected by experience, such as "being hit on the head" or "having your cortex surgically rewired" (Fodor 1981, p. 275). Fodor does not say in more positive terms what makes a process rational, but it seems safe to assume that the idea is that in rational concept learning the perceived *contents* of the training data are the cause of the acquisition of a grasp of the new concept, as against other (nonrational) routes which bypass the training data (such as being hit on the head) or which depend on it in some weaker way (e.g., as soon as you hear anything at all, you find the concept 'mother' has been triggered in your mind—here, the content was not given in the training data; it merely required some nudge from the environment to bring it into play). Fodor's key claim is that the only model we have of a rational process of concept learning is one in which we use evidence given in training cases to assess various internally constructed hypotheses concerning the content of some new concept. For example, if you have to learn the meaning of 'FLURG', you construct a hypothesis of the form "Something is an instance of 'FLURG' if and only if P," where P is filled in in some way suggested by your experiences to date. Then you check your hypothesis by seeing if future cases fit it. Once you have found a way of unpacking P which fits all the cases you are encountering, you have completed the process of rational content assignment. In short: "concept learning involves . . . the formulation and confirmation of hypotheses about the identity of the concept being learned." (Fodor 1981, p. 267) But the sense in which such a model is properly termed 'weak' is now manifest. As Fodor (1981, p. 269) puts it:

> On this view, learning the concept FLURG is learning that a certain hypothesis is true; viz. the hypothesis that the concept FLURG is the concept of something that is green or square. But learning that the hypothesis is true is in turn said to be a matter of entertaining that hypothesis and comparing it with the data. But that hypothesis itself *contains* the concept GREEN OR SQUARE. Now, surely, if a concept is available to you for hypothesis formation, then you *have* that concept. And if you have to have a concept in order to perform the concept-learning task, then what goes on in the concept-learning task cannot be the learning of that concept. So the concept-learning task is not a task in which concepts are learned.

Concept learning thus understood involves only *weak* representational change, insofar as it does not result in any increase in the *representational power* of the system. To learn the "new" concept at all, on the generate-and-test model, you must already possess the representational resources to express its content. The potential repertoire of the system is fixed by the repertoire available for expressing hypotheses. Because (for obvious reasons) this cannot itself have been acquired by the generate-and-test method, Fodor concludes that it must be innate. More on this in a moment. First, we must guard against an all-too-easy misreading of Fodor's claim.

Fodor's image of rational representational change is weak insofar as it depicts the products of such change as necessarily falling within the expressive scope of the original representational base. It is weak, I repeat, insofar as it depicts rational representational change as limited by a *preceding* and *representational* base. Notice how this goes beyond the mere fact that the evolution of a system is constrained by its original potential. The latter is trivially true. As Christiansen and Chater (1992, p. 245) note, "potential of *any* sort cannot increase . . . for a system to learn or do anything, it must necessarily have had the potential to learn or do it in the first place." But this is not Fodor's point. The point is that concept learning (according to Fodor) can only consist in the triggering of innate representational atoms or the deployment of such atoms in generate-and-test style learning. Either way, the basic representational power of the system remains unaltered—its representational scope is fixed by the innate representational repertoire. This fixing of expressive scope in virtue of an innate representational repertoire is the distinctive and nontrivial feature of Fodor's story.

What goes into this innate repertoire is not our immediate concern. But it is just worth mentioning that in Fodor's view (1981, pp. 279–292) a great many of the concepts in our repertoire (not just basic sensory concepts such as 'red' and 'square', but almost *all* our concepts, including highly abstract ones) are among the brute representational *atoms* that require triggering by a modicum of timely experience but are not learned by any rational process. It is in this sense that most concepts are said by Fodor to be *unstructured*. (By contrast, I shall later depict concepts as highly structured (though transitory and fluid) information complexes.)

Fodor thus depicts all rational processes of representational change as (i) involving an innate representational base, (ii) exploiting the training environment only as either a source of triggering experiences (for the base) or a source and a test bed for conjectures (for the rest), and hence (iii) being fundamentally conservative (as representational power never really increases). Connectionist approaches invite us, I believe, to think again. By shifting much more weight onto the training environment, the connectionist is able to treat learning as essentially rational (according to our earlier definition) yet as capable of genuinely transforming the representational capacities of the system. To see how, let us briefly contrast the connectionist stories concerning (i) and (ii) above.

Regarding the putative innate representational base, we should note first that many connectionist models acquire domain knowledge without the benefit of any such resource. These are the models which begin with a set of random connection weights and learn about a domain "from scratch." Famous examples include NETtalk (Sejnowski and Rosenberg 1986) and the past-tense learning network (Rumelhart and McClelland 1986b). It is true that the initial choices of architecture, number of units and layers, etc. amount to the building in of a little knowledge (more of this in the next chapter) but this is not at all akin to the provision of an innate base of atomic symbols ready for combination into hypotheses to be tested against the evidence. The only real candidate for such a complex symbolic base is not the overall architecture but the connection weights. And there is a *sense* (though not, as we will see, a very interesting one) in which the weights do participate in a generate-and-test procedure: ". . . the hypotheses are embedded in the weights of the network, the test is the measure of network performance (such as sum-squared error), and the procedure for generating new hypotheses, given the successes or failures of past hypotheses, is given by the learning algorithm" (Christiansen and Chater 1992, p. 244). The point, however, is that the initial weights (assuming a random starting point) are not usefully seen as constituting a set of *representational elements* (ask yourself what such weights represent!) and, *a fortiori*, the subsequent learning of the network is not usefully understood as constrained by the representational limitations of an initial "language." Christiansen and Chater (p. 245) miss this and depict such networks as falling under the umbrella of Fodor's argument—but such is the case only if one opts for the trivial reading of Fodor's nativist claim (viz., that a system cannot exceed its original potential), which we rejected above. Fodor's real position is that representational potential is determined by an innate *representational* base—and, thus understood, random-start connectionist models constitute a notable exception to the claim.

The random-start case is a useful existence proof of the ability of some systems to engage in something like rational concept acquisition without an innate representational base. Such systems do not acquire knowledge by accident (e.g. a bang on the head), by simple maturation, or by external rewiring. Instead, what they learn is a consequence of the *contents* of the training cases. The process is thus a rational one in the sense in which I (and, I think, Fodor) use the term.

The existence proof is useful, but we should not be carried away into thinking that connectionism must buy into a *tabula rasa* model of knowledge acquisition. Such a model would be implausible on well-documented empirical grounds (Baillargeon 1987; Spelke 1991;

Johnson and Morton 1991; Leslie 1984). The precise way in which knowledge about (e.g.) physics, faces, and language may be built in remains an open question, but one obvious option is for evolution to preset some or all of the weights so as to embody some initial domain knowledge.[7] Even so, we no longer need hold that this knowledge limits future learning in anything like the way Fodor imagines, for it does not constitute a set of representational resources in terms of which any target knowledge must already be expressible if it is ever to be acquired. If some target knowledge lies outside the expressive repertoire of the inbuilt representations, it may still be acquired (if the system's basic resources are adequate and local minima are avoided) in the same way as it would be in the random-start case. Correlatively, if some of the inbuilt knowledge turned out to be false or misleading in the domain as evidenced by later training data, the system can undo the preset weightings and try again[8] (Rumelhart and McClelland 1986a, p. 141). Finally, the distributed nature of the method of encoding knowledge (i.e., encoding it across a whole set of weights) allows us to make sense of *partial innate knowledge*—viz., a system might encode "90% or 10% of any innate idea" (Bates and Elman 1992, p. 17). This ability to model degrees of innateness of ideas is hailed by Bates and Elman as potentially constituting "connectionism's greatest contribution to developmental cognitive neuroscience" (ibid.). Whether this is so or not, it certainly does seem to be the case that connectionist approaches offer a rich and varied apparatus for dealing with questions of innate knowledge and the developmental trajectory of learning (see chapters 6–9), and that they do so without the implausible and overly constraining hypothesis of an innate symbol system whose representational resources are fixed once and for all.

The second point of contrast concerns the environment and the training data, the effects of which are severely downplayed in Fodor's approach. The various inputs to the system may trigger dormant innate representations, or they may contribute to the choice of a hypothesis concerning target meanings, or they may be used to test such hypotheses. In all cases, however, the training data subserve a full-fledged, preexisting, unchanging representational economy—an economy which, from the outset, possesses its complete representational repertoire *and* is organized as a systematic symbol system. In connectionist approaches, the training environment plays a much greater role. Such approaches do not build systematicity in as a basic feature of their processing, for they do not exploit concatenative symbol systems. Instead (as I shall argue at length in chapter 7), systematicity—if such models are to show it at all—must emerge as a *product* of the *knowledge* acquired by the system as a result of its training. The training environment, for good or ill, is a major determinant of both the knowledge and the processing profile acquired by a network. For example, many classical models depict the use of rule systems in various linguistic tasks (e.g., pronunciation and past-tense formation) as dependent on a distinct processing resource which is innately given (though it does not emerge until a certain point in the maturational cycle). Connectionist approaches, by contrast, can display the emergence of a rule system as a product of training in a single network. (For a nice discussion, see Marchman 1992.) A further interesting prospect is that much of what is currently attributed to *innate* modular structure in the brain might in fact be achieved by a process of highly input-sensitive learning which results in degrees of *functional modularity*—that is, sets of units "which are powerfully interconnected among themselves and relatively weakly connected to units outside the set" (Rumelhart and McClelland 1986a, p. 141). The effects of localized damage to the hardware (the brain) might, as a result, vary according to variation in the "modularizing" learning experiences of the individual. And damage to the same area at different times during the course of learning might produce quite different effects (Marchman 1992; Bates and Elman 1992).

More crucial than all this, however, is the way continued training can bring about qualitative changes in the performance of a network. I have already touched on one example of this: the case in which a single connectionist mechanism which begins as a rote memorizer of past tenses can, as a result of continued training, begin quite suddenly to exhibit knowledge of the rule for the regular past tense[9] (while still retaining knowledge of irregular cases, subject to an initial U-curve effect—see Plunkett and Marchman 1991). The suddenness of the transition is direct evidence of the ability of these systems to model *stages* in cognitive development; thus, we read that "performance in the network reveals a *critical mass* effect. . . . That is to say, the transition from a state of rote representation to a state of systematic representation [involves] . . . a sudden transition between the two modes of representation when the training set reaches a given critical size." (Plunkett and Sinha 1991, pp. 30–31) In a similar vein, Bates and Elman (1992, p. 15) note that "in trying to achieve stability across a large number of superimposed, distributed patterns [a] network may hit on a solution that was 'hidden' in bits and pieces of the data; the solution may be transformed and generalized across the system as a whole, resulting in what must be viewed as a qualitative shift."

Fully worked out examples of such qualitative shifts will be presented below. For now, we need only note that the *root* of this ability (the ability, as I shall put it, to develop new significant virtual machines) lies in the deep interpenetration of knowledge and processing characteristics which is fundamental to connectionist approaches. Processing in these systems involves the use of connection weights to create (or re-create) patterns of activation yielding desired outputs. But these weights just *are* the network's store of knowledge, and new knowledge has to be stored superpositionally (i.e., by amending existing weights). Changes in the knowledge base and in the processing characteristics thus go hand in hand. As McClelland, Rumelhart, and Hinton (1986, p. 32) put it: "The representation of the knowledge is set up in such a way that the knowledge necessarily influences the course of processing. Using knowledge in processing is no longer a matter of finding the relevant information in memory and bringing it to bear: it is part and parcel of the processing itself."

Critical-mass effects are thus to be expected, for we are dealing with highly data-driven systems whose processing profiles are an immediate consequence of their state of superposed stored knowledge. A few extra items of data can restructure the output profile completely. The great promise of connectionism in this respect is thus to offer a detailed understanding of how the combination of this distinctive mode of processing and storage and the stream of environmental inputs can yield qualitative increments in performance of the kind which have so long been at the heart of psychological theories of cognitive development.

On Text and Process

The radical connectionist vision is pretty much the antithesis of Fodor's vision. Fodor depicts the mind as a static representational storehouse, subserved by innate modules and evincing qualitative representational change only if it occurs as part of a fixed maturational program. Connectionist approaches allow for quite subtle types of innate knowledge but do not restrict learning to manipulations of a fixed representational base. They allow us to explore modularization as a knowledge-driven process, and they encourage the investigation of strong representational change as a product of genuine learning. What Fodor sees as the starting point of our mental life (a store of context-free, recombinable representational atoms) the connectionist sees as (at best) the endpoint of a sustained developmental process.[10] Each approach has its attendant attractions and problems, but the unique selling point of the connectionist vision has at last fully emerged. It is the ability to build representational fluidity and representational change into the heart of its approach to cognitive modeling. Where the classicist thinks of mind as essentially *text*, the connectionist thinks of it as highly environment-coupled *process*. To complete this conceptual shift, the connectionist needs to find new ways of analyzing and understanding models. Unlike the classicist, the connectionist cannot simply inspect the contents of language-like data structures. It is to this problem, and its various solutions, that we now turn.

Chapter 3

What Networks Know

The Tank and the Sun

Once upon a time, a connectionist network was trained to detect the presence of tanks in photographs.[1] It was able, after training on a corpus of tank and nontank photographs, to respond affirmatively to the presence of tanks even in difficult cases (such as where a tank was partially occluded by a bush). It even generalized its success so as to deal nicely with a batch of photos which had been held back from the training data. It seemed, then, to have learned about tank shapes. To test this, the Stanford Research Institute (where the net was developed) then tried it on a whole new batch of photos. The result was complete failure. What had gone wrong? After some investigation it transpired that the net, in learning to categorize the original set of photos, had become sensitive not to tank shape at all but to the difference in light and density between the bush-only photos and the photos involving tanks—a predictor contributed to by the unfortunate fact that all the photos involving tanks had been taken in the morning, with the sun high in the sky, and all the nontank photos had been snapped in the afternoon.

The moral: Don't be too quick to assume that a network, even an apparently successful one, has actually fixed on the features on which you wanted it to fix. An up-and-running network is an opaque beast which requires further analysis if we are to understand what it is actually doing and why. One purpose of this chapter is to introduce several means of performing such *post hoc* analyses and to contrast the kinds of information they provide. This is an essential preliminary to our use of such techniques, in subsequent chapters, to try to understand the nature and the limits of the kinds of knowledge acquired by specific networks.

But the discussion has more than pedagogic interest, and for two reasons. First, there is a difficult issue concerning the ability of connectionist approaches to actually explain (as opposed to merely reproducing) cognitive phenomena. This issue, it is argued, is intimately linked to the idea of achieving a Marr level 1, or competence-theoretic (see below), understanding of a domain. Second, the various kinds of *post hoc* analysis continue to illuminate the sense in which connectionist approaches are process driven, for in essence the analyses must take various kinds of dynamic network properties and transform them into static symbolic descriptions. This is not an undiluted blessing, as it can lead us to hallucinate familiar, manipulable symbolic items where none exist.

Levels of Explanation

Explanation, it seems, is a many-leveled thing. A single phenomenon may be subsumed under a panoply of increasingly general explanatory schemas. On the swings and roundabouts of explanation, we trade the detailed descriptive and explanatory power of lower levels for a satisfying width of application at higher levels. And at each such level there are virtues and vices; some explanations may be available only at a certain level; but individual cases thus subsumed may vary in ways explicable only by descending the ladder of explanatory generality.

For example, the Darwinian (or neo-Darwinian) theory of natural selection is pitched at a very high level of generality. It pictures some very general circumstances under which "blind" selection can yield apparently teleological (or purposeful) evolutionary change. What is required for this miracle to occur is differential reproduction according to fitness and some mechanism of transmission of characteristics to progeny. This is an extremely general and potent idea. The virtue of this top-level explanation, then, lies in its covering an open-ended set of cases in which very different actual mechanisms (e.g., of transmission) may be involved. In this way it defines an *equivalence class* of mechanisms—that is, a set of mechanisms which may be disparate in many ways but which are united by their ability to satisfy the Darwinian demands.

The natural accompaniment to virtue is, of course, vice, and the vice of the general Darwinian account is readily apparent. We don't yet know, in any given case, *how* the Darwinian demands are satisfied. That is to say, we don't yet have the foggiest idea of the actual mechanism of heritability and transmission in any given case. Moreover, there may well be facts about some specific class of cases (for example, recessive characteristics in Mendel's peas) which are not predicted by the general Darwinian theory. This gives us still further reason to seek a more specific and detailed account.

Mendelian genetics offers just such an account. It posits a class of theoretical entities (genes, as they are now called) controlling each trait, and it describes the way such entities must combine to explain various observed facts concerning evolution in successive generations of pea plants. The specification includes, for example, the idea of pairs of genes (genotypes) in which one gene may be dominant, thus explaining the facts about recessive characteristics. (For an accessible account of evolutionary theory and Mendelian genetics, see Ridley 1985.)

Between any two levels (Darwinian and Mendelian genetics, for example) there will almost certainly be other, theoretically significant levels. Thus, Mendelian inheritance is in fact an instance of a more general mechanism called Weismannist inheritance (Ridley 1985, p. 23). But Weismannist inheritance is still less general than Darwinian inheritance. Weismannism carves off a theoretically unified subset of general Darwinian cases, and Mendelism carves off a theoretically unified subset of Weismannism. At each stage the equivalence class is strategically redefined to exclude a number of previous members. We can visualize this as a gradual shrinking of the size of the equivalence class (although this may not be strictly true, since each new case has a possible infinity of members and so they are, in a trivial sense, identical in size).

Mendelian genetics provides an interesting case for one further reason. It was originally conceived as neatly specifying the details of lower-level DNA-based inheritance (that is, of the hardware realization of an inheritance mechanism). As Dennett (1988b, p. 385) puts it, Mendelian genes were seen as specifying "the language of inheritance, straightforwardly realized in hunks of DNA." This corresponds to what I shall term the *classicist vision* of the relation between a certain level of abstract theorizing in cognitive science (competence theorizing) and actual processing strategies.

But in fact, according to Dennett (1988b, p. 385), "there are theoretically important mismatches between the language of 'bean-bag genetics' and the molecular and developmental details—mismatches serious enough to suggest that, all things considered, there don't turn out to be genes (classically understood) at all." This looks like (and is regarded by Dennett as) an analogue of the connectionist's view of the fate of the constructs of a classical competence theory.

Be that as it may, the point for now is simply that, beneath the level of Mendelian genetics, there is some further level of physical implementation (with who knows what in between), and this completes our descent down the ladder of explanatory generality. We start at the top level (level 1) with the general Darwinian theory defining a large and varied equivalence class of instantiating mechanisms. We descend to a more detailed specification of a subclass of mechanisms (Mendelian theory) and thence, one way or another, to the details of the implementation of those mechanisms in DNA. The effect is a kind of triangulation of the actual details of actual earth animals' inheritance from much broader explanatory principles governing whole sets of possible worlds.

Explanation in cognitive science, as conceptualized by Marr, by Chomsky, and by Newell and Simon, has a similar multi-layer structure. For a given task or class of tasks (vision, parsing, etc.) there will be a top-level story which comprises "an abstract formulation of *what* is being computed and *why*," a lower-level one which specifies a particular algorithm for carrying out the computation, and (still lower) an account of how that algorithm is to be realized by physical hardware. To illustrate this, Marr (1977, p. 129) gives the example of Fourier analysis. At the top level we have the general idea of a Fourier analysis. This can be realized by several different algorithms, and each algorithm in turn can be implemented in many different kinds of hardware organization.

There is an important gap between the "official" account of the top level (level 1, as Marr calls it) and the actual practice of giving "level 1" theories. Although the official line is that a level-1 account specifies only the what and the why of a computation, this specification can be progressively refined so as to define a more informative (i.e., more restrictive) equivalence class. This more refined version of level-1 theorizing (which yet falls short of a full algorithmic account) has been persuasively depicted by Peacocke (1986) under the title of level 1.5.

The contrast Peacocke highlights is between an equivalence class generated by defining a function *in extension* (i.e., by its results—the *what*, in Marr's terms) and a more restrictive (and informative) equivalence class generated by specifying the *body of* information upon which an algorithm draws. Thus, to adapt one of Peacocke's own examples, suppose the goal of a computation is to compute depth D and physical size P from retinal size R. And suppose, in addition, that this computation is to occur inside a restricted universe of values of D, P, and R. Specifying the function in extension merely tells us that, whenever the system is given some D and some P as input, it should yield some specified R as output. One way of doing this is to store the set of legal values of R for every combination of values of D and P—a simple lookup table. A second way is to process data in accordance with the equation $P = D \times R$. In saying that the system draws on the information that $P = D \times R$, we are, as Peacocke insists, doing more than specifying a function in extension. The lookup table does not draw on that information, yet it falls within the equivalence class generated by the function in extension specification. But we are doing less than specifying a particular algorithm, since there will be many ways of computing the equation in question (e.g., using different algorithms for multiplication).

It is this grain of analysis (what Peacocke calls level 1.5) that I will have in mind when I speak, in the remainder of this chapter, of a competence theory. This seems to accord at least with the practice of Chomsky, who coined the term *competence theory* to describe the pitch of his own distinctive investigations into the structure of linguistic knowledge. And it may well accord with Marr's actual practice at "level 1" (though not with the official dogma).

A Chomskian linguistic competence theory does far more than specify a function in extension. It seeks to answer (at a level of abstraction from the physical mechanisms of the brain and from specific algorithms) the question "What constitutes knowledge of language?" In so doing it seeks a "framework of principles and elements common to attainable human languages" (Chomsky 1986, p. 3). And (in its most recent incarnation) it characterizes that framework as a quite specific "system of principles associated with certain parameters of variation and a markedness system with several components of its own" (ibid., p. 221). It does not matter, for the purposes of this chapter, just what principles and parameters Chomsky actually suggests. We should merely note that, if a competence theory is as definite and structured as a Chomskian model (and it's his term, after all), then it is more like a level-1.5 analysis than a simple level-1 account, for it describes, at a certain level of abstraction, the structure of a form of processing (by specifying the information drawn on by the processes), and hence it helps "guide the search for mechanisms" (ibid.). In short, it is more like Mendelian genetics than General Darwinism. Rather than being merely descriptive of a class of results, it is meant also to be suggestive of the processing structure of a class of mechanisms that includes human beings.

The Classical Cascade

A "suggestive" competence theory, then, leads a double life: It specifies the function to be computed *and* it specifies the body of knowledge or information used by some class of algorithms. In classical cognitive science these two roles can easily be discharged simultaneously, for the competence theory is just an articulated set of rules and principles defined over symbolic data structures. Since classical cognitive science relies on a symbol-processing architecture, it is natural (at level 2) to represent the data structures (e.g., structural descriptions of sentences) directly and then carry out the processing by the explicit *or* tacit representation of the rules and principles defined (in the competence theory) to operate on those structures. Thus, given a structural description of an inflected verb as comprising a stem and an ending, the classicist can go on to define a level-2 computational process to take the stem and add *-ed* to form the past tense (or whatever). The classicist, then, is (by virtue of using a symbol-processing architecture to implement level-2 algorithms) uniquely well placed to preserve a very close relation between a competence theory and its level-2 implementations. Indeed, it begins to seem as if that close relation is what *constitutes* a classical approach. Thus, Dennett (1987, p. 227) visualizes the classicist dream as involving a "triumphant cascade through Marr's three levels." This classicist vision is clearly exemplified in Syntactic Image–style models in which the objects of computation are syntactically structured representations and the computational processes consist of logico-manipulative operations defined to apply to such items in virtue of their structure. (See, e.g., Fodor and Pylyshyn 1988, pp. 12–13.)

The computational processes, in any such case, can be described by transition or derivation rules defined over syntactically structured representations. For example:

If (A and B) then (A).

If (A and B) then (B).

If (stem + ending) then (stem + -ed).

The items in parentheses are structural descriptions which will pick out open-ended classes of classical representations. The if-then specifies the operation. But recall that the classicist, under the terms of the act, is *not* committed to the systems *explicitly* representing the if-then clause. All that need be explicit (see chapter 1) is the structured description upon which it operates. Thus, a machine could be hardwired so as to take expressions of the form

(A and B)

and transform them into the expression

(A) and (B).

The derivation rules may thus be implicit, or *tacit*, but the data structures must be explicit. On this matter, Fodor and Pylyshyn (1988, p. 61) are rightly insistent: "Classical machines can be *rule implicit* with respect to their programs. . . . What *does* need to be explicit in a classical machine is not its program but the symbols that it writes on its tapes (or stores in its registers). These, however, correspond not to the machine's rules of state transition but to its data structures." As an example, they point out that the grammar posited by a linguistic theory need not be explicitly represented in a classical machine, but the *structural descriptions of sentences* over which the grammar is defined (in terms of verb stems, subclauses, etc.) must be. A successful "classical cascade" from a linguistic competence theory to a level-2 processing story can thus tolerate having the rules of the grammar built into the machine. Thus, the attempts to characterize the classicist/connectionist contrast solely by reference to the explicitness or the nonexplicitness of rules are shown to be in error.

Damming the Classical Cascade

Connectionist models of the superpositional, distributed stripe, characterized in chapter 2, depart from the classical vision in two related ways. First, they make do without stable computational objects ("symbols") which stand (in a positive, context-free way) for the objects and features fixed on by the competence theory. Second, they do not operate by the application of (tacit or explicit) rules defined to apply to structures of such objects—how could they, given that no such objects exist? Instead of seeing a good competence-theoretic story as a guide to the true processing story concerned, the connectionist takes what I shall call an *externalist* attitude toward such stories, seeing them as descriptive of what gets done (that is, of the *abilities* of the system) but resisting the temptation to identify the symbolic structures mentioned in the competence theory with the data objects over which an internal-processing story is to be defined.

Numerous example cases are to be found in the literature on connectionism. Early examples include the Ohm's Law network (Smolensky 1988), in which a network's problem-solving behavior is nicely tracked by a competence-theoretic story which posits symbolic representations of features such as voltage, current, and resistance and which ascribes to the network knowledge (which could be tacit or explicit) of rules defined over such features (for example, Ohm's Law: Voltage = Current × Resistance). Despite the success (*qua* external description) of such a characterization of what the network knows, Smolensky shows that the net does not exploit *general* representations of voltage, etc. Instead, it commands a myriad of more microscopic representations which capture qualitative relations among states of the circuit (e.g., 'increased value at point X yields decrease at point Y'). The combined action of these microscopic knowledge items roughly mimics the effects of explicitly representing voltage, current, and resistance and the relations among them. Knowledge of Ohm's

Law is thus distributed across the multiple microscopic knowledge items. Similarly, the Rooms network described by Rumelhart, Smolensky, McClelland, and Hinton (1986) behaves as if it commands discrete schemas for various prototypical rooms; in fact, however, it encodes a multiplicity of micro-representations of co-occurrence of room features (such as cooker and sink), and the combined action of these yields the schema-like overall behavior. What is critical in all these cases is that, because the network's *actual* knowledge representation exhibits a finer-grained and less prearticulated structure than anything mentioned in the competence theory, the net can be very flexible in dealing with the domain. Such networks can, as Smolensky (1988) stresses, respond sensibly when faced with situations (for example, a mixed bathroom-bedroom scenario, or an illegal combination of values of current and voltage at certain locations) which fall outside the scope of the coarser rule and symbol descriptions which nonetheless capture central subsets of the net's behaviors.

In a revealing note, Smolensky (1988, p. 246) casts the point in terms highly appropriate to the present discussion. The characterization of competence as a set of derivation rules applied to a symbol system can be viewed, as Smolensky suggests, as providing a *grammar* for generating the high-harmony (maximal-soft-constraint-satisfaction) states of a system. Thus, a competence theory emerges as a body of laws which serve to pick out the states into which the system will settle under certain ideal conditions. This, then, is the full externalist attitude toward a competence theory: A competence theory is a kind of grammar which fixes on certain stable states of the system. As such, it is, in a central range of cases, descriptively adequate. But it need not reveal what Smolensky calls the *dynamics*—that is, the actual processing strategies of the system. This observation is echoed in a recent discussion of a network for visual word recognition and pronunciation in which Seidenberg (1989, p. 67) comments that "the fact that it is easier to describe the model in terms of rules or rule-like behavior should not mask the fact that the explanation for the observed empirical phenomena derives from an understanding of how the computation is actually performed. How the knowledge of spelling-sound correspondence is actually encoded and used is critical, not the fact that it is easier to summarize what the model does in language that abstracts away from those characteristics."

A further issue here turns on the context sensitivity of connectionist representation (recall chapter 2 above). Even when it is correct, in a sense (see the next section), to describe a network as representing some conceptual-level item (like, notoriously, coffee), it is still not the case that the system commands a stable, context-free symbol which *means* coffee and is the object of inner manipulative processes. Instead, different coalitions of hidden units (typically) will represent coffee according to local context. By replacing the conceptual-level symbol 'coffee' with a shifting coalition of microfeatures (the so-called dimension shift), such systems deprive themselves of the structured mental representations which are deployed in a classical competence theory and in a classical symbol-processing (level-2) account. Likewise, there is no stable representational entity in the simple Ohm's Law network which stands for resistance (just as in the infamous past-tense network there is no stable, recurrent entity which stands for 'verb stem' (see Rumelhart and McClelland 1986b; Pinker and Prince 1988; Clark 1989a).

To sum up: Classical competence theories seem to capture (at best) some central patterns in the processing of distributed, superpositional networks. However, it would be a mistake to view such networks as actually encoding (tacitly or otherwise) the rules enshrined in the competence theory. Typically, they do not do so, since they do not compute by manipulating symbols which stand for the items mentioned in the competence theory. And even in those cases where, in some sense, a representation of the item in question exists, it will not take the form of a context-free symbol; rather, it will be an abstraction across a variety of different (but related) concrete states (such as hidden-unit patterns).[2]

Explanatory Inversion in Connectionist Cognitive Science

But now a danger looms. The connectionist has just denied that any top-level classical competence theory can be richly suggestive of the level-2 processing strategies of the connectionist network which carries out a given cognitive task. This now looks to be a doubly embarrassing loss, for the classical competence theory performed two tasks: It figured in a picture of the proper form of investigations in cognitive science (i.e., delineate the task at the level of competence theorizing and then write algorithms to carry it out), and it figured in a picture of what *explanation* in cognitive science involved. Just having a working program was not, in itself, to be regarded as having an explanation of how we perform a given cognitive task. Rather, we wanted some high-level understanding of what constraints the program was meeting and why they had to be met—an understanding naturally provided by giving the top level competence theory which a given *class* of programs could be seen to implement. The unavailability of the classical competence theory thus threatens to render connectionist models *nonexplanatory* in a very deep sense, and it leaves the actual *methodology* of connectionist investigations obscure.

As a brief illustration of the problem, consider an example of Good Old-Fashioned Explanation in Cognitive Science (GOFEICS—apologies to John Haugeland). Take Naive Physics, the attempt to discover the knowledge which enables a mobile, embodied being to negotiate its way around a complex physical universe. A well-known instance of this general project is Hayes' (1985) work on the naive physics of liquids, which involved trying to compile a "taxonomy of the possible states liquids can be in" and formulating a set of rules concerning movement, change, and liquid geometry. The final theory in this case included specifications of 15 states of liquid and 74 numbered rules or axioms written out in predicate calculus. This amounts to a detailed competence specification, which might eventually be given full algorithmic form. Indeed, Hayes is quite explicit about the high level of the investigative project, insisting that it is a mistake to seek a working program too soon. The explanatory strategy of naive physics is thus a paradigm example of the official classical methodology. First, seek a high-level competence theory involving symbolic representations and a set of state-transition rules. Then write algorithms implementing the competence theory, secure in the knowledge that you have a precise higher-level understanding of the requirements which the algorithms meet and hence a real grasp of why they are capable of carrying out the task in question. The connectionist lacks this security, not being able to proceed by formulating a detailed classical competence theory and then neatly implementing it on a classical symbol-processing architecture.

Hence the problem: How *should* the connectionist proceed, and what constitutes the higher-level understanding of the processing which one needs in order to claim to have really explained how a task is performed? What is needed, it seems, is some kind of connectionist analogue to the classical competence-theoretic level of explanation.

I believe that such an analogue exists. But it remains invisible until we perform a kind of Copernican revolution in our picture of explanation in cognitive science. The connectionist effectively inverts the usual temporal and methodological order of explanation, much as Copernicus inverted the usual astronomical model of his day. In connectionist theorizing, the high-level understanding will be made to revolve around a working program which has learned how to negotiate some cognitive terrain. This inverts the official classical ordering, in which the high-level understanding (competence theory) comes first and closely guides the search for algorithms. To make this clear, and to see how the connectionist's high-level theory will depart from the form of a classical competence theory, I propose first to take a look at a famous example: Sejnowski's NETtalk project.

NETtalk is a large, distributed connectionist model which aims to investigate part of the process of turning written input (words) into phonemic output (sounds or speech). The network architecture comprises a set of input units, which are stimulated by seven letters of text at a time; a set of hidden units; and a set of output units, which code for phonemes. The output is fed into a voice synthesizer, which produces the actual speech sounds.

The network began with a random distribution of hidden unit weights and connections (within chosen parameters); it had no "idea" of any rules of text-to-phoneme conversion. Its task was to learn, by repeated exposure to training instances, to negotiate its way around this particularly tricky cognitive domain (tricky because of irregularities, subregularities, and the context sensitivity of text-to-phoneme conversion). And learning proceeded in the standard way: by a backpropagation learning rule, which caused the system to minutely adjust its connection weights in a way which would tend toward the correct output. This procedure is repeated many thousands of times. As a result, the system slowly and audibly learns to pronounce English text, moving from babble to half-recognizable words and on to a highly creditable final performance. For a full account, see Rosenberg and Sejnowski 1987 and Sejnowski and Rosenberg 1986, 1987a, 1987b.

Consider now the methodology of the NETtalk project. It begins, to be sure, by invoking the results of some fairly rich prior analysis of the domain. This is reflected in the author's choice of input representation (for example, the choice of a seven-letter window, and a certain coding for letters and punctuation), in the choice of output representation (the coding for phonemes) and in the choice of hidden-unit architecture (e.g., the number of hidden units and the type of learning rule). These choices highlight the continued importance of some degree of prior task analysis in connectionist modeling. However, they are a far cry from any fully articulated competence theory of text-to-phoneme conversion. What is noticeably lacking is any set of special-purpose state-transition rules defined over the input and output representations. Instead, the system will be set the task of learning a set of weights capable of mediating the desired state transitions. For this reason I shall characterize the connectionist as beginning her investigations with a level-0.5 "task analysis," as opposed to a level-1 (or 1.5) competence theory. However, the level-0.5 specification, though less than a full-blown symbolic competence theory, may still embody a psychologically unrealistic amount of prior information, for when a person learns to perform a task he or she does not know, in advance, how many hidden units to allocate (too many and you form an uninformative "lookup tree," too few and you fail to deal with the data), or the best way to represent the solution. In this sense, the level-0.5 specification may be doing more of the problem-solving work than some connectionists would like to admit. For present purposes, however, the point is just that the level-0.5 model forms the basis upon which, courtesy of the powerful connectionist learning rules, the system comes to be able (after much training) to negotiate the targeted cognitive terrain. At this point, the connectionist has in hand a working system—a full-scale level-3 implementation.

If we were to stop there, we would have a useful toy but very little in the way of increased understanding of the phenomenon of text-to-phoneme conversion. Of course, the connectionist doesn't stop there. From the up-and-running level-3 implementation, she must now work backwards to a higher-level understanding of the task. This is Marr through the looking glass. How is this higher-level understanding to be obtained? There are a variety of strategies in use, and many more to be discovered. I shall mention just three.

First, there is simple *watching*, but at a microscopic level. Given a particular input, the connectionist can see the patterns of unit activity (in the hidden units) which result. (This, at any rate, will be the case if the network is simulated on a conventional machine which can keep a record of such activity.)

Second, there is *network pathology*. While it is obviously unethical to deliberately damage human brains to help us see what role subassemblies of cells play in various tasks, it seems far more acceptable to deliberately lesion artificial neural networks. (See, e.g., Patterson, Seidenberg, and McClelland 1989; Hinton and Shallice 1989; Bechtel and Abrahamson 1991, chapter 8.)

Third (and perhaps most significant), the connectionist can generate a picture of the way in which the system has learned to divide up the cognitive space it is trying to negotiate. This picture, given by techniques such as principal-components analysis and hierarchical cluster analysis, seems to me to offer the closest connectionist analogue to a high-level, competence-theoretic understanding.

Cluster analysis is an attempt to answer the question "What kinds of representation have become encoded in the network's hidden units?" This is a hard question, since the representations will in general be of somewhat complex, unobvious, dimension-shifted features. To see how cluster analysis works, consider the task of the network to be that of setting the weights of hidden units in a way which will enable it to perform a kind of set partitioning. The goal is for the hidden units to respond in distinctive ways when, and only when, the input is such as to deserve a distinctive output. Thus, in text-to-phoneme conversion we want the hidden units to perform very differently when given 'the' as input than they would if given 'sail' as input, but we want them to perform identically if given 'sail' and 'sale' as inputs. So the hidden units' task is to partition a space (defined by the number of such units and their possible levels of activation) in a way which is geared to the job at hand. A very simple system, such as the rock/mine network described in Churchland 1989, may need only to partition the space defined by its hidden units into two major subvolumes: one distinctive pattern for inputs signifying mines and one for those signifying rocks. The complexities of text-phoneme conversion being what they are, NETtalk must partition its hidden-unit space more subtly (in fact, there must be a distinctive pattern for each of the 79 possible letter-to-phoneme pairings). Cluster analysis, as carried out by Rosenberg and Sejnowski (1987), in effect constructs a hierarchy of partitions on top of this base level of 79 distinctive stable patterns of hidden-unit activation. The hierarchy is constructed by taking each of the 79 patterns and pairing it with its closest neighbor—that is, with the pattern which has the most in common with it. These pairings act as the building blocks for the next stage of analysis, in which an average activation profile (between the members of the original pair) is calculated and paired with *its* nearest neighbor drawn from the pool of secondary figures generated by averaging each of the original pairs. The process is repeated until the final pair is generated. This represents the grossest division of the hidden-unit space which the network learned—a division which in the case of NETtalk turned out to correspond to the division between vowels and consonants (see figure 3.1).

Cluster analysis thus provides a kind of picture of the shape of the space of the possible hidden-unit activations which power the network's performance. By reflecting on the various dimensions of this space (i.e., the various clusterings), the theorist can hope to obtain some insight into what the system is doing. It may, for example, turn out to be highly sensitive to some subregularity which had hitherto been unnoticed or considered unimportant.

As a second and less well-known example, consider Sanger's (1989) analysis of a simplified version of NETtalk called Micro-NETtalk. The general architecture of Micro-NETtalk, illustrated in figure 3.2, has 18 input units divided into two groups of nine. Each input unit represents a letter. The units in the first group of nine stand for letters in position 1 of a two-letter sequence; those in the second group of nine stand for letters in position 2. An input string consists of the activa-

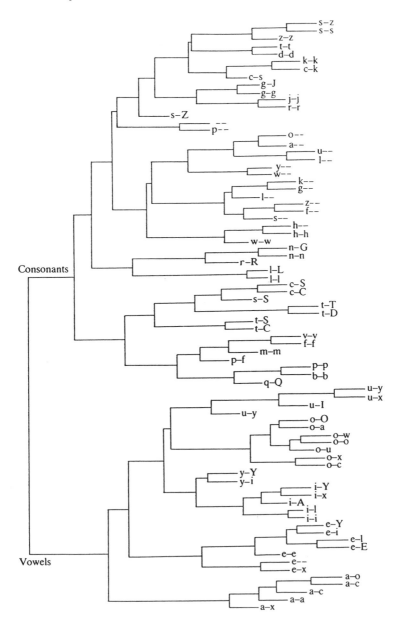

Figure 3.1
Hierarchy of partitions on hidden-unit vector space: results of a cluster analysis of
NETtalk. (From Churchland 1989, after Rosenberg and Sejnowski 1987; used with
permission.)

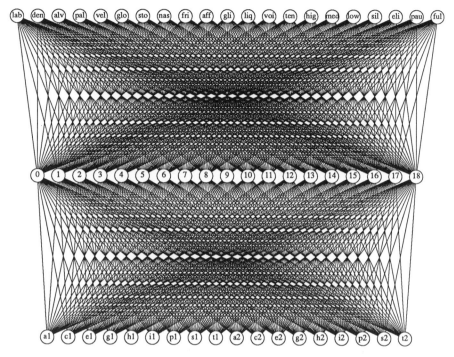

Figure 3.2
Micro-NETtalk architecture. (From Sanger 1989, with permission.)

tion of one letter from each group. There are 19 hidden units and 21 output units. The output units, which stand for phonetic features as displayed in table 3.1, are referred to by the abbreviations listed (e.g., lab for labial).

The goal of Micro-NETtalk (like that of its big sister) is to learn to negotiate the domain of English text-to-phoneme conversion. Patterns of output unit activation are systematically interpreted as coding for phonemes. Obviously Micro-NETtalk aims at competence in only a subset of the transformations characteristic of the entire domain. The network was trained by the backpropagation method, and a satisfying level of competence was achieved.

At this point the specter of explanatory inversion is manifest. We have a successful network, but no detailed understanding of why it works. Sanger therefore introduces a type of *post hoc* analysis which he terms *contribution analysis*. Contribution analysis reveals, for a given input, the extent to which a combination of a given hidden unit and the weighting on its link to the output units is implicated in the network's output behavior. That is, it measures the importance of a

Table 3.1
Phonetic features.

Unit	Feature	Feature type
lab	labial	
den	dental	
alv	alveolar	
pal	palatal	position in mouth
vel	velar	
glo	glottal	
sto	stop	
nas	nasal	
fri	fricative	
aff	affricative	
gli	glide	phoneme type
liq	liquid	
voi	voiced	
ten	tensed	
hig	high	
med	medium	vowel frequency
low	low	
sil	silent	
eli	elide	
pau	pause	punctuation
ful	full stop	

combination of weighting and hidden unit to the network's output.[3] Each possible combination of input features, hidden unit, and output unit thus has an associated contribution measure. In Micro-NETtalk that comes to 21,945 contributions! Fortunately, a careful choice of statistical methods (in fact, a principal-components analysis) allows the extraction of the interesting data. These methods enabled Sanger to produce two types of data: the group of patterns of hidden units which contribute to the activation of specific output units and the group of patterns of output units to which a specific hidden unit contributes. The first grouping unveils the semantics of distributed hidden-unit patterns; the second unveils the local semantics of individual hidden units.

The results of the first analysis are shown in table 3.2. The output feature 'med' was seen to be activated principally by the hidden units 9, 13, and 11. In general, it seems that Micro-NETtalk learned *distributed* representations at the hidden-unit layer; that is to say, it learned to represent single output features by the activity of multiple hidden units. Notice also that in one or two cases a single pattern of hidden units is associated with two output features. Thus, 'glo' and 'gli' are

Table 3.2
Hidden-unit patterns (19 hidden units). (From Sanger 1989, with
permission.)

Feature	Hidden units	Input presentations
lab	12 13	ei_i ea_i ee_i ec_E ep_E et_E eg_E pp_p eh_E it_I es_E ic_I ig_I ip_I pa_p ph_f is_I pi_p pe_p
den	9	et_E ec_E eh_E eg_E ep_E es_E at_@ ap_@ ac_@ ag_@ as_@
alv	6	si_s st_s sa_s se_s sc_s sp_s ci_s ss_s ce_s ie_A ia_A ps_s
pal	7	ch_C sh_S ah_a
	7	sh_S ch_C ah_a
	6 15 11	se_s si_s
vel	0	gs_g gg_g gp_g ga_g ct_k cc_k gi_g ge_J ca_k cs_k
glo	8	hi_h ha_h
sto	16	pp_p gs_g ca_k pa_p gg_g cc_k gi_g gp_g cs_k ga_g pi_p pe_p ct_k
nas	2 0 13	ge_J
fri	18	si_s se_s sa_s st_s sp_s sc-s ss_s ps_s ci_s ce_s sh_S ph_f
aff	6 18 5 15	se_s si_s ci_s ce_s sp_s sc_s sh_S ss_s sa_s st_s
	0 7 2	gg_g gt_-gp_g gs_g gh_-
gli	8	hi_h ha_h
liq	0 3 2	cc_k gs_g gg_g cs_k gp_g ct_k ga_g gt_-gh_-gi_g ca_k
voi	2 0	gs_g gg_g gp_g ge_J ga_g gi_g
ten	15 10	ai_e ae_e ie_A ee_i ei_i ia_A ea_i ah_a
hig	12	it_I ic_I ig_I ip_I is_I ea_i ei_i ee_i
med	9 13 11	et_E ec_E eh_E ep_E eg_E es_E ai_e ae_e ia_A ie_A
low	10 11 9	at__@ ap_@ ac_@ ag_@ as_@ ah_a
sil	12 1	gh_-gt_-
	10	ae_e
	1	gh_-gt_-
eli	12 1	gh_-gt_-
	10	ae_e
	1	gh_-gt_-
pau	0 3 2	cc_k gs_g gg_g cs_k gp_g ct_k ga_g gt_-gh_-gi_g ca_k
ful	0 3 2	cc_k gs_g gg_g cs_k gp_g ct_k ga_g gt_-gh_-gi_g ca_k

both catered for by the same pattern (in this case, the single hidden unit 8) in the hidden units. Here the net has been quite canny and has noticed that the output units 'glo' and 'gli' are each active for just the same pair of inputs: 'hi__h' and 'ha__h'. It is thus safe to treat them identically.

In the results of the second analysis (table 3.3) we see evidence of what Sanger calls *orderliness* in the network's creation of patterns. Thus, hidden unit 0 is active for inputs resulting in the phonemes 'k', 'g', and 'J', while unit 8 handles the 'h' phoneme and so on. There is (as previously discovered by the cluster analysis of NETtalk) a robust separation between units handling vowels and units handling consonants, although some hidden units (e.g., 6) do both. Cases of the latter kind are explained by the resemblance of the targeted phonemes (in this case 's' and 'A') along some dimension (in this case both are alveolar phonemes).

Sanger (1989, pp. 127–131) goes on to show that contribution analysis can be used systematically to chart the effects of varying the number of hidden units and suggests that it could also be extended so as to *modify* networks by destroying units and weights whose contributions are zero, superfluous, or small.

Micro-NETtalk thus illustrates in some concrete detail the various ways in which a *post hoc* statistical analysis can help us understand the kinds of representation (both distributed and local) which enable a network to negotiate a given domain successfully. Such analyses, I claim, constitute the nearest connectionist analogue to a classical competence theory. Like a competence theory, they provide a level of understanding higher than (i.e., more general than) the algorithmic level. The "algorithmic" specification, for a connectionist, must be a specification of the network configuration, the unit rules, and the connection strengths. But there is a many-one mapping between such algorithmic specifications and, e.g., a particular cluster analysis. For example, a network which started out with a different random set of weights could, after training, exhibit the *same* partitioning profile (and hence could have an identical cluster analysis) but do so using a very different set of individual weights. Unlike a classical competence theory, however, the cluster analysis will typically not look like a set of state-transition rules defined over conceptual-level entities. Instead, it will be more like a kind of geometric picture of the shape of a piece of cognitive terrain. Those theorists who think that a high-level explanation must be like a set of sentences and rules may find this hard to adjust to.

This route to a kind of competence-theoretic understanding inverts the traditional strategy of classical cognitive science. The connection-

Table 3.3
Hidden-unit responsibilities (19 hidden units). (From Sanger 1989, with permission.)

Hidden unit	Features	Input presentations
0	vel	gp_g gg_g ga_g gs_g ct_k gi_g cc_k ca_k ge_J cs_k
	med	gt_- at_@ ac_@_@ ap_@ gh_- ag_@
1	med	ah_a ch_C sh_S gh_- gt_- at_@
	sil eli	gh_- gt_-
2	lab	gs_g gg_g gp_g gi_g ga_g ge_J
3	nas med ten	cc_k gp_g gg_g ca_k cs_k ga_g gs_g
4	voi	ct_k
5	fri alv	ss_s st_s sc_s si_s se_s sp_s sa_s ps_s ci_s ce_s
6	alv	si_s se_s sa_s st_s sp_s sc_s ci_s ce_s ss_s ie_A ia_A
7	sto vel den	si_s se_s sp_s ci_s sh_S ce_s sc_s ss_s
8	gli glo	hi_h ha_h
9	den	et_E ep_E ec_E es_E eg_E eh_E
10	sto	es_E as_@ ap_@ ag_@ ac_@ is_I at_@ ep_E eg_E ai_e ae_e ip_I ig_I ec_E ic_I ah_a ea_i eh_E ei_i ee_i ia_A ie_A et_E it_I ps_s
11	vel sto alv	at_@ ac_@ as_@ ag_@ ap_@ eh_E et_E ai_e ae_e ah_a ec_E gh_- es_E ph_f eg_E ep_E sh_S gt_-
12	lab vel	et_E ec_E eh_E eg_E ep_E es_E it_I ea_i ei_i ic_I pp_p ee_i ph_f ig_I ip_I is_I
13	fri low lab	ei_i ea_i ee_i ep_E et_E ec_E ec_E ip_I eg_E it_I ic_I pi_p ig_I pa_p pe_p eh_E es_E pp_p ia_A ie_A is_I ai_e ae_e
14	hig	ip_I it_I ic_I ig_I is_I
15	sto	se_s si_s sa_s ce_s
	ten	ee_i ei_i ae_e ai_e ea_i ie_A ia_A ah_a
16	sto	cs_k cc_k gs_g ca_k pp_p pi_p pa_p gg_g gp_g gi_g pe_p ga_g ct_k
17	lab	eh_E et_E ec_E ep_E eg_E
18	fri	se_s ps_s si_s sc_s ss_s st_s sp_s sa_s ce_s ph_f ci_s sh_S
bias	sto lab	ce_s ci_s sc_s ss_s sa_s se_s si_s sp_s st_s st_s ps_s sh_S ph_f

ist achieves a high-level understanding of a cognitive task by reflecting on, and tinkering with, a network which has *learned* to perform the task in question. Unlike the classical, Marr-inspired theorist, the connectionist does not begin with a well-worked-out (sentential, symbolic) competence theory and then give it algorithmic flesh. Instead, she begins at level 0.5, trains a network, and then seeks to grasp the high-level principles it has come to embody. This is a great boon for cognitive science, which has been dogged by the related evils of ad-hocery and sententialism. Forced to formulate competence theories as sets of rules defined over classical, symbolic data structures, theorists have plucked principles out of thin air to help organize their work. Connectionist methodology, by contrast, allows the task demands to trace themselves and thus suggest the shape of the space in a way uncontaminated by the demands of standard symbolic formulation. We thus avoid imposing the form of our conscious, sentential thought on our models of cognitive processing—an imposition which was generally as unsuccessful in practice as it was evolutionarily bizarre (see Clark 1989a, chapter 4).

Beyond Cluster Analysis

An interpreted *post hoc* analysis, I have suggested, provides an example of the sort of analogue to competence-theoretic storytelling which is needed to discharge connectionism's explanatory obligations. But such analogues, I shall now argue, must be treated with a certain degree of caution. There are two reasons for this:

(1) Such analyses typically transform dynamic processing characteristics of a network (such as its tendency to respond to groups of related inputs by generating similar patterns of hidden-unit activity) into static symbol structures (such as a tree with symbolically labeled nodes). But in so doing they lose information concerning the representational trajectories which link the various inner states, and they paper over differences between closely related activation vectors—differences which will nonetheless make a difference to future processing.
(2) Such analyses foster the illusion that the system has generated internal symbols which stand for the various items or features cited as (e.g.) cluster labels and which are thus potential objects of further computational activity.

In short, such analyses can make it seem as if a net knows less than it does (by losing information about net dynamics), and, conversely, they can make it look as if it knows more than it does (by fostering an illusion of fully manipulable symbols). The second issue is taken up at length in the next chapter. For the present, let us concentrate on the sense in which cluster-analysis approaches may actually underestimate what a network "knows."

The worry that cluster analysis suppresses important details of what a network "knows" can be brought out by asking why a network which succumbs to a symbolic cluster analysis is not *thereby* revealed as a mere units-and-weights implementation of a classical symbol-manipulating system. Part of the answer is that the "symbols" thus unearthed are abstractions over sets of much more highly structured distributed representations. As a result, the system's actual on-line representations interact (both with one another and with new inputs) in complex ways which depend on this distributed constituent structure. The large-scale patterns which succumb to semantic interpretation thus do not exhaust the semantic nuances encoded by the distributed representations. Such nuances will not be re-created in a system which defines its computational operations only over syntactic entities corresponding to the large-scale patterns. Thus, insofar as all the phenomena a cognitive psychologist cares about can be explained in terms of computational properties which can be displayed by a conventional symbolic program, the fact that that program is implemented as a neural network would be of no consequence. But if much of the interesting behavior depends crucially on the non-symbolically-specifiable fine-grained structure of particular vectors of weights, a symbolic model will offer at best a rough guide to some facets of the system's behavior. We may make sense of the success of such systems in part by seeking a symbolic understanding of the significance of large-scale patterns; however, insofar as a model which merely implemented that symbolic understanding would fail to exhibit all the fine-grained behavior we need, we may conclude that the network is not a mere implementation of such a model. This is true, in particular, of all networks which involve both distributed representations and a nonlinear evolution equation. The evolution equation is the law governing the interaction of the units in the network. Such an equation is linear if the units' activity is simply determined by the weighted sum of its inputs. In the linear case, it turns out (Smolensky 1986b, pp. 411–413) that the distributed representations could be replaced by local ones without making any difference to the normal behavior of the system. There is, as Smolensky (1986b, p. 411) puts it, "an exact isomorphism between the lower and high levels of description." In nonlinear systems (i.e., ones in which the evolution equation is more complex), this is not the case. In these systems (of which almost all interesting connectionist networks are examples), "flipping" the distributed representations into local ones would compromise the normal performance of the system.

Another way of illuminating the sense in which abstracting away from what Churchland (1989, p. 178) calls the "subconceptual combinatorial elements" suppresses useful explanatory information is to focus on the understanding of representational change. That angle is nicely pursued in Churchland's chapter 9, where it is argued that the theoretically fundamental level of description of networks must be pitched at the level of individual units and weights and not at the level of the partitions (i.e., boundaries) between groups of similar activation patterns revealed by cluster analysis.[4] The reason is this: "While differently weighted systems can embody the same partitions and thus display the same output performance on any given input, they will still *learn* quite differently in the face of a protracted sequence of new and problematic inputs. This is because the learning algorithm that drives the system to new points in weight-space does not care about the relatively global partitions that have been made in activation space. . . . The laws of cognitive evolution, therefore, do not operate primarily on the level of the partitions. . . ." (Churchland 1989, p. 77) The point is well taken. But it does not, I think, signal Cluster's Last Stand. Granted, if we wish (as we often will) to understand the evolution of a network *during learning*, we will need access to information which is lost in standard cluster analyses. For other purposes, however, we may need precisely the level of detail which the cluster analysis provides. In opting at times for a level of analysis which groups particular activation profiles into equivalence classes via cluster analysis, we naturally trade specificity for generality. Just as pure Darwinism leaves recessive characteristics unexplained but highlights general principles covering a class of evolutionary mechanisms, so cluster analysis leaves details of cognitive evolution unexplained but highlights the gross sensitivity which enables a class of networks to negotiate a given cognitive terrain successfully. Such high-level understandings seem essential if connectionism is to be deeply explanatory of cognitive performance.

Moreover, it is increasingly clear that the understanding of connectionist networks (on which their role as cognitive models surely depends) is going to require a multiplicity of different kinds of *post hoc* analysis, some statistical and some more directly interventionist. I have already mentioned the technique of lesioning artificial neural nets and the various additional kinds of statistical survey carried out by Sanger. Sanger's "contribution analysis," in fact, involved a technique which goes some way toward addressing the issues of cognitive evolution just raised. The technique is to perform a principal components analysis on a trained network and to use this to illuminate the representational trajectory of the network during processing.

In a nice example of this, Elman (1991b, p. 106) comments that a weakness of hierarchical cluster analysis is that, despite providing a useful picture of the static similarity structure of a network's representational space, it "tends to de-emphasize the dynamics involved in processing. Some states may have significance not simply in terms of their similarity to other states, but with regard to the ways in which they constrain movement into subsequent state space. . . ." To see what this means, Elman invites us to consider three sentences:

(a) The *boy* broke the window.

(b) The *rock* broke the window.

(c) The *window* broke.

Recall from chapter 2 above the simple recurrent network whose task is to predict succeeding words. If it is to cope successfully with these three cases, it will need to know that the word 'window' appears in all three sentences. In line with our previous discussions, this sameness will be reflected in the close similarity (reflected in actual cluster analyses of the network—see Elman (1991b) between the active hidden-unit vectors in each case. But there is also a significant difference between cases a and b, on the one hand, and case c. In case c the word 'window' occurs in a position in which it could not terminate the overall sentence or clause, whereas in cases a and b it acts as a terminator. The potential successor states are thus quite different in the two kinds of case. In one case, the potential successors are any states associated with the onset of new sentences. In the other case, the potential successors are any states associated with the conclusion of the clause. (See Elman 1991c for a second example of the same kind.) If the network is able to succeed (as it does) at the prediction task, it must be encoding information of this type. Yet such information (information concerning how a given network state N constrains the movement of the network into successor state N_{+1}) is "papered over" by the standard cluster analysis, which tells us nothing about the *temporal* information-processing profile of a network. What we need, then, is an analysis which can shed light on how "network dynamics (encode) grammatical knowledge" (Elman 1991b, p. 106). This is where principal-components analysis comes in.

Principal-components analysis (PCA) is a statistical technique (closely related to cluster analysis) in which each member of the training set is processed by a trained network in which learning has been "turned off." The hidden-unit response for each item is recorded; however, instead of just clustering together the most similar responses, PCA seeks a new description of the network's state space (e.g., a 70-dimensional space in a network with 70 hidden units). Each possible location in 70-dimensional weight space (each eigenvector) is treated as a dimension itself, and the amount of *variance* (i.e., the number of statistically significant correlations in the training data) accounted for by that dimension (that eigenvector) is calculated. The result is a picture showing which overall points in 70-dimensional space are doing the most work in enabling the network to deal successfully with the training set.[5] The eigenvector which accounts for the greatest amount of variance is labeled the "first principal component," the one which accounts for the second is labeled the "second principal component," and so on. The network's processing of a given sentence can then be displayed relative to one or more of these new dimensions, and the trajectory through this (now much more restricted and understandable) space can be inspected.

Suppose the network is presented with the following four sentences, and the hidden-unit pattern which follows the presentation of each word is recorded.[6]

(d) Boys hear boys.

(e) Boy hears boys.

(f) Boy who boys chase chases boy.

(g) Boys who boys chase chase boy.

Given a precalculated PCA for the network, we can then follow the processing of each sentence relative to one or more of the principal components. The sentences differ in the number (singular or plural) of the main-clause subject, and it becomes evident from examination of the processing profiles of the sentences relative to several of the principal components that this information is being handled largely by the second principal component. Moreover, it can be seen that the information concerning number is not preserved once a main verb (e.g., the second occurrence of 'chase' in cases f and g) has been processed. As Elman (1991b, p. 108) comments, this must be because, in the artificial grammar he used, number information was never relevant beyond that point. The network's progression through the state space defined by the second principal component, for each of the sentences in question, is displayed in figures 3.3 (which plots sentences d and e) and 3.4 (which plots f and g). Such graphs allow us to inspect the way a network's current activation state constrains its movement into subsequent states, relative to particular dimensions

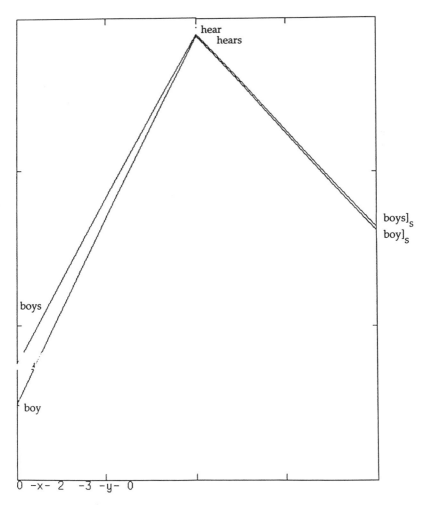

Figure 3.3
Trajectories through state space for sentences d and e. Each point marks the position along the second principal component of hidden-unit space after the indicated word has been input. Magnitude of second principal component is measured along the ordinate; time (i.e., order of word in sentence) is measured along the abscissa. (From Elman 1991b, with permission.)

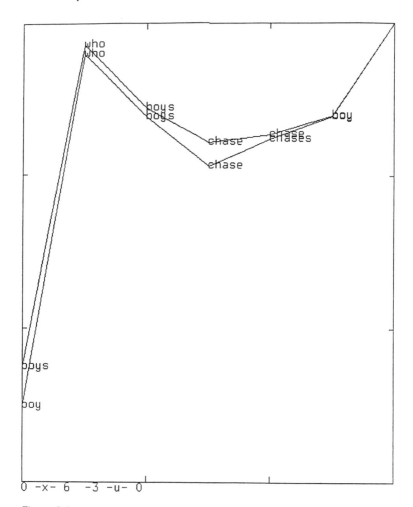

Figure 3.4
Trajectories through state space during processing of sentences f and g. (From
Elman 1991b, with permission.)

of interest. They thus provide a window onto some of the knowledge implicit in the processing dynamics of a given network. To that extent, they constitute a step toward filling in the informational lacuna.

More negatively, it should be stressed that what PCA gives us is at best a means of examining the dynamic representational properties of a mature, trained network. It does not give us any comparable understanding of how an overall assignment of weights at time t, during training, will constrain the network's ability to move into other positions in the weight space at time $t + 1$. That is, PCA does not allow us to probe the issues of learning and conceptual change which originally motivated Churchland's comments. Such change over developmental time is a key area which connectionist approaches have the potential to illuminate (see especially chapters 7–9 below). The construction of powerful techniques to display and interpret such processes of change must therefore be a high-priority item on the connectionist agenda.

The Need for Multiple Analyses

The endeavor of the connectionist cognitive scientist is methodologically both sound and problematic. It is sound because, by bypassing the direct implementation of a classical competence theory, the connectionist avoids the error of projecting a coarse symbolic analysis of the problem domain back onto the cognitive mechanism itself. It is problematic because, by thus eschewing the "classical cascade," the connectionist gains an explanatory obligation. She must discover what the network knows and display its use of such knowledge in the actual processing of inputs. To refuse this explanatory obligation is to risk practical disaster (recall the tank and the sun) as well as to give up on the idea of a genuinely cognitive science. The trouble is that to accept the obligation is often to engage in some systematic distortion of the facts (concerning exactly what the network "knows"). For example, one favored kind of *post hoc* analysis—cluster analysis—turns out to suppress knowledge implicit in the processing dynamics of a network over time. The best cure is to develop and use *multiple* different and complementary kinds of network analysis (including the more "physical" options provided by studies of artificial lesions, pruning and adding units and weights, etc.). The final call, however, is for caution: Connectionism reconfigures content in dynamic ways which can often outstrip our attempts to capture it in a piece of static, text-like code. Buyer beware!

Chapter 4

What Networks Don't Know

Hallucinating Knowledge

We saw in the previous chapter how the symbolic *post hoc* analysis of networks can mislead by failing to reflect information implicit in the processing dynamics of the network over time. Such underestimates of what a network knows are matched by a comparable kind of overestimate which results from the hallucination of a stable and manipulable symbol or data object where none exists. It is the purpose of the present chapter to clarify the nature of this alleged overestimate and to tie the issues thus raised to central questions concerning the special nature of knowledge of *concepts*.

I begin by introducing some worries about the nature of the knowledge acquired by a typical, old-fashioned (three-layer, feedforward, backpropagation-trained) connectionist network. I take as a famous and well-understood example Sejnowski and Rosenberg's NETtalk. NETtalk, I argue, is a system which knows how to negotiate a certain problem domain, and we, as external theorists, can analyze its behavior in a way which invokes a set of conceptual-level categories (such as 'vowel' and 'consonant'). Nonetheless, its knowledge is only partially (and somewhat misleadingly) described in these terms; there is an important sense in which it lacks the general idea of a vowel. I go on to argue that the knowledge attained by such simple networks is analogous to what Cussins (1990) has termed "nonconceptual content." The issue of the transition from nonconceptualized to conceptualized thought therefore looms. I then introduce a speculative theory—Annette Karmiloff-Smith's Representational Redescription Hypothesis—which addresses this issue directly by asking how knowledge which was once merely implicit (in a sense to be elaborated) becomes increasingly manipulable and usable by the system as a result of processes of internal representational change. Further evidence for such a view, drawn from studies of the development of expertise, is then presented.

The developmental hypothesis is suggestive, but its precise computational implications remain unclear. The main conclusion is, however, a philosophical one: Whatever the final outcome of the debate over mechanisms, certain implications for the analysis of content remain. Genuinely contentful thought requires a system to have both nonconceptual and conceptual knowledge of its world. The nonconceptual knowledge is the epistemological bedrock which puts the system in contact with the world its thoughts are meant to concern. It is, in the terminology of Harnad (1990), the source of the *grounding* of its inner representational repertoire. But full-blooded thought ascription imposes a further demand which requires the wider interanimation of a being's cognitive abilities.

What NETtalk Doesn't Know

NETtalk is a three-layer backpropagation-trained connectionist network which learned successfully to negotiate the domain of text-to-speech transformations (see chapter 3). By the end of its training regime, the network produced (via a speech synthesizer) quite accurate and intelligible output—an impressive achievement indeed. But what does NETtalk actually know?

Naturally, NETtalk does not in any sense understand what it is saying. But that is not the point. Likewise, I might learn roughly how to pronounce Chinese sequences without understanding them. Nonetheless, NETtalk has gone from babble to an output which is lawfully disciplined with respect to its inputs. This strongly suggests that it has learned something. The question is, what?

As we saw in the previous chapter, merely having an up-and-running connectionist system (such as NETtalk) does not, in and of itself, do much to advance our understanding of how its target domain is being negotiated. This is because the system is trained, not programmed as a result of some detailed task analysis of a traditional nature. So something has to be done to arrive at a picture of what NETtalk knows. One possibility, as we saw, is to examine the network using a statistical technique such as cluster analysis. The cluster analysis of NETtalk unearthed similarities of hidden-unit response to p's and b's and, proceeding up the hierarchy of pairings of pairs of pairings, to all vowels and to all consonants. In some sense, then, NETtalk had learned to respond *very* similarly to p and b inputs and quite similarly to all vowel inputs. In short, it seemed to have learned the structure of a classical discrimination tree for the text-to-phoneme pairing task. This was quite a striking result. The net had learned to treat a, e, i, o, and u as in some respect similar. So it knows about vowels. Or does it?

What cannot be doubted is that it knows its way around in a domain which we external theorists characterize by abstractions such as 'vowel' and 'consonant'. I shall now argue that there is an important sense in which those abstractions, useful (or even essential) as they are in helping us helping us to see what NETtalk is doing, are not available to NETtalk itself.

It will help to begin with a somewhat simpler example.[1] Consider a network whose task is to learn to assess applications for bank loans. Imagine that a certain bank has a massed body of data concerning loan applicants over a five-year period. The data include sex, age, job, income, address, and so on. And suppose the bank also has a record of which applicants paid their loans back as arranged. The bank uses some of the data to train a neural net to weigh the various factors and output Yes or No to a loan request. Its job is to learn to output Yes in response to input data which (as it turned out) described loanworthy applicants (those who repaid their loans as arranged). Imagine that the training is successful and that the net is then tested on a subset of the original data which had been kept back and not used in the training sessions. The net, let us suppose, does a better job of assessing these applicants than the bank's loan officers. What we have, it seems, is a wonderful tool for assessing loanworthiness.

Imagine now that the network was trained using data from a buoyant economy. Now suppose that we want to generate a network to perform the same task in a depressed economy. And suppose also (as is in fact the case) that the indicators of loanworthiness are systematically altered in the latter case—for example, in a buoyant economy a high income counts for more than a steady job, whereas in a depressed economy the reverse is true. But many of the other factors stay the same. There is no straightforward method of isolating resources in the original network so as to leave intact the bulk of the network's knowledge but reverse the priorities assigned to income and job. In short, despite the large overlap in the knowledge required to perform the two variants of the task, a net trained on one variant is not thereby well placed to succeed in a systematically altered domain. Of course the notion of being 'well placed' is somewhat vague here, but it is meant to cover two cases: the *self-diagnostic* case, in which the system itself (using its own internal resources) spots the overlap between the two problem domains and adjusts its own weights in some suitable way, and the *externally diagnosed* case, in which an external theorist spots the overlap and seeks to modify the old system for the new domain. In both cases the difficulty is the same. It is often the case that (for any fairly interesting problem solved by a highly distributed net) we have no way of directly exploiting the weightings which characterize the original net so as to deploy all and only the relevant pieces of the original network's knowledge as part of a solution to a different but partially related problem.

One more example should help fix the problem. In the Ohm's Law network described in chapter 3, knowledge of symbolic rules was replaced by knowledge of a multitude of softer constraints whose interaction yielded behaviors which in most (but not all) cases were the same as those which would result from application of the symbolic rule. Nonetheless, the reliance on soft constraints bought an enviable robustness and a certain kind of versatility. But now consider the imaginary case in which the laws governing the circuitry domain undergo a *systematic* change. Suppose, for example, that we seek to model an imaginary world in which R = C × V, or that the relation between resistance and voltage is strictly inverted so that in every case where voltage would normally increase by an amount *p* it now drops by the same amount. Now we have the problem of amending the network to deal with the newly defined domains. As it turns out, the very fact which was responsible for the network's flexibility within the static domain is now a source of inflexibility in the plastic (i.e., systematically alterable) domains. The network has no variables which stand for voltage and resistance as such; hence, it is not open to us, or to an overseeing system, simply to reach in and alter or reverse a stored representation of the relationship between such variables. Instead it is necessary to retrain (or reprogram by hand) the network in a global and nonobvious fashion. And the result, of course, will be a network which is again adapted to a static domain but is not able to accommodate further systematic changes easily.

The underlying issue is exactly the same as in the bank-loans case. To exploit the original knowledge in the altered domain you need to represent the original domain as comprising a set of *potentially independently variable* entities and relations. But distributed connectionism build the relations into the representations of the entities. In so doing, it makes it difficult (to say the least) to vary the relations while retaining a representation of the entities.

The sense in which NETtalk *lacks* knowledge of (e.g.) vowels should now be apparent. Suppose we had in mind some other task involving vowel recognition, such as getting a network to output Yes if an input was a vowel and No if it was not. There is no simple and direct way to exploit the knowledge embodied in NETtalk so as to achieve this goal, for NETtalk's knowledge of the vowel/consonant divide is highly task specific. It is fully intertwined with its ability to use the knowledge to perform the text-to-speech transformation. (This is, if you like, the dark side of the deep interpenetration of knowledge and processing described in chapter 2.) Despite the labeling motivated by the cluster analysis of the network, there is a real sense in which it lacks the "general idea" of a vowel. This is not to claim, of course, that new and fancier networks that would overcome some of these difficulties could not be constructed. It is just a caution to beware the labels associated with various *post hoc* analyses. They are a useful guide, but they can mislead too.

What simple ("first-order") networks lack, we may say, is the ability to learn *structure-transforming* (ST) generalizations. The idea is best appreciated by contrast with what may be termed *structure-preserving* (SP) generalizations. Generalization is the process by which a system is able to use knowledge acquired over a finite set of training cases to intelligently influence its treatment of new cases from outside the training set. SP generalization involves applying the knowledge gained in the training cases *unchanged* to deal with new situations. For example, if you learned to add -*ed* to a verb stem to form the past tense, then it is an SP generalization of the training cases to add -*ed* to some new and never-before-encountered stem. ST generalizations, by contrast, involve not just the application of the old knowledge to new cases but the systematic adaptation of the original problem-solving capacity to fit a new kind of case. It would be an ST generalization of the past-tense knowledge to take the past-tense form and remove the -*ed* suffix so as to unveil the stem.

Net Knowledge and Nonconceptual Content

The observations concerning NETtalk (and simple connectionist systems in general) find an interesting parallel in some recent philosophical work concerning nonconceptual content. Nonconceptual content is defined (Cussins 1990, p. 383) as content which consists of nonconceptual properties, and a nonconceptual property is one which is "canonically characterized . . . by means of concepts which are such that an organism *need not have* those concepts in order to satisfy the property" (ibid.). A conceptual property, by contrast, is one which is characterized by means of concepts which the organism *must have* if it is to satisfy the property in question.

Cussins gives the following as illustrations. Consider first the property of 'thinking of someone as a bachelor'. We would specify the property using the concepts 'male', 'adult', and 'unmarried', and no system could count as thinking of someone *as* a bachelor *unless* it was able to regard him as falling under those concepts. That makes 'thinking of someone as a bachelor' a *conceptual* property.

But conceptual content, according to Cussins, is not the only kind of content. There are also, he argues (1990, p. 383) psychological states which (unlike ones involving conceptual content) "must be canonically specified by means of concepts that the subject need not have." Consider the experience of hearing a sound *as* coming from a certain place. How are we to characterize the content of this experience? It might occur to us to say that someone hears a sound as coming from the south. But this is, in a way, to fail to capture the content. For we might then imagine that two people both hear a sound *as* coming from the south but they turn their heads or move in different directions because one thinks that south is *that way* whereas the other does not. The point, then, following Evans (1982), is that the content is in fact *constitutively* tied to a way of orienting oneself in the world. To hear a sound *as* coming from a certain place inescapably involves being disposed to move or orient oneself in a certain way in response.

But now consider a theorist's description of that orienting behavior, or that way of moving. The description will inevitably involve concepts which the organism *need not itself have* in order to hear the sound *as* coming from such and such a place. We can imagine a device or an animal which orients itself as a result of such experience and yet lacks even the concepts involved in the general content description which relates the content to a way of moving or orienting itself. It may have no concept of movement or orientation!

A second example, which Cussins draws from Charles Taylor, concerns the concept 'up'. Our idea of up may need to be analyzed in terms of basic abilities of movement and action, which may in turn be unpacked using concepts such as 'sensitivity to a gravitational field'. But you certainly don't need to possess those concepts to be in states characterized as, e.g., believing you are upside down. (See Cussins 1990, p. 398.)

In sum: The idea is that some contents properly *consist in* being able to negotiate a certain domain. As Cussins (1990, p. 395) puts it, "It is the idea that certain contents consist in a means of finding one's way in the world (tracking the object, say) being available to the subject in his or her experience, even though it may not be available to the subject conceptually, and, indeed, the subject may be incapable of expressing in words what this way of moving is." This should recall vividly the discussion of NETtalk above, for NETtalk is a nice case of a system which "knows its way around" in a certain domain yet lacks, in an important sense, the concepts we might use (say, in our cluster analysis) to describe *what* it knows. First-order connectionist networks are thus ideal contenders for systems capable of supporting nonconceptual content. (This is not necessarily to say that NETtalk really has states which are contentful, albeit nonconceptually so. Rather, one could say that such a network, if certain other unspecified conditions were met, would *then* enjoy such states.)

Moreover, the idea of nonconceptual content seems well suited to describing the cognitive states of many animals. Consider the sandfish *(Scincus scincus)*, a lizard which buries itself in the sand and detects vibrations caused by prey on the surface. When an insect on the surface is thus located, the sandfish emerges, with fatal accuracy, to take its dinner. The sandfish thus negotiates a domain which we describe using concepts like 'insect' and 'vibration', but the sandfish need not literally have any such concepts. We can imagine it as a small network capable of partitioning an input space of vibrations in a way which, under cluster analysis, would yield groupings for 'insect at bearing X', 'insect at bearing Y', and so on, yet lacking any explicit representation of insects and bearings (just as NETtalk was seen to lack any explicit representation of 'vowel').

What we then need to understand, according to Cussins, is how, from a basis of nonconceptual awareness of the world, a creature can slowly come to satisfy (or more nearly satisfy) the constraints we impose on the ascription of *conceptual* contents. What constraints are these? If I describe a frog as spotting a fly, what determines whether I have the right to regard this as a specification of a conceptual or a nonconceptual content? Cussins offers a rather intricate account in which one of the leading ideas is that to have a conceptual content requires more than a mere causal or informational link to the state of the world implicated in the description of the content. To have (properly) the concept 'fly' involves more than being able to find your way around (like a frog) in a fly-infested domain. It involves having a whole web of concepts in which your concept of a fly is embedded. In particular, it involves having your fly concept at the disposal of any other conceptual abilities you have. This consciously echoes Evans' generality constraint, which insists that to truly possess a concept 'a' you must be able to think of a in all the (semantically sensible) combinations into which it could enter with other concepts you possess. Thus, if you can *really* think Fa, and *really* think Gb, you must (as a matter of stipulation) be able to think Fb and Ga. But a frog may be able to have the proto-thought 'there is a fly over there' and some other types of proto-thought and yet be quite incapable of having any other kind of thought about flies. And what this shows, according to the generality constraint, is that it lacks the concept of a fly. Thus, the content of the frog's experience cannot be a *conceptual* content 'there is a fly over there'; it must instead be a nonconceptual content (which doesn't require that it have the concept 'fly' at all) which Cussins

(1990, 423) suggests we might express as 'there-is-a-fly-over-there'. The hyphenation marks the fact that the content is unstructured. Conceptual content, by contrast, is structured content in which each element implicated in the specification of the thought has a separate significance for the creature and can enter freely into combinations with elements of the creature's other thoughts.

The move from unstructured to structured contents is, as Cussins sees it, a move from perspective-dependent to more objective representations of the world. The frog lacks the general idea of a fly as a part of an objective world that can be related to that world in a wide variety of ways (e.g. being dead, being alive, being nearby, being far away, being crunchy). It knows about flies only from a single and limited perspective: that of 'spotting and eating'. By contrast, a system which met the generality constraint with respect to its ideas of flies would have to be able to think about flies in a much wider variety of ways. This is seen as constituting the move towards objectivity. The task of psychological explanation, then, will be to display "psycho-computational transformations defined over nonconceptual contents which have the effect of reducing the perspective-dependence of the contents" (Cussins 1990, p. 424).

In short: The deep explanatory lacuna is an essentially *developmental* one concerning the transition from special-purpose problem solutions to the highly flexible and interanimated knowledge characteristic of grasp of a concept. How might such a transition be achieved?

The Representational Redescription Hypothesis

In an influential series of papers publications, Annette Karmiloff-Smith (1979, 1986, 1987, 1992a) has argued for a phase-like picture of human cognitive development. Unlike most other animals, humans, she holds, are compelled by endogenous forces to go beyond simple success in a domain and to seek a more abstract representation of the strategies which brought success. As she puts it, we go beyond "behavioral mastery" and *redescribe* our functioning procedures in a series of higher-level languages. This redescription (which may culminate in conscious, verbal access to a higher-level redescription) enables the organism to get more mileage out of information which, in a certain sense, it already possesses, courtesy of the functioning procedure. The core of the proposal involves the idea that knowledge which was once merely implicit in a system's actual ability to negotiate some problem domain becomes an object for the system and hence can be redescribed in various ways. These redescriptions have the effect of making the knowledge available in a format which facilitates interaction with other kinds of knowledge which the organism possesses, as well as making it more easily manipulable in its own right. These twin effects yield the increasingly open-ended flexibility of use that characterizes conceptual thought.

The parallel with the above discussion of NETtalk is immediate. NETtalk (like the sandfish) has a functioning procedure. It has a kind of behavioral mastery in the domain. But it has not gone beyond that mastery. It (like the sandfish) is locked into the first phase of Karmiloff-Smith's picture. The complete picture involves a number of phases, some of which will be detailed later. For now, we need only stress the coarsest detail.

> *Basic Mastery* The system has a means of negotiating the problem domain. But the procedure is heavily dependent on external inputs and, as far as the organism is concerned, unstructured.

> *Higher-Level Redescriptions* The functioning procedure is treated as a new problem domain and is thus theorized *about* (unconsciously) by the organism. This theorizing results in the organism redescribing the procedure underlying its basic mastery in a series of higher-level languages.

(See Karmiloff-Smith 1986, pp. 102–103.)

Karmiloff-Smith has tested the broad lines of the hypothesis in a number of experiments involving widely varied problem domains, ranging from knowledge of the article system (Karmiloff-Smith 1979, 1986) to knowledge of physical causality (Karmiloff-Smith 1987). I shall describe a single, illustrative experiment concerning children's drawing. The experiment, detailed in Karmiloff-Smith 1992a, involved children of two age groups: 4–6 and 8–10 years. They were asked to draw familiar, much-practiced items, such as a house or a person, and then to draw deviant versions, such as a 'funny house' (or a 'house that doesn't exist' and so on). Various locutions were used, and precautions were taken to ensure that the instructions were understood. The hypothesis was that at first the children would have a basic mastery in the drawing domains but would not have developed higher-level redescriptions of this and hence would exhibit various limitations in their drawing behavior.

Children of all ages were able to draw a basic house. The interesting data concerns a small number of younger children who seemed unable to draw deviant versions, such as a 'funny house' (which suggests a pure 'basic mastery' kind of competence) and, perhaps more important, the striking differences in *kind* among the alterations to the basic house or person drawings exhibited by children of different ages (which suggests various constraints operative at different phases of redescription).

Figures 4.1–4.4 show some of the structure within the class of successful attempts. The following pattern of types of change were revealed:

(a) shape and size of elements changed
(b) shape of whole changed
(c) deletion of elements
(d) insertion of new elements
(e) position/orientation changed
(f) insertion of cross-category elements.

It turned out that children of all ages (in the successful class) were able to make changes of types a–c, but only children in the older group (8–10 years) were generally able to make changes of types d–f (Karmiloff-Smith 1990, 1992a). How is this to be explained? One hypothesis is that the younger children simply hadn't thought of the subtler changes. A more interesting hypothesis is that the younger children, because of the way their knowledge was represented, had great difficulty making such changes. To decide between these two hypotheses, a followup experiment was conducted. Eight of the younger subjects who had made only changes of types a–c were asked to draw two pictures involving the other two types of change made spontaneously by the older children. One drawing was to be of a man with two heads (an insertion change) the other of a house with wings (a cross-category change). All eight of these children rapidly and fluently drew the house with wings, but seven out of the eight made a revealing "error" in the other task: Instead of drawing a man with two heads, they drew one body and one head, drew a second head, and then "went on laboriously and very slowly to draw

Figure 4.1
Deletions. Left: child, age 5 years, 3 months. Right: child, age 9 years. (From Karmiloff-Smith 1990. Reprinted with permission of Elsevier Science Publishers B.V.)

Figure 4.2
Insertions of elements from same category. Left: child, age 8 years, 7 months. Right: child, age 9 years, 6 months. (From Karmiloff-Smith 1990. Reprinted with permission of Elsevier Science Publishers B.V.)

Figure 4.3
Changes in position or orientation. Left: child, age 9 years, 8 months. Right: child, age 10 years, 11 months. (From Karmiloff-Smith 1990. Reprinted with permission of Elsevier Science Publishers B.V.)

Figure 4.4
Insertions of elements from other categories: Left: child, age 8 years, 3 months. Right: child, age 10 years, 9 months. (From Karmiloff-Smith 1990. Reprinted with permission of Elsevier Science Publishers B.V.)

two bodies, two arms and two legs on each body, etc. And they kept starting again because they were dissatisfied with their results. They had some difficulties even in simply copying a model provided by the experimenter. By contrast, when 8–10-year-olds spontaneously drew a man with two heads (interrupting sequential order to insert a new subroutine for drawing a second head), they drew a single body with the speed of their usual drawing procedure." (Karmiloff-Smith 1992a, p. 160)

The failure to fluently produce a two-headed figure is *prima facie* evidence that it is not simple lack of imagination which underlies the differences between the two age groups. But the winged house then begins to look anomalous. Karmiloff-Smith suggests that to explain the data we need to consider the constraints that operate at the first level of representational redescription. At this point, she speculates, the initial procedure responsible for basic mastery in the domain has been redescribed as a "sequentially fixed list," thus (as it were) inheriting a constraint from the bare "procedural" level. Such redescription is said to enable the child to "introduce variables on size and shape" (Karmiloff-Smith 1990, p.17). But the constraint on sequential order of elements remains. In the case of the man with two heads, the child is required to interrupt this sequential order; this is very hard to achieve. By contrast, adding wings to a completed house-drawing sequence is relatively easy. Thus, the key data concern the relative ease of production (ibid., p.19).

On the basis of the followup experiment, then, Karmiloff-Smith postulates the following structure within the class of successful attempts at "funny-X drawing": first, a phase in which redescription is relatively sequentially constrained (the younger children are capable of fluently drawing a winged house but not a two-headed man); second, a phase in which the sequential constraint is lifted (the older children are capable of fluent drawing without midroutine insertions).

Note that Karmiloff-Smith's model is not intended as a model of stages in child development; rather, it is intended as a model of recurrent phases which attend even adult learning. Thus, she suggests (1990, p. 25) that adult learning in a phonological-awareness task fits the model she proposes, as does the acquisition of musical skills (for example, learning to play the piano, where one begins by learning to play a piece in sequence, starting at the beginning, and one then progresses to being able to start in the middle of the piece and (perhaps) ends up able to play variations on a theme, changing all aspects of the sequential order, introducing insertions, and so forth (ibid., pp. 26, 27). In addition, the "sequential constraint" example is merely illustrative. The idea is that the first-pass redescriptions will all impose a *multitude* of constraints on how the information may be put to use, and that later stages of redescription progressively relax these constraints, whatever they were.

The redescription hypothesis is, I believe, suggestive but overstated, at least in its original formulations. The mechanism of change that it posits (viz., the subsequent analysis of an existing solution to prompt a new and deeper understanding) is very rationalistic. Although it seems clear that there is indeed a progression from simple to more complex and powerful domain knowledge, it is by no means certain that such a progression need be rooted in the kind of highly self-analytic processes (conscious or unconscious) which are implied by the talk of redescription. Some alternative possibilities are pursued in chapters 6–9 below. Nevertheless, the following aspects of Karmiloff-Smith's work remain true and important: her insistence that the process of learning should not be brought to a halt by success (i.e., by the achievement of a desired input-output mapping), her insistence that an inner drive to generate ever more powerful and extendable problem solutions constitutes a distinctive and central part of the human cognitive achievement, and her commitment to the careful microdevelopmental study of real cases in which local, weak problem solutions (which she calls "procedures") give way to a specifiable series of more powerful ones. Such microdevelopmental studies will, I predict, become increasingly important as a clue to the kinds of internal computational process and external scaffolding (see chapter 7) which, together, make flexible human cognition possible.

Expertise

Karmiloff-Smith's conjectures find a suggestive counterpart in recent studies of expertise. Holyoak (1991) describes the history of the study of expertise in terms of three generations of model. First-generation models of expertise pictured the expert as someone "particularly skilled at general heuristic search" (Holyoak 1991, p. 301). Such models were doomed by the increasingly obvious role of specialized domain knowledge and inference patterns in expert success. Second-generation models took the lesson to heart and depicted the development of expertise as a process of "knowledge compilation." The idea here is that the novice proceeds piecemeal through a series of steps which (if they are successful) become "chunked" into single computational acts as the novice turns into an expert. Examples of such models include those of Anderson (1983, 1987) and Shiffrin and Schneider (1977). The knowledge-compilation paradigm seems to have been adopted, in a slightly new guise, by connectionists such as Smolensky (1988). Smolensky presents a model in which the true expert is fluent in virtue of having a fully trained connectionist network capable of negotiating the task domain and in which the novice uses linguistically encoded knowledge (processed by a special device which Smolensky calls the Conscious Rule Interpreter) to rapidly gain a limited ability in the domain through conscious rehearsal of rules and heuristics ('lean into the wind', 'never change gears while turning a corner', and so on). In short, the novice-to-expert transition is depicted as the transition from reliance on symbolic sentential knowledge structures to reliance on a trained network. The transition is achieved, of course, by the kind of continued practice or experience in the domain that is necessary to train a pattern-recognition network. The expert is then able to negotiate the domain by means of what Dreyfus and Dreyfus (1986) termed a "process of holistic recognition of similarity." The kind of knowledge thus encoded may, they claim, "defy complete verbal description" (p. 32). There is certainly something compelling about such a characterization of expertise, and Dreyfus and Dreyfus give convincing and detailed examples from (e.g.) chess playing to support their analysis. Moreover, unpacking the story of holistic similarity recognition by reference to the fluent, nonsentential, experience-based pattern-recognition abilities of connectionist systems lends it much needed mechanistic credibility (for a detailed defense along these lines, see Bechtel and Abrahamsen 1991, pp. 155–175). Nonetheless the mechanistic story cannot stop there, for the kind of expertise achieved by familiar connectionist pattern completion devices is, as we saw, characteristically limited and nonextendable. Yet the true expert is capable not just of fluent holistic problem solving in the original domain, but also of applying her knowledge in new but related domains and of rapidly amending localized areas of her skills in response to new task demands. Holyoak (1991) summarizes a set of recent studies of such skills which, he says, are simply anomalous with respect to the knowledge-compilation model of expertise. Two worth mentioning here are *condition-action recoupling* and *cross-domain transfer*.

Condition-Action Recoupling
Allard and Starkes (1991) note that skilled motor performers are fluent at adjusting to *altered* condition-action pairings. Thus, for example, an expert player of video games can rapidly adjust to the use of a new type of controller mechanism, whereas a less expert player is affected much more by such a change. In short: "The greater the skill level of the performer, the less the performance decrement when

the doing side of the performance must be modified." (Allard and Starkes 1991)

Cross-Domain Transfer

Expert skills also show a tendency to allow relatively easy transfer to certain new domains. A particularly nice example, for our purposes, concerns microsurgical expertise. Microsurgery is conducted using microscopic instruments and a foot-pedal-controlled microscope (the pedals adjust focus and magnification). A competent microsurgeon was asked to perform a radically new task using the microsurgical instruments and techniques: to write her name and some low-frequency words ('gentry', 'dactyl', 'ingot', and 'ironic') using microsurgical forceps. She had never attempted such "microwriting" before, but, as figure 4.5 shows, she succeeded admirably. Her microwriting also showed the same handwriting style as her macrowriting (except that at 40× magnification she was forced to adjust the pressure exerted so as to avoid getting tangled up with individual fibers of the paper). What this example shows is that it is possible "to construct skilled performance from currently existing elements even when the elements have never been practiced together" (Allard and Starkes 1991, p. 148).

Transfer of learning and recombination of elements of existing skills thus seem to go together. Transfer often requires separating out various parts of a "single" skill and reinvoking selected parts in a new environment alongside other skill fragments, which may preexist or may have to be acquired from scratch. In a related vein, Holyoak (1991, p. 307) reports work by Dörner and Schölkopf (1991) which shows that "experienced executives were more successful than college students in coping with an unfamiliar problem involving management of a complex dynamic environment." Holyoak cites a number of related findings and concludes (p. 308) that "all of these demonstrations of relatively flexible transfer seem to require explanations that go beyond a characterization of expertise as the product of increasingly specialized domain knowledge." In response to these and other difficulties, Holyoak is led to endorse a distinction that seems closely related to the issues concerning extendability. This is the distinction between *routine* and *adaptive* expertise, first suggested by Hatano and Inagaki (1986). Holyoak (p. 310) reports the distinction as follows: "Whereas routine experts are able to quickly and accurately solve familiar types of problems, they have only modest capabilities in dealing with novel types of problem. Adaptive experts, on the other hand, may be able to invent new procedures derived from their expert knowledge."

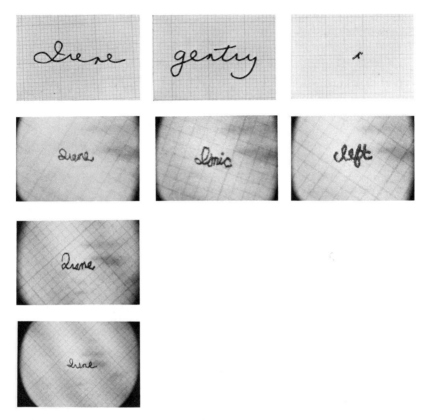

Figure 4.5
Microwriting of high- and low-frequency words by an intermediate microsurgeon (IP) at magnifications of 16×, 25×, and 40×. Top three are actual size (two normal followed by one at 40×). Magnification of next three words is 40×; that of next lower name is 25×; that of bottom name is 16×. (Original slides provided by J. Starkes.)

The puzzle, of course, is this: What is it about the underlying representational format that allows the adaptive expert to perform such feats of partial, selective knowledge transfer? In the cases of microwriting and video games, Allard and Starkes conclude that the cognitive part of each task (tactics and strategy in the video game, letterforms and writing style in microwriting) is represented separately from the motor-skill component (the motor commands to move the controller or the pen). Hence, they argue, it is possible for the expert to preserve the cognitive component and recouple a new motor component onto it. They are thus led to claim that there are "independent databases for knowing and doing" (Allard and Starkes 1991, p. 147).

Such a conclusion is not forced upon us by the data. What the data demand is not a firm separation of knowing and doing but a general *modularization* of the solution to a given problem. That is, the data demand that, whenever possible, the expert will separate a single overall skill into a series of independently usable subskills. No *intrinsic* separation of motor and cognitive elements is then necessary. The general process of "modularize whenever possible" will still result in the independent encoding of such elements. In addition, we would be led to expect (and we in fact find) that modular structure will characterize even the cognitive or the motor elements alone, allowing flexible transfer of parts of each. Thus, someone skilled at the strategy of Pac-Man can usefully deploy some fragments of that skill in a new but related game (using the same controller). Likewise, a skilled jive dancer can learn a new floor step (the basic pattern of foot movements between "real" moves) and immediately integrate this new motor routine into an existing motor sequence of turns, spins and air steps. Such phenomena indicate that reuseable structure exists *within* each of Allard and Starkes' two components.

Thus, the novice to expert shift is best seen, I suggest, as a process in which a relatively unstructured initial solution to a problem is replaced by more highly modularized encodings. This clearly supports Karmiloff-Smith's vision of a process of redescription. But, as was mooted at the close of the preceding section, we should beware of conceiving of such a process in overly rationalistic (code-oriented) terms. Instead, we shall later see how (for example) a modular network architecture can automatically decompose a problem into a set of relatively independent subproblems, assigning a distinct subnet to each. Such an encoding may involve nothing like strings of classical recombinable *symbols,* and yet nonetheless it may provide for just the kind of wider exploitation of achieved knowledge I have been stressing.

The possibility of adaptive expertise may also mark an important boundary in the natural order. A variety of findings by Brown et al. (1983) show a robust cognitive separation between such forms of life as very young infants and fishes, on the one hand, and older children and some higher animals (e.g., some monkeys) on the other. This separation concerns the relative abilities of these organisms to succeed at *transferring* the abstract principles used to solve one kind of problem to a related but different kind of problem. What some adult humans can do and fishes can't, it seems, is map a highly abstract picture of the structure of a particular problem solution onto a new domain. Thus, it is frequently suggested (in this case by Halford (1989, p. 134)) that "a major difference between young and old learners is their ability to access and flexibly use competencies they possess. The findings of phytogenetic and developmental research are . . . consistent. It appears to be the ability to acquire an abstract principle, demonstrated by interproblem transfer, that best discriminates between different groups of participants."

Thus, connectionist modelers should look very seriously at the literature on cognitive development, expertise, and transfer of learning. In our terms, the crucial issue will be whether the flexibility of use and the potential for knowledge transferral that characterize the true expert can be modeled without resort to the kinds of representation that characterize classical nondistributed connectionist systems. More succinct: Does secondary manipulability require classical symbols and concatenative encoding? The question is empirical, open, and pressing. We will return to it in chapter 6.

Conclusions: Concepts versus Information

The arguments and observations presented in this chapter placed the idea of the multiple usability of stored information at center stage. Simple connectionist networks were seen to be characteristically limited in their capacities to further exploit existing information, even if (e.g.) the partitionings of their hidden-unit space were properly seen as embodying precisely the information required for some new task. Human development, while including phases in which acquired knowledge is similarly task bound, was seen frequently to involve a subsequent loosening up in which the knowledge became more widely deployable. Related phenomena were reported in a brief discussion of the growth of expertise. From a more philosophical perspective, it now seems that the intuitive distinction between having *information* about a domain and having a *belief* about it turns in part on the idea that a belief is a cognitive state involving the apprehension of its component *concepts*, and that grasp of a concept requires some kind of open-ended usability such that the concept could figure in any of a host of other kinds of cognitive episodes. Two empirical questions now arise: What kind of inner processing economy is needed to subserve the kind of flexible use of information just described? By what computational means is the transition to increasingly flexible uses of information achieved? These questions, and with them the issue of the current state of connectionist modeling of concepts, will occupy us for the next several chapters.

Chapter 5

Concept, Category, and Prototype

Concepts as Pattern-Recognition Devices

Historically, much of the study of concepts has consisted in the study of one of the clearest *functions* of concepts, namely categorization. A concept functions as a categorization device by enabling the person who has it to assign instances (of, e.g., individual dogs) to the category ('dog') and to make inferences about newly encountered individuals on the basis of stored knowledge about properties of the class. Thus understood, concepts may be said to be "essentially pattern-recognition devices" (Smith and Medin 1981, p. 8). Such a view of concepts offers a standing invitation to the connectionist, for connectionist models, as we saw above, are especially well suited to perform such categorization tasks. Several quite impressive models of concepts, thus conceived, have been put forth. Such models constitute (or so I shall argue) significant progress of a sort. They capitalize on the special features of connectionist knowledge representation (semantic metric, context sensitivity, generalizability) isolated in chapter 2, and they can be studied in useful microdevelopmental detail. A major task of the present chapter is to display this natural affinity between connectionist approaches and categorization phenomena and to raise some further questions concerning the extension of such treatments to increasingly abstract or theoretical categories.

The obvious lacuna in the connectionist treatment then rears its head. Such models take us a long way in the understanding of categorization phenomena, but they seem ill suited to address the role of concepts as elements of structured thoughts. Yet this role (recall the focus on multiple usability of information in chapter 4) seems essential to the intuitive notion of grasping a concept.

The lacuna is real, but the prognosis, I shall suggest, is not all bad. Connectionists have begun to develop several ways of dealing with structure. And, more negatively, the classical solution has its own (high) price. By the close of the present chapter, the way should be clear to pursue the connectionist solution on its own terms.

From Definitions to Prototypes

We can begin with a brief and selective tour of the cognitive psychological literature on concepts. The most prominent feature of the psychological landscape is the distinction between classical and probabilistic models of knowledge of concepts. The most straightforward instance of a classical approach would be the idea that the kind of knowledge we have when we grasp a concept such as 'pigeon' or 'chair' is knowledge of some necessary and sufficient defining conditions allowing us to test for membership of the category by testing for the presence or absence of the features cited. To take one of the few examples where such an account seems to work (but see pp. 66–70 of Lakoff 1987 for doubts even about such "simple" cases), grasp of the concept 'bachelor' might be thought to consist in knowing that it is necessary and sufficient for being a bachelor that someone is an unmarried, adult, eligible male. Correct application of the concept then depends merely on checking to see whether these conditions are met.

The classical view, however, looks to be undermined in two important respects. First, for many of our concepts there simply are no necessary and sufficient conditions to be discovered. The standard case here is Wittgenstein's example of the concept 'game'. There seem to be no set of features whose presence is both necessary and sufficient to fix an activity as a game. Instead, games are related to one another by a series of partially overlapping characteristics. Thus, just as the members of a human family may all resemble one another without there being any features which they all share (instead, one has the father's nose, another has his chin, and so on), so too many pairs of games have features in common (the use of balls, bats, goals, competition, teams, etc.) without there being any core set of features which are present in all of them. Second, our judgments of category membership (whether or not a concept is applicable to a given case) are scalar (Rosch 1975; Rosch and Mervis 1975; Rosch 1978). That is to say, we often judge an instance P as falling under a concept Q *to a greater or lesser extent* (e.g., a dog is a better example of a pet than a tortoise is, and a robin is a better example of a bird than a pigeon is). This result would be anomalous if the psychological mechanisms by which we judge category membership involved simply testing for the presence of the defining features picked out by some set of necessary and sufficient conditions, for such features will either be present or absent and hence there will be no metric by which to gauge goodness of example; the concept will either apply or fail to apply simpliciter. (Such objections are suggestive but by no means conclusive. For some modern defenses of the classical view, see Armstrong et al. 1983 and Osherson and Smith 1981.)

Widespread dissatisfaction with the classical view led many theorists to adopt what Smith and Medin (1981) call the *probabilistic view.* As its name suggests, this approach replaced the idea of defining properties with that of the probable properties for a member of a given class. A probabilistic view accounts for graded class membership, since the "better" members will be those which exhibit more of the characteristic properties. There are various ways of further developing a basic probabilistic approach. One such way is to suppose that a category is represented by stored traces of actual exemplars— viz., instances of objects which fall under it (Brooks 1978; Medin and Schaffer 1978). If we suppose that there exist some especially salient instances (or "paradigms"), then graded membership is explained by distance from them. An increasingly popular alternative account (see various essays in Smith and Medin 1981) proposes that, instead of representing several concrete instances in memory, we judge category membership by degree of similarity to an abstract *prototype,* which need not be identical with any real-world object or situation. Thus (recall chapter 2 above), our several experiences with individual dogs and their various attributes may lead us to abstract out of those experiences an average profile (or "central tendency") such that we subsequently come to judge doghood by judging the similarity of newly encountered cases to the central tendency. Thus, a typical prototype model may represent instances as sets of attributes (properties or features) with some numeric measure of both the importance of the attribute to that concept (sometimes called its weight[1]) and the extent to which the attribute is present. The set of attributes present and their weights will then be somehow summed (e.g., by simply adding up the numeric measures—the so-called linear combination rule), and a threshold will be introduced such that instances below a certain value are partitioned out of the category while those above it are judged to fall within the category. Graded membership is then achieved by ranking according to the number of points achieved on the numeric scale: a kind of clapometer effect.[2] A good survey of these various approaches is given by Hampton (1991, 1992). As Hampton points out, such models can allow variations in "goodness of membership" while maintaining (courtesy of the threshold) the idea that even low-goodness members are still full-fledged instances of the category. An ostrich is a full-fledged bird, even if a rather poor example of one.

The important question to ask of any prototype model (see Hampton 1991, 1992; Keil 1987; Murphy and Medin 1985) is "Where do the attribute weights come from?" This question introduces the important topic of theoretical knowledge.

One simple thought is that the weight of an attribute (the extent of its contribution to determining category membership) is a direct function of the number of times that attribute is found in exemplars of the category. As it stands, this won't do. It may well be the case that almost every dog you have ever encountered has four legs, but that hardly makes the presence of the four-legs attribute a useful tool for discriminating dogs from nondogs. (Cats have four legs too.) The simplest workable proposal is probably to opt for *correlated* attributes—viz., clusters of properties which have tended to co-occur in the instances of doghood to which you have been exposed. The trouble here is that the measure remains a purely statistical one. The prototype will be nothing but the center of a statistically driven state space in which the overall tendencies of attribute co-occurrence (the "central tendency" of the category members) fix the abstract prototype which organizes future judgments. A variety of difficulties face such purely statistical approaches. The major drawback is that such approaches seem to ignore the role of theoretical knowledge in informing judgments of category membership. Thus (to give the now-classic example), the judgment that an animal is a skunk will depend not merely on attribute similarity relative to a central tendency but also on biological facts such as whether it had skunk parents—a hamster in a raccoon suit simply won't do. Keil (1987, p. 180) calls this shift (from an attribute-based model to a theory-based model) the "characteristic-to-defining shift" and comments that children progress from "a relatively even weighting of many features that co-occur frequently with a category to a heavy emphasis on just one or two primary features or fundamental organizing dimensions. At some point they seem to assume the presence of such dimensions and actively look for them."

Of course, *suitable* weighting of *suitable* attributes will explain these cases. But the worry is that we cannot *derive* those weightings simply by a process of statistical extraction of characteristic features. Instead, the attribute weightings which come to power the similarity metric and indeed the choice of attributes themselves, look to be consequences of acquired theoretical knowledge about the domain.

On reflection, it seems fairly obvious that at least some of our concepts must, in this sense, be driven by theory. We are capable, after all, of forming abstract concepts, and concepts of unencountered (even unencounterable) situations and objects. Such cases cannot be explained by the extraction of a central tendency from a class of sound exemplars. Moreover, there is the important question (Medin and

Wattenmaker 1987) of what makes a category *psychologically* cohesive. Not all possible partitionings of the world, even if they are quite learnable by statistical attribute correlation, appeal to us. It might be thought that broadly evolutionary considerations are sufficient to solve this puzzle, and so they may be for the basic preferences which drive early learning (Markman 1987; Mervis 1987). But once the child has more resources available, she can make sense of a category whose members are (seemingly implausibly) children, jewelry, oil paintings, and pets if she is given the context fixer "things to take out of one's home during a fire." (See Barsalou 1987 and below.) These seem to be clear-cut cases in which theoretical understanding drives a sense of category membership, and they lead quite nicely to a particular recent proposal which I wish to consider in some detail: Barsalou's notion of concepts as temporary context-reflecting constructs.

Do We Ever Create the Same Concept Twice?

Heraclitus famously claimed that we can never step into the same river twice. Lawrence Barsalou makes a similar claim about concepts. Barsalou seeks to challenge the received picture of a concept as a basically invariant structure which explains set membership and typicality judgments. His skepticism is based on a series of results which show that such typicality judgements (the Rosch-style graded membership cases discussed above) are surprisingly unstable across contexts. To explain such instability, he proposes that concepts ("occurrent psychological states which drive categorization and typicality judgments") are constructed "on the hoof" and embody context-responsive subsets of the information stored in long-term memory. The result is that "the same concept is rarely, if ever, constructed for a category" (Barsalou 1987, p. 101). Barsalou's position combines what I take to be an important insight (concerning instability and context variability) with a revealingly unhappy terminological choice (the reading of 'concept'). Both are central to the concerns of this book, so let us examine his proposal in a little depth.

Barsalou begins by noting the ubiquity and power of our graded typicality judgments. Such judgments are ubiquitous insofar as there seem to be no categories or concepts that are exempt from the scalar grading effect. Everything from basic taxonomic concepts ('fruit', 'furniture') through abstract and formal concepts ('odd number', 'square') to *ad hoc* categories ('ways to escape being killed by the Mafia') and on to goal-directed categories ('things to eat on a diet') has been shown to display graded structure. (For details see Rosch 1973; Armstrong et al. 1983; Lakoff 1986; Barsalou 1985; Barsalou

1983.) And these gradations are psychologically potent insofar as they are also correlated with response times (the more typical cases are more quickly categorized) and with ease of acquisition. Typicality judgments, then, must be taken seriously. But on what might they depend?

One answer, which we toyed with above, would be that the typicality ratings are calculated relative to the central tendency (statistical center) of a state space of exemplars. But if *simplistic* central tendencies were the sole operative factor, it would be hard to explain a range of results involving goal-derived categories, linguistically fixed context, points of view, and *ad hoc* categories.[3]

Goal-Derived Categories
Here the notion of *centralness* and that of *goodness of exemplar* come apart. Thus, the rank ordering of exemplars of 'things to eat on a diet' seems to reflect, not closeness to the central tendency of actual cases (e.g., 'having 10 calories'), but closeness to an *ideal* ('having no calories') which may only rarely be instantiated.

Linguistically Fixed Context
Linguistic context can invert rank orderings. For example, in the context of *milking*, cows and goats are judged to be better exemplars of animals than horses and mules; however, in the context of riding these ratings are reversed (Roth and Shoben 1983).

Points of View
Ordinary subjects are quite capable of changing their normal rank orderings if asked to perform a task from someone else's point of view. Switching from the American to the Chinese point of view results in a reordering of eagles and peacocks as good exemplars of birds.

Ad hoc Categories
Subjects prove capable of rank ordering examples even for novel ("ad hoc") categories such as 'things that could fall on your head', and 'items to save from a burning building'.

The lesson to learn from such cases, according to Barsalou, is that the concepts on which we rely to drive our categorizations and our judgments of typicality (more accurately, goodness of exemplar) are not static structures stored in long-term memory. It is a mistake, he writes, to assume "that there are invariant cognitive structures associated with categories that we should be trying to discover. . . . Invariant representations of categories do not exist in human cognitive systems. Instead, invariant representations of categories are analytic fictions created by those who study them." (Barsalou 1987, p. 114) The reason is straightforward: Given the evidence of graded structure even in *ad hoc*, goal-derived, and other viewpoint-relative cases, it seems implausible to suppose that the gradations are built into some preexisting conceptual unit or prototype that has been simply extracted whole out of long-term memory. Instead, our categorization abilities look to be fully *productive*: we are masters of a probable infinity of fully graded category judgments corresponding to an infinity of possible goals and contexts. Since the brain is simply too small to hold an infinity of static representations (one per category in context), it follows that the representations must be constructed on the hoof, and in ways which are highly flexible and context sensitive. If we were to identify the *concepts* with the instantaneous inner representations which drive performance on (e.g.) grading-of-exemplar tests, it would follow that the folk picture (in which a single concept drives performance in many contexts) was misleading. Barsalou (1987, p. 116) makes precisely this proposal when he explicitly signals his intent to use 'concept' to "refer to the particular information used to represent a category . . . on a particular occasion." Although one may, of course, use a technical term in any way one likes (as long as it is defined), this usage does not strike me as altogether happy; this tendency to use 'concept' to indicate an instantaneous internal state (which can thus be implicated in the very simplest of causal stories) extends an unholy invitation to eliminativism. For now, I shall keep my distance from the Barsalou usage by writing 'concept (= occurrent state)' whenever the extended usage is in question.

Barsalou's claim is, thus, that "graded structure changes across contexts because different category concepts (= occurrent states) are used in different contexts for the same category" (1987, p. 117). The concept (= occurrent state) 'animal' will thus include expectations of tame domestic pets if activated in a 'suburban resident' context (i.e., if subjects are asked to take a suburban resident's point of view), and expectations of large wild creatures if activated in a wilderness context. Long-term memory is seen as a vast information store out of which specially tailored, contextually idiosyncratic category concepts (= occurrent states) are generated as the need arises. It is important to get a clear sense of the picture that Barsalou is opposing here. Of course, all theorists agree that context can affect our *use* of information. The question is whether there is a fixed body of information which constitutes a subject's long-term representation of (e.g.) 'bird' and is called up (and then selectively used) whenever the subject is entertaining bird thoughts. Cognitive psychological attempts to define *property lists* for daily concepts, or to limn the characteristics of *the* bird prototype (etc.), all assume the existence of invariant, integrated structures corresponding to context-free concepts. The Barsalou proposal is that such invariant structures are useful fictions created by the theorist. This is not to deny that some features *may* figure in all the cases corresponding to some folk concepts. It is, as Barsalou (1987, p. 123) puts it, *obligatory* to build 'smells' into a skunk representation. But such obligatory information is by no means a 'classical core', since it may fall well short of constituting necessary and sufficient (or even necessary) conditions of correct application, and the obligatory contents may vary between different masters of the concept (ibid.).

This story ends with a difficult twist. It may have seemed that Barsalou's proposal amounted to this: that the mind contains stable, long-term, context-independent representations of information about features and properties (like 'wild' and 'large' for the wilderness-context category concept) and merely constructs the composite category concept (= occurrent state) on the hoof, according to circumstances. But there is an immediate and profound difficulty here: All these features and properties are concepts too. Thus, the 'wheel' feature of a car category concept is itself a concept with context-sensitive dimensions. The truly radical proposal, mooted but not developed by Barsalou (but recall the discussion of context sensitivity in chapter 2 above) is thus that all the semantically interpretable elements are constructed on the hoof—viz., that there are *no* "fundamental units used to build property and concept representations that remain invariant across contexts," and that "instability may generally characterize the circuitry of the nervous system" (Barsalou 1987, p. 129).

In sum: The full Barsalou proposal is that the concepts (= occurrent states) that power categorization and graded membership judgments are constructed, according to contextual demand, in working memory. Neither the concept itself nor the features and properties associated with it need be present as long-standing representational states bearing context-invariant contents.

Connectionist Models of Categorization

Many categorization phenomena succumb rather nicely to connectionist treatments, for several key phenomena emerge as direct results of *fundamental* properties of connectionist representation and retrieval techniques. To get a sense of this, consider two specific models found in the recent literature: the Plunkett-Sinha model and the Schyns model.

Plunkett and Sinha's Model of Concept Formation and Vocabulary Growth
Plunkett and Sinha (1991) trained a four-layer, fully feedforward network to associate images with labels. The images consisted of distorted versions of each of 32 random dot patterns which had been designated as prototypes for the purpose of the simulation (the same procedure as was used for the "dog prototype" example detailed in chapter 2 above). Some of the individual images thus created were more distorted (i.e., involved the displacement of more dots) than others. No prototypical patterns were used in the actual training of the network. Input to the network was a distributed representation of the random dot patterns (created by a stage of "retinal preprocessing") alongside (in a separate input channel) a representation of a label for each pattern. The labels were 32-bit orthogonal vectors which embodied no information about the relative similarity of the images (that is, they were arbitrary names).

The net was trained to autoassociate label/image inputs with identical label/image outputs (that is: given a particular pattern over the input units, its task was to learn to re-create the same pattern across a matching bank of output units). The task is far from trivial, as the path from input to output involves various stages—including one at which the information coded as input across two separate banks (one of 30 units and one of 32) must be integrated in a single compressed (50-unit) representation before it can activate the output units. This compression and integration results in what Plunkett and Sinha call a *composite* representation, in which image and label information are intertwined. It is because the net creates this composite representation that it is able eventually to reproduce the label when given only the image as input (production) and, conversely, to show that it "knows" what the label means by producing the image when given only the label as input (comprehension). The overall architecture is shown in figure 5.1.

Training involved a repeated three-phase cycle whose elements were

> presentation of image as input with image *alone* as target output,
> presentation of a label for the previous image as input, with the label as target output, and
> joint presentation of image and label with full image/label pair as target output.

At each phase, weight adjustment proceeded by backpropagation of error down the appropriate input channel (first and second cases) or channels (third case).

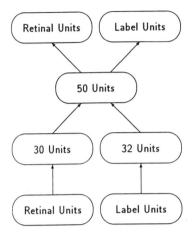

Figure 5.1
Network for processing images and labels. (From Plunkett and Sinha 1991, with permission.)

The network produced a variety of psychologically interesting effects. Some key effects were

  prototype extraction,
  a vocabulary spurt, and
  a comprehension/production asymmetry.

The prototype-extraction effect is just what we would expect in view of the discussion in the first section of chapter 2. Exposure to the various deformed instances led the network to knowledge of the unseen prototype. This is evident from the fact that when the prototype image was given as input the naming performance was actually better than the naming performance on the specific distortions used in training. (For quantitative data see Plunkett and Sinha 1991, pp. 41–42.) The reason is, as usual, that the network's use of superpositional storage techniques leads it to strongly represent the central tendency of the various exemplars—and this central tendency is, naturally, the unseen prototype from which the exemplars were systematically generated.

Less anticipated, perhaps, is the network's tendency to undergo a vocabulary spurt—a period in which the ability to produce correct labels undergoes a sudden dramatic increase.[4] This is a phenomenon that has been noted in child development (Bates, Bretherton, and Snyder 1988) and evidenced in the network's learning pattern over time. The network's ability to produce appropriate labels was initially low and then, after 20–30 training cycles, exhibited a large and fairly sudden improvement. Such changes in the qualitative behavior are in fact quite common, despite the continuous nature of the gradient-descent learning algorithms which drive representational change.[5]

The comprehension/production asymmetry (also reported in the developmental literature—see E. Clark 1983) consisted in the network's finding the label → image task much easier to master than the image → label task. This is because the labels—being arbitrary, orthogonal vectors—are a better clue to the images than the images are to the labels. The label-image mapping is one-to-many, whereas the image-label mapping is many-to-one (and hence harder to isolate). And the images, being partially overlapping vectors, are subject to mutual interference effects, whereas the labels—being orthogonal—are not. An interesting side issue here is that the net's ability to learn the image clusterings does not depend on the pairings of sets of images with labels. (The commonalities between various image vectors are real enough to power the grouping of sets of vectors independently of the provision of labels.) But the presentation of labels speeds up the ability to learn the right image clusterings. This is because the common label can be used by the network as a clue to the "natural clusterings of the distortions in the image plane" (Plunkett and Sinha 1991, p. 47). Linguistic labels are thus not essential for the acquisition of knowledge of categories; however, when labels are provided such knowledge is acquired more rapidly.

Schyns' Modular Neural Network Model of Concept Acquisition
Schyns (1991) presents a somewhat different approach. Using a variant of a self-organizing Kohonen network (see Kohonen 1984), Schyns implements a *categorization* module, which is then augmented by a more familiar autoassociative *naming* module. The general behavior of the model is, however, quite similar to that of the previous one. The categorization process is entirely unsupervised and basically involves competition among groups of output units to respond to relevant (i.e. distinctive) features of input patterns. The task is (as in Plunkett and Sinha's model) to take distorted instances of unseen prototypes as input and to learn to cluster the instances derived from a given prototype together. The network learns to do this, and for the now familiar reasons—viz., "because the categories are composed of variations around a prototype, in the long term, the variations cancel out, and the weight vectors pick out the center of the input subspaces, the prototypes" (Schyns 1991, p. 477). Schyns then augments the categorization module with a *naming* module. The task of this module is to learn to autoassociate the pairing of a conceptual inter-

pretation of an input instance (the output of the categorization module) and a name. The net learns to do this and, upon subsequent testing, exhibits a shorter mean reaction time for the naming of prototypes than for the naming of deformed instances. Once again this is because the network creates a powerful attractor corresponding to the central tendency of the input clusters—viz., the prototype.

Schyns also found that the presence of naming information, though not essential to category learning, is able to facilitate the learning of new categories if it is given. This effect too is noted in the Plunkett-Sinha simulation.

Schyns goes on to consider the learning of new prototypes and the structure of the development of varying degrees of expertise in regard to different categories. For present purposes, however, the lesson is that there seems to be a reassuring robustness about a connectionist approach to categorization and naming phenomena. Quite basic properties of connectionist models (superpositional storage and the development of representational spaces with a built-in semantic metric) give rise to the rich and psychologically realistic patterns of development highlighted above. In particular, the deep natural affinity between connectionist approaches and prototype-based models (proposed as explanations of our ability to make graded judgments of category membership) has been clearly displayed. Nonetheless, the fact that connectionist models learn prototype-style representations does not yet fully explain either the Rosch or the Barsalou results reported above.

To see why, consider first the basic phenomenon of graded category-membership judgments. It is evident that any cognitive model which involves learning a prototype representation *and* for which we can define a metric on which to judge distance from that prototype will provide the right kind of information to allow us to predict judgments of graded membership. Connectionist networks of the kind described fit the bill to a degree, for they come to embody an activation space which has a large number of dimensions, and we (the external theorist) can judge how close to a prototype-constituting peak in such a space a given activation profile lies. Many standard systems do not, however, actually *make* the graded membership judgments which we have heard so much about. Nonetheless, the information needed to do so seems to be available. What is required is a system which knows about the biggest peaks in its activation space (e.g., the activation pattern for a *typical* bedroom) and can then judge that the activation profile caused by the 'bedroom-with-sofa' input is farther from that peak than is, say, a 'bedroom-without-bedside-light' profile. In a sense, this information is already present in a standard "central tendency"-extracting network. To exploit it requires some further apparatus, however. This is the first of two flaws to which we should be alert. Let us call it the *problem of accessibility.*

Recall the dog-recognition network. There is, as we saw, a sense in which that network makes its judgments (about whether to partition a given input into the dog category or the nondog category) according to distance from the statistical center of the example-driven state space—that is, according to distance from the central tendency of its knowledge about dogs. Nonetheless, as Robins (1989) points out, the network's capacity to deploy information about the center of that state space (its "dog hot spot," as Paul Churchland likes to say) is limited. All the network can do is *complete* to the prototypical pattern when given, as input, an adequate cue. And this must be either a sufficiently large fragment of the prototypical pattern itself or a name (say 'dog') which the system has been taught to strongly associate with that pattern. The latter approach yields a somewhat emaciated sense of prototype learning, since it makes "both category formation and categorization processes . . . completely determined by externally selected labels (manipulated by the experimenter)" (Robins 1989, p. 349), whereas the former procedure restricts the network's *use* of prototype knowledge to a somewhat trivial "prototype in, prototype out" retrieval system (ibid.).

To help overcome such difficulties, Robins proposes a model in which the network stores information about the "centrality distribution" of units. This is information concerning the extent to which a given unit (say) is typically (in the history of the network) coactive with the other currently active units. This allows it to judge how typical an instance of (e.g.) *dog* it is representing on a given occasion, and to "know," without cuing, what the most typical dog pattern consists in.

Legendre, Miyata, and Smolensky (1990a,b) also discuss graded judgments in their work on harmonic grammar. In particular, they develop a network which learns to classify French verbs as accusative and nonaccusative, and they deliberately set out to model the further fact that "some verbs are more unaccusative than others." This work exploits Smolensky's (1986a, pp. 206–208) idea of a "harmony measure" which increases as the number of self-consistent complexes of features activated by a given input increases. With the aid of the harmony metric, the Legendre-Miyata-Smolensky model can be used to predict "not only the polarity of acceptability judgments but also their strength" (Legendre et al. 1990a, p. 5).

But what happens if we go beyond the Rosch-style results and ask how a connectionist model could cope with Barsalou's data? Consider the ability to make graded membership judgments concerning *ad hoc* categories. To be concrete, suppose that we are told to grade a variety of cases as exemplars of the *ad hoc* category 'bedroom-with-a-sofa-in-it'. What is needed, it appears, is for the system to complete a pattern on the basis of that description alone (yielding, let us assume, the "large fancy bedroom" description reported in chapter 2), then to somehow mark that *"ad hoc* hot spot," then to complete a pattern in response to a variety of example cases (e.g., 'small room with bed and sofa'), and finally to judge the goodness of the exemplars in terms of their relative distances from the *"ad hoc* hot spot." Robins' system, if I understand it correctly, stores only long-term coactivation information and so would not be able to perform this task, which demands recall of one-off activation patterns.

Thus, by no means is it cut and dried that connectionist models will immediately capture the Barsalou phenomena. Nonetheless, the combination of prototype-style encoding and context-sensitive recall certainly means that the right information is available within the system. It is just its exploitation *by* the system which seems to demand some further work. Potentially more serious, however, is the accusation that, even if such information were fully accessible, it would hardly amount to a model of fluid human categorization, since such categorization is often theory-driven whereas all that connectionist models do is extract statistical central-tendency information. We must now turn to this objection.

A Common Complaint

The idea of a distinction between theory and statistics is important because many different failings of connectionist models are attributed to their "merely statistical" nature, yet it is elusive because the idea of the statistics/theory divide is underspecified. With greater precision, however, it becomes clear that the case against connectionism is far from compelling.

The "common complaint," in essence, is that connectionist models are compromised by their use of statistical surrogates for essentially non-statistical knowledge. Recall the story of the skunk. There is, we saw, a stage at which children make what Keil (1987) called a "characteristic to defining shift" in their bases for categorization. Thus, only a very young child will agree that a skunk in a raccoon suit is a raccoon. Older children, once they are told about the suit, will categorize the animal as a skunk. In other words, the child is no longer impressed by the sheer number of surface similarities between a real raccoon and a cunningly disguised skunk. Instead, she seems to be deploying a normative criterion which insists that surface features alone cannot make something a raccoon.

The point here is that, according to Keil, adult human concepts involve not just knowledge of feature correlation but also (and more profoundly) an *explanation* of the correlations. That is, the correlations are required to make sense within some kind of causal model. This embedding of the knowledge in a causal or explanatory model of some kind results in our categorization judgments' being, in a real sense, informed by some theory of the domain. The shift in children's cognitive strategies (from a feature-correlative to a theory-based approach) has, Keil (1987) remarks, been noticed by such otherwise diverse psychologists as Vygotsky, Piaget, Bruner, and Werner. Such a shift may also be seen as a holistic-to-analytic shift, insofar as it involves "a decreasing attention over time to all the attributes that typically co-occur with a category and an increasing focus on only a certain subset of attributes" (Keil 1987, p. 14).

A further angle on the shift is suggested (and pointed out by Keil) in the work of Garner (1974), who notes that in the early stages of development certain features may be treated as inextricable from one another, whereas later they are regarded as genuinely separate features such that one of them can be treated as salient for a given classification task while others are disregarded (for example, someone might find it hard to treat hue and saturation as separate from color and yet find it easy to treat color as separable from shape (Keil 1987, p. 11). A variety of experiments (Kemler and Smith 1978; Smith 1981; Kemler 1983) have shown that the ability to isolate salient dimensions develops as children get older. If we cast this in the terms of our earlier discussions, it will be clear that standard connectionist models of our judgments of similarity (such as that objects X and Y both fall into category P) depict them as fundamentally *integral* (i.e., X and Y are both judged according to their closeness to a prototypical P, which is the extracted central tendency of a set of exemplars of P). Here *all* the features which were statistically common in the exemplar classes will be considered by the system as it decides whether or not to assimilate a new input to a given prototype. More theory-based approaches, by contrast, are supposed to allow you to disregard certain features even if they were statistically salient in the exemplar set. On the face of it, connectionist/prototype models look congenitally unable to do this. But all is not as it seems, as we shall see.

In defense of connectionism I propose to push the simple idea that the theory of the domain might just *be* a set of weights in a connectionist network. To make this plausible, I will need to address not only the representation of such a theory but also its acquisition.

It is possible for connectionist systems to learn to ignore statistically salient regularities in a training set. Consider Mozer and Smolensky's technique for the "skeletonization" of networks. The idea here is to use an automatic procedure which takes a successful "trained" network and computes a "measure" of relevance that identifies which input or hidden units are most critical to performance and then automatically deletes the least relevant units. It turns out (Mozer and Smolensky 1989, pp. 4–5) that this can improve the system's ability to generalize, speed up its learning, and yield a network whose behavior can be understood "in terms of a small number of rules instead of an enormous number of parameters." This is because the process has the nice property of beginning to loosen the system's ties to the total statistical profile of the training set. For example, in one of the cases discussed by Mozer and Smolensky, a network which originally embodies a sensitivity to both a number of partial cues (statistically salient in the training data) and a number of sufficient cues was able to purge itself of all but the sensitivity to a single sufficient cue. This moves the network in the direction of real knowledge of a rule for the domain and shows one way in which connectionist systems may partially overcome the problem of oversensitivity to the statistical properties of the training set.

More important, however, it is in any case quite unfair to restrict the prototype models considered to ones involving only basic, perceptual feature spaces. Thus, we may concede that central tendency information defined directly over perceptual features does not confer the ability to classify skunks in raccoon suits as nonraccoons. But we should insist that the connectionist is *not* committed to the use of only low-level perceptual features to define the state space. In principle, the connectionist can help herself to any of the features chosen by the experimenter. Thus, we could easily have an input node for 'has raccoon parents' and, by suitable training, ensure that nonactivation of that node was sufficient to inhibit any raccoon categorization. What is perhaps a little harder to see is how a network might discover such a normative feature for itself—that is, how it might be forced to generate novel and highly theoretical representations at the hidden unit level. But it is not obvious that generating a 'has raccoon parents' feature is a *qualitatively* different kind of task from, e.g., a network's generation of a representation of 'animate' or 'vowel' as a classifying principle. And such learning is commonly achieved by fairly simple networks. Of course, we could not expect a network whose input descriptions are limited to perceptual features to generate such a representation. But presumably any realistic psychological model of the formation of a raccoon recognition space will allow as input any information to which a child is normally privy, including functional and genealogical information.

In short: Although the development of highly theoreticized prototype spaces is murky, there is no reason to believe that the cause of the trouble is the connectionist's "central-tendency extraction" approach. Once we allow a cascade of layers of units, and a wide variety of types of information as inputs, it seems quite possible to imagine multi-dimensional feature spaces which do indeed rate 'has raccoon parents' as an important (perhaps even necessary) condition of raccoonhood, and which do so by the usual connectionist means of statistical central tendency extraction over a well-chosen set of training instances.

Networks which build in nonlinearities (e.g., a squashing function at the hidden-unit layer) have, in any case, the ability to push and pull the representational space so that similar inputs need not lead to similar outputs. Such nets can learn to treat very similar inputs in quite different ways if the task demands it. Thus, the shortcomings of devices such as linear pattern associators (as used in the original past-tense model of McClelland and Rumelhart (1986)) should not be mistaken for fundamental shortcomings.

For all these reasons, the picture of pattern associators as indiscriminate sponges condemned to be sensitive to irrelevant and misleading correlations among the training inputs is too simplistic. Multi-layer nonlinear networks may develop highly abstract feature spaces in which continued processing is oblivious to many features of the concrete input. Such feature spaces may be the homes of a variety of different orders of prototype-based representation. Paul Churchland (1989) describes what he calls property-cluster prototypes (ones which consist of typically co-occurrent properties), etiological prototypes (which add a notion of prototypical sequence of events and hence make contact with causal stories), practical prototypes (concerning means-end reasoning), superordinate prototypes (the centers of state spaces whose members are themselves prototypes), social-interaction prototypes, and motivational prototypes ("typical configurations of desires, beliefs and preferences").[6]

In the light of this discussion, we can see that the problem of theoreticity is to some extent a pseudo-problem—hardly surprising, since nonlinear networks can provably encode any possible categorization function. The question of how highly theoretical features are

learned out of what must in the first instance be perceptual information remains, however, a tricky one. (For some discussion, see
Churchland (forthcoming).)

The Ubiquity of Theory

There is a picture[7] of the development of concepts which goes like
this: Children begin by creating 'concepts' which consist of atheoretical, statistically driven clusters of associated surface features. They
then progress, in a way which involves a qualitative shift in their
mode of knowledge representation, to a causal or otherwise theoretical understanding of what makes a given item or event fall under a
given concept. Such a picture must, however, be handled with considerable care. The reason lies with an accumulating body of evidence
which suggests that even very young children may organize their
knowledge around certain principles and beliefs; it is just that these
are often very different from ours, and commensurately harder to
spot. For example, Carey (1985) suggests that although 4-year-olds
lack the fully developed biological theories which allow older children to rule out the possibility of a skunks having raccoons as its
babies, it does not follow that a 4-year-old's judgments are in no way
determined by a theory. She presents convincing evidence that there
is a theory at work, and that it involves behavioral and psychological
features rather than hidden biological ones. Relative to such a theory,
there is no reason to rule out the possibility of a skunk's having raccoon babies. Similarly, Smith, Carey, and Wiser (1985) suggest that
young children do indeed have theories of weight and density, but
that these theories differ from those of adults.[8]

In all these cases, the point of speaking of a theory seems to be that
the principles which make up the theory can "override characteristic
features" (Keil 1989, p. 251). On this understanding, it is clear that
any system which can use stored knowledge to reject or modify a
judgment it would otherwise have made (on the basis of a perceptual
input) counts as deploying some kind of theory of the domain. This
makes it very clear that (as was argued in the previous section) a set
of weights in a connectionist network can indeed constitute a theory,
for such networks use the connection weights (tuned by previous experience) to store knowledge which can then be used to amplify and
correct incoming data. In a very real sense, a system[9] which is given
a degraded letter T as input, and which uses its weights to judge that
the input (despite, e.g., a space in the middle of the downward bar)
is indeed the letter T, is deploying a theory of the domain.

At this point it might be objected that this is precisely to miss the point, for the important difference is between

> (a) systems which amplify and correct incoming data purely on the basis of previous experience of feature clusters

and

> (b) systems which amplify and correct incoming data on the basis of a deep (e.g. causal) understanding of a domain.

Thus we can, if we like, speak of a-type systems as deploying a *theory*, but that theory is different in kind from the theories implicated in the success of b-type systems.

In what might this difference really consist? Consider the case of a network which has been exposed to the correlation of whining and injury in cats and dogs. It is then given a different 'injured animal' input, and it predicts whining. It has never been exposed to the correlation of this animal and whining. Are we now looking at an a case, or at a b case? And what of a system which assimilates an input to a stored prototype of stellar collapse? (See Churchland 1989, p. 210.) At the level of the computational mechanism, it seems, there may be no distinction. What is different in each case is surely the knowledge involved. What we seem to find in the literature on children's cognitive development is not evidence (or not direct evidence) of a shift in inner representational format but evidence of a shift toward judgments based on larger and more varied bodies of knowledge. Thus, as children's knowledge of biology increases, so too does their ability to judge category membership in terms of this knowledge. Insofar as the biological angle provides a more robust and successful way for the child to bring her judgments into line with those of the surrounding linguistic community, she will come to rely on that knowledge more and more. The natural image is of a process of integration (the child learns more and tries to form a consistent world view encompassing this growing body of knowledge) and crystallization (the child discovers which bits of her knowledge are most powerful in bringing her judgments into line with those of the surrounding community, and comes to rely on these in relevant cases). Such an image is, I think, pretty close to that endorsed by Keil (1989). In summarizing the upshot of his investigations, Keil (1989, p. 254) suggests that "increasingly rich domain-specific knowledge structures, especially those that form coherent causal belief systems, are a guiding force in moving children away from holistic, atheoretical modes of construal." Modulo the uneasy distinction between nontheoretical and theoretical knowledge, there is nothing here which the connectionist need dispute.

Connectionist approaches to categorization thus need not be fatally embarrassed by the phenomenon of "theory-driven" categorization. There is, however, a tougher problem waiting in the wings.

Concepts as Elements of Structured Thoughts

Connectionist approaches clearly have enormous potential as models of categorization and naming. But the function of a concept, intuitively understood, is not restricted to its role as a pattern-recognition device. Instead, we think of concepts as (also) being the building blocks of structured thoughts. And therein lies a problem. It is a much-publicized failing of standard prototype-style approaches to knowledge representation that there is no good theory of *prototype combination*. Yet without such a theory, it seems that prototype-style representations, however useful they may be for explaining categorization phenomena (such as graded judgments), cannot also explain the role of concepts as building blocks of structured thoughts. In the absence of such a function, it may look as if what is modeled in much connectionist work on "concepts" is in fact nonconceptual (see chapter 4) knowledge of *categories*. If so, then the prototype representation threatens to be at best a supplementary data structure existing *in addition* to some more easily recombinable (language-of-thought-style) resources. Recalling our earlier discussion, it is surely natural to regard some of the case which Barsalou described as evidence of abilities of *ad hoc* categorization ('things which could fall on your head', etc.) as in fact cases in which categorization judgments flow from the content of a *structured thought*. It is surely stretching our sense of category to treat 'things to eat whose names begin with B and which have fewer than 17 calories per average portion' as a category in any psychologically interesting sense. Categorization in such cases cannot easily be treated as a case of the deployment of prototype knowledge. To see why, consider the classic problems of *prototype combination*.

The problem is that the simple combination of prototype-style knowledge structures seldom captures the content of a complex expression. Imagine that you have prototype-style representations of 'diamond' and of 'worthless'.[10] You then encounter a new phrase: 'worthless diamond'. How are you to understand it? Conjoining the prototypical properties of 'diamond' and 'worthless' will yield an incoherent mess. But if we don't combine the prototypes of the elements of the complex expression, what can we do? We surely cannot tolerate the explosion of prototypes which would result from insisting that we also have a representation of a prototypical worthless diamond! There just can't be a distinct prototype for every complex expression. As Fodor (1981, p. 297) rightly notes, "there may, for, example be prototypical cities (London, Athens, Rome, New York); there may even be prototypical *American Cities* (New York, Chicago, Los Angeles); but there are surely not prototypical *American cities situated on the east coast just a little south of Tennessee*." Complex thoughts, in short, don't have prototypes. It follows, Fodor claims, that, despite the undoubted psychological reality of prototype structures (see Fodor 1981, p. 293), such structures do not play the role of the building blocks of complex contents.

One small disagreement with the flow of Fodor's argument can already be registered. He assumes that prototype combination, if it is to occur, must consist in the linear addition of the properties of each contributing prototype. But why saddle prototype combination with such a simple mechanism? (For a similar objection, see Samet and Flanagan 1989, p. 202.) Even the simplest connectionist incarnations of prototype-style representations embody a more complex combinatoric mechanism than that. The network which stores prototype-style representations of 'bedroom' and 'living room' and is able to represent a 'large, fancy bedroom' as a result does not do so by simply combining the properties of the two "constituent" prototypes. Instead, the webs of knowledge structure associated with each "hot spot" engage in a delicate process of mutual activation and inhibition. As a result, the 'large, fancy bedroom' representation does *not* include all the standard bedroom and living room items. The process is thus much more intelligent than one of simple feature addition. In short, Fodor's objection is already slightly off the mark, since the connectionist version of prototype representation (at least) is not a simple property list but is rather a complex of interlocking microrepresentational elements well suited to engage with certain other such complexes.

An important limitation on the above result should, however, be noted. It is that the conceptual combination concerned is possible only because the two items (bedroom and living room) were already represented in a single space with a unifying "semantic metric" (see chapter 2). Thus, the kind of conceptual combination which consists in finding a midpoint in an existing representational space may not be a good model for the apparently open-ended kinds of conceptual combination which distinguish higher thought.

In fairness, then, it cannot seriously be doubted that there is some major problem for connectionist approaches hereabouts. An ability to perform certain domain-restricted operations of informational integration is one thing, but the ability to entertain any one of an infinity of potential thoughts involving the systematic recombination of grasped meanings is another. (Recall the critical discussion of multiple useability of information in chapter 4.) No connectionist has, I believe, a convincing story to tell about these matters. However, there are some positive things to be said about the progress that connectionists have made in dealing with structure. And there are some negative things to be said about the extent to which the classical "solution" to the problem is really a solution at all. Finally, there are some philosophical misgivings to be aired concerning the way the problem is being posed.

Philosophical misgivings first. The problem, as posed by Fodor and others, builds in a certain conception of the nature of the solution. The problem is seen as one of the recombination of fixed representational *vehicles* (recall the "compositional principle of context invariance" from chapter 1 above). But why suppose that what is invariant across different complex thoughts which (we say) involve a common concept is a specific, static inner representational vehicle? The commonality may be much less concrete than that. Perhaps the two thoughts involve *different* inner vehicles which nonetheless occupy closely related regions of a representational space, or perhaps they involve quite distant regions of such a space but regions whose activation involves a partially common trajectory through activation space (see, e.g., Butler 1991). Such options, in which the idea of a representational vehicle is broadened and temporalized, are pursued in chapters 6–9 below. The moral will be that connectionists *do* have promising avenues for dealing with structured cognition. But these avenues are quite radically unlike the fixed "representational atoms and recombination" approach that characterizes much orthodox AI.

More negatively, it is in any case unclear that the classical solution to the problem of structured thoughts is as powerful as it is usually painted. In the next section, I rehearse a case for caution.

The Irony of Central Processing

> While some interesting things have been learned about the psychology of input analysis—primarily about language and vision—the psychology of thought has proved quite intractable. (Fodor 1983, p. 126)

> The cost of not having a Language of Thought is not having a theory of thinking. (Fodor 1987, p. 147)

In discussing the ability of classical and connectionist approaches to address the issue of structured thought, there are two issues to be considered. The first, as we just saw, is: How are new complex thoughts built up from existing knowledge structures? But there is a second, equally pressing, question: How is the *right* complex thought generated at the right time? This latter problem is one of the greatest stumbling blocks for what we earlier termed the syntactic vision. To see why, we should reflect on the ironic Tale of Central Processing.

Consider Fodor 1983, a compact and decisive demonstration of the inadequacy of the syntactic vision as an account of so-called central processing. Central processing, in this usage, means the system or systems involved in belief fixation, rational thought, and inference—the very system(s) which would be the locus of what Fodor (1987) called "episodes of mental causation." The claim, in 1983, was that classical, symbolic AI had made great progress in the understanding of noncentral systems—largely domain-specific *input* systems (see, e.g., Fodor 1983, p. 103). But two properties distinguished the processing achieved by such systems from that achieved by the central system, and these properties were both highly resistant to the classical treatment. These were the properties of being Quinean and being isotropic. A Quinean system is one in which "the degree of confirmation assigned to any given hypothesis is sensitive to properties of the entire belief system" (Fodor 1983, p. 107). An isotropic system is one in which any part of the knowledge encoded can turn out to be relevant to the system's decisions about what to believe (see Fodor 1983, p. 105). The two properties are obviously closely bound up. Together, they characterize systems in which information processing is profoundly *global*. And much of what goes on in central processing, according to Fodor, has just this global character. When we choose whether or not to accept a new belief, we do so both by allowing that *any* other belief we hold could in principle be relevant to the decision (isotropic) and by allowing the decision to turn also on the collective impact of the sum of our other beliefs (Quinean). Moreover, all forms of *analogical* reasoning, by effecting the "transfer of information among cognitive domains previously assumed to be mutually irrelevant" (Fodor 1983, p. 107), are themselves evidence of the fundamentally isotropic nature of central processing. These kinds of *global* information processing, Fodor believes, are distinctive of "higher cognition." Yet they have not succumbed to the advances of classical AI and cognitive science. And for a very good reason: Such globally sensitive processing runs classical systems very quickly into well-known problems of combinatorial explosion, for there are no fixed sets of beliefs, markable out in advance, among which the relevant ones can be assumed to hide. But the problem of searching among the contents of the entire belief set is simply intractable in classical models; the amount of time and/or computation required increases exponentially with the number of items to be taken into account. One instance of this, noted by Fodor, is the so-called *frame* problem in AI—viz., how to update the *right subset* of a system's beliefs as new information is received. The frame problem, Fodor claims, is just one instance of the general inability of classical AI to model globally sensitive information processing. Indeed, so pessimistic does Fodor become about the whole situation that he proclaims his infamous "first law of the nonexistence of cognitive science": "The more global . . . a cognitive process is, the less anybody understands it." (Fodor 1983, p. 107)

Classical AI, to sum this all up, is depicted by Fodor (1983) as a research program which has done well in helping us model a variety of input systems and peripheral modular processing but which has failed to illuminate the domain of *real thought* (i.e. belief fixation and central processing). How strange, then that the upshot of Fodor and Pylyshyn 1988 seems to be that, although connectionist models might (perhaps) help us understand various peripheral, perceptual processing devices, the classical approach must be preferred in the domain of "real" thought, since real thoughts (like the thought that Mary loves John) form a systematic set and the best explanation of such systematicity lies in our supposing them to be underpinned by classical processing strategies. Strange, too, that Fodor (1987, pp. 143–147) stresses the commitments of actual cognitive models to symbol manipulating approaches (using examples drawn from the processing of language-parsing *input* devices) as part of an argument in favor of a symbolic model of real thoughts (i.e., central processing). There is no mention of the fact that all the successful models, it seems, are targeted on the fundamentally different class of nonglobal computational processes.

Strangeness is not, of course, to be confused with inconsistency. It is quite consistent to hold that classical AI faces fundamental problems in dealing with the global processes characteristic of central processing and that classical AI is especially well placed to deal with the systematicity of contents characteristic of central processing. Still, to completely reject connectionism for its alleged failure to explain productivity and systematicity while simultaneously believing that the classical alternative fails to explain an *equally deep* feature of central processing seems a trifle partisan—the more so since (to a degree) the acknowledged strengths of the connectionist approach lie in its ability to make computationally tractable the task of globally sensitive information processing. The fixation of belief, insofar as it is to be sensitive to both the individual and the collective properties of a large body of information, is surely a prime case for a connectionist treatment. Such systems excel at simultaneously satisfying large numbers of constraints, and the time taken to perform such a task does not increase exponentially as the number of constraints increases. (For a nice treatment, see Oaksford and Chater 1991.)

To sum up: It is simply not clear that the classical approach actually solves the full-fledged problem of the productivity of thought. It gives a neat account of the structural relations between (putative) vehicles of thought. But the price of that account seems to be an equally deep problem concerning *actual* on-line production: It is no longer clear how the right thought complex is produced at the right time. Connectionist approaches show promise here, since they store knowledge in ways which make the large-scale interanimation of knowledge a natural and unforced part of the process of retrieval.

What Symbols Don't Buy You

Connectionist approaches, we saw, have clear potential as models of basic (nonconceptual) categorization phenomena. From the fundamental properties of superpositional storage of distributed representations we can predict the ubiquity of graded judgments, other prototype effects, and rampant context sensitivity, as well as several finer-grained developmental phenomena to be examined in subsequent chapters. There remain, however, some pressing problems. In particular, we need to see in some detail how to *learn* the kinds of higher level feature spaces required to represent the knowledge involved in our grasp of certain contents. Although, as we have seen, connectionist models can learn to rely on quite sophisticated features (vowelhood, animacy, etc.), it remains unclear exactly how the progression from sensory inputs in childhood to a grasp of stellar collapse in later life must go!

The major worry, however, was seen to concern the extension of the model of categorization phenomena to encompass real knowledge of concepts. An emerging theme of the present treatment is that knowledge of concepts is intimately tied up with abilities of *informational integration* (the ability to exploit knowledge gained in one domain in an indefinite variety of other cognitive contexts). Classical approaches give the illusion of holding out a ready-made solution to this problem, since they exploit a base of representational elements (symbols) which are perfectly suited to enter into recombinative operations. But the classical solution is ultimately shallow, since there are well-documented and very profound problems in the *exploitation* of knowledge thus coded. The mere act of opting for a rule-and-symbol approach does not, in the end, buy you much if the appropriate symbol structures cannot be generated at the right time.

It would be nice to think that connectionism was better off here, but the dialectical situation is at best a standoff. Although the connectionist fairs slightly better at fast, globally sensitive, and contextually nuanced information retrieval, she still lacks any general account of conceptual combination (succeeding only, it seems, when the combined content lies within a single, preexisting representational space). To avoid disappointment, I should confess right away that I shall present no such fully general account in the succeeding chapters. Instead, I shall simply try to recast the problem of structured thought in a somewhat different way and then show that significant progress has been made. The first hope is to fully transcend the beguiling image of stored knowledge as structured inner text, and to embrace a vision in which data and processing coevolve and in which the goal of understanding strong representational change is paramount. The shape of cognitive science thus reoriented is sketched in part II.

PART II

From Code to Process

Chapter 6

The Presence of a Symbol

Of Codes and Constituents

The Syntactic Image (chapter 1) depicts the mind as a locus of static, context-invariant symbols whose recombinatorial antics provide for the various phenomena (productivity, systematicity, etc.) of structured thought. Connectionist approaches, by relying on fluid, context-involving, prototype-style representations, are not, on the face of it, very plausible candidates as models of such structured thought. But appearances, as we know, can be deceptive. It turns out that such approaches can indeed make significant headway with the kinds of problem just described. Such headway is obscured, however, by our tendency to conceive the whole question of structure and structured thought in classically infected (symbol-and-text-based) ways.

In the immediately following section, I recall the classical syntactic picture and show how it yields a particular image of structure and explicitness. In the third section I discuss a recent account (van Gelder 1990) of some ways in which certain connectionist models achieve structure sensitive processing without relying on syntactic structure of the kind described in the second section. In the fourth section I ask what happens to the notion of explicit representation in the absence of the familiar syntactic story, and I pursue the suggestion (Kirsh 1991) that it should be reconstructed as a comment on the ease of usability of information. Both van Gelder and Kirsh leave out the important functional characteristic (highlighted in chapters 4 and 5 above) of multiple usability of information. I raise this issue in the fifth section, where I argue that some recent developments in the use of modular connectionist architectures begin to show us how to meet such a demand without falling back into the textual paradigm. I conclude the chapter by noting an implication of the process-orientated approach: that questions about structure and explicitness often have no answer independent of a particular environmental embedding.

The Syntactic Image (Again)

It is common enough to encounter talk about internal representations' being structured and/or explicit. Such talk comes easily as long
as we can trade on the image of *tokens* in an *internal recombinative code.*
This is part of the Syntactic Image of mind.

According to the Syntactic Image (see chapter 1), our representations consist of tokenings in an inner code which has primitive elements which get combined and transformed according to rules. The
example which drives this image is the familiar case of *logics* and *artificial grammars,*[1] in which a base class of primitive elements are operated upon according to well-specified rules; e.g., in propositional
calculus you can take base elements P, Q, and R and combine them
into some complex expression like

$$((P \text{ \& } Q) \lor R)$$

and then operate on that expression in certain legal ways, such as by
transforming it into

$$-(- (P \text{ \& } Q) \text{ \& } -R).$$

Such logics exemplify one of the key properties of the Syntactic Image—viz. constituency relations: the complex expressions have tokens of the component expressions (and ultimately of base-class
atoms) as *real parts,* and these parts are *transportable* in the sense that
they can reappear (as syntactically identical tokens) in other expressions. It is these properties of constituency and transportability which
make Language of Thought (LOT) systems naturally systematic, insofar as their basic mode of operation is one of decomposition and
recombination. Given such a Syntactic/LOT style model, the notions
of structure and explicitness can be nicely specified. A content is implicit if it is not currently tokened but is one which would be expressed by a symbol sequence which can be reached by a string
of legal transformations on a sequence or sequences of symbols
which *are* currently tokened by the system. All contents expressed
by sequences of symbols which are currently[2] tokened count as
explicit,[3] and an internal representation is *structured* insofar as it is
built out of a (legal) complex of atomic elements in a way which
allows the manipulating system to transform the complex structure
in ways sensitive to the elements (atomic or molecular) which it
comprises.

But what purchase (if any) can we get on these properties once we
step outside the familiar bounds of the Syntactic Image?

Functional Compositionality

Consider first the question of structure. A structured internal representation must (trivially) have parts, and these parts must (trivially) be representational (otherwise what you get is, at most, an unstructured representation with a structured vehicle—e.g., one realized in a highly but not semantically structured assembly of physical atoms). A structured internal representation must thus *in some sense* be a product of the combination of representational parts. But in what sense? Van Gelder (1990) has usefully distinguished two broad ways in which such structuring might be achieved. The first, familiar to us from the Syntactic Image, is by *concatenative encoding*. If we take an external formalism like propositional logic, concatenative encoding consists in the spatial juxtaposition of simple informational elements to create complex structures—for example, (P & Q) is placed alongside (R ∨ S) in the complex expression

[(P & Q) ∨ (R ∨ S)].

Classical symbolic computation relies on a nonspatial form of such concatenative encoding in which tokens of symbolic expressions are combined into tokens of complex ones by an intricate system of internal signposts (e.g., pointers) which "(provide) a way of linking or ordering successive constituents without altering them in any way as it forms the compound expression. Thus tokens of the symbol 'P' are the same whether appearing standing alone, P, or in the context of an expression such as (P & Q)" (van Gelder 1990, p. 360).

Concatenative encoding, then, need not be literally spatial, but it must "preserve tokens of an expression's constituents (and the sequential relations among tokens) in the expression itself" (ibid., p. 360). Fodor and Pylyshyn's (1988) talk of complex expressions' having simple ones as literal parts and of the real transportability of symbolic expressions is probably best understood as a commitment to concatenative encoding.

But consider once again our general notion of a structured representation—viz. one which embeds individually usable items of information. It is clear that it is (at least in principle) possible that a representation might have this property without being concatenative in the sense just described. The alternative is to find some way of combining and utilizing informational elements which does not involve the preservation of tokens of these elements in the complex representations themselves. This is the option which van Gelder calls *functional compositionality*. Functional compositionality exists wherever there is a robust and general means of moving from simple to complex representations and back again. All concatenative encoding is functionally compositional in virtue of providing such means, but not all functionally compositional encoding is concatenative. Connectionism provides a useful example case of such an alternative approach to dealing with structure.

In one respect, familiar connectionist systems exhibit more semantic structuring of their representational states than classical Fodorian systems. In another respect, first-generation systems, at least, exhibit less such structuring. This is because all (distributed) connectionist encoding takes advantage of the fine-grained similarity space made available by the learning of *nonarbitrary* representations and their storage in a single network. But first-generation systems were unable to recover or exploit distinct informational elements in the systematic manner characteristic of truly *compositional* encoding and processing schemes. Fortunately, there now exist several "second-generation" methods which make possible the recovery or exploitation of distinct structural elements from noncatenative connectionist representations.

Let us unpack all this. There is an important sense in which even the representations created by first-generation connectionist systems have structure. They have structure insofar as a network will learn a representation of, say, dog as a tendency to create certain kinds of activation pattern in response to input cues. These patterns will not (as we saw in chapter 2) always be syntactically identical, since the particular pattern (vector) generated will be heavily context-dependent. The good news about this is that it allows the pattern (the occurrent representation of dog) to reflect significant semantic structure, such as the state of the dog (hungry, sleeping), its size, and so on. Moreover, semantically related states of affairs will often (given the operation of the learning algorithm) come to be encoded by partially overlapping activation vectors. The representations formed are thus in an important sense nonarbitrary; *what* internal resources are deployed to signify a given content is determined in part by the content in question. The properties of generalization and graceful degradation are direct consequences of the natural similarity metric which characterizes the semantic space defined by a given network. (Dyer (1990) calls this similarity space a *microsemantics*.)

The bad news is that the provision of nonarbitrary microsemantic structure does not yet provide us with a means of *systematically operating* on the representations embedded in the larger structure. This lack of a mechanism for the systematic processing (e.g. transformation) of complex representational structures was once thought to constitute a fatal limitation on the abilities of connectionist systems, for a great deal of human cognition (especially language processing) seems to involve such processing. A variety of techniques, however, have now been developed which allow for structure-sensitive processing without a return to concatenative (strict token-preserving) encoding. The most famous of these is probably Smolensky's tensor-product encoding (see Smolensky 1991 and pp. 371–374 of van Gelder 1990). The crucial step here is that the theorist must decompose the target knowledge into *roles* and *fillers*—for example, to represent the ordered string ⟨A,B,C⟩ you decompose the knowledge into knowledge of position in sequence (role) and letter which has that position (filler). Each knowledge item then gets a vectorial representation, and the fillers are bound to their roles by a kind of vector multiplication. The technique is useful because there exist methods of operating on the resultant products so as to recover (to a degree of tolerance) the original constituents. Nonetheless, the approach is nonconcatenative, since "the vectors which result from . . . successive role/filler bondings are not syntactically structured; they do not contain tokens of the primary constituents (i.e. the primitive vectors assigned to the original roles and fillers) in any sense other than that there are processes that can generate those constituents given the compound representation. Close examination of a tensor product representation of a complex structure fails to reveal the vectors that represent the parts of that structure considered independently." (van Gelder 1990, p. 373)

A second approach to representing structure is illustrated by Chalmers' (1990) model of active-to-passive transformations.[4] The model uses representations developed by a RAAM (Recursive Auto Associative Memory) architecture due to Pollack (1988). This consists of a three-layer feedforward network with a small number of hidden units and with larger and equal numbers of input and output units (e.g. 39 input, 13 hidden, 39 output). The net is taught to develop *compressed distributed representations* of sentence-structure trees. Thus, it may be fed inputs coding for the contents of three terminal nodes on a sentence-structure tree by dividing the input units into groups of four and using one group per terminal node. The network is required to reproduce the input tree at the output layer. It uses the back-propagation learning rule to learn a compressed distributed representation of the 39-unit input structure at the hidden-unit layer (13 units). These hidden-unit patterns are also fed to the network as inputs, thus forcing it to "autoassociate on higher order structures" (Chalmers 1990, p. 55). The upshot is a network which can decode compressed representations of sentence structure trees of arbitrary depth.[5] To perform the decoding, you give the compressed representation directly to the hidden-unit layer and read an expanded version at the output layer. If the expanded version contains only terminal tree structures, the decoding is complete. If it does not, any nonterminal structures must again be fed in to the hidden-unit layer until they are discharged.

Chalmers trained a RAAM architecture to encode tree structures representing sentences of active (but see note 4) form (e.g., John love Michael) and passive form (e.g., Michael is love by John). Forty sentences of each type were used. As expected, the network learned to decode at the output layer the compressed representations of the sentences which it formed at the hidden-unit layer. Chalmers then went on to train a further network to take as input the compressed (hidden-unit layer) representation of active sentences and to give as output the compressed representation of its passive (or at least inverted) correlate. The point of this exercise was to show that a standard network could be taught to transform the RAAM representation in ways sensitive to its constituent structure. The experiment was a success. The new network learned the transformation of the training cases and was then able to perform quite well even on new sentences. Thus, new active sentences, once compressed by the RAAM network, were transformed into appropriate "passives." The network is thus able to perform structure-sensitive transformations on items (the RAAM representations) which do not consist in concatenative tokenings of the structural elements being operated on. The network is thus an existence proof of the practical possibility of what van Gelder called *functional compositionality*. In fact, it is more than that, since functional compositionality is consistent with the need to decode the (functionally compositional) representation before operating on the constituents (as in Pollack 1988), whereas Chalmers' work shows that systematic structure-sensitive processing is possible without proceeding via the step of decomposition.

Chalmers (1990, p. 60) claims that the experiment shows that "not only is compositional structure *encoded* implicitly in a pattern of activation, but this implicit structure can be *utilized* by the familiar connectionist devices of feedforward/back-propagation in a meaningful way. Such a conclusion is by no means obvious *a priori*—it might well have turned out that the structure was 'buried too deeply' to be directly used, and that all useful processing would have had to proceed first through the step of extraction."

In what sense, however, is such compositional structure supposed to be merely *implicitly* encoded in the RAAM representation? One possibility is that 'implicit', so used, means merely that *it is not obvious to us*, on inspecting the RAAM representation, that it encodes the particular structure it does. Thus we read in Blank, Meeden, and Marshall 1991 (p. 12) that "the encodings produced by a RAAM do not explicitly reflect the structure they represent. Understanding the implicit structure in the representations often requires the use of analytical techniques such as cluster analysis and principal component analysis."

This sense of 'implicit' has little to do with the issue of what knowledge ought to be counted as implicit or explicit *to the machine*. What it captures instead is the rather uninteresting notion of what is explicit (i.e., easily visible) to us. Could it be, then, that the notion of a *concatenative* encoding is actually the shallower notion of one which *looks concatenative to us*—that the distinction between functional and concatenative compositionality turns not on intrinsic properties of the representation but on how easily we human theorists can discern the structure of component parts within it? In particular, if (as the quote from Blank et al. suggests) the structural elements are visible via some *post hoc* analytical technique such as cluster analysis or principal-components analysis, then surely syntactic tokens of the structural elements *do* exist in the system; it is just that they are visible only at a level of syntactic structure substantially higher than that of a units-and-weights description. Nonetheless, an important point of contrast remains, insofar as the classical style of (concatenative) encoding is 100% symbol preserving. That is to say, the symbols are completely unaffected by their composition with other symbols. Connectionist modes of composition, by contrast, are symbol altering. What gets stored as part of a larger structure is not a straight copy of an original syntactic part. This (genuine) sense in which connectionist encoding in nonconcatenative seems, however, to have no obvious bearing on the implicit/explicit question. There is no obvious reason why a symbol-altering composition should not, nonetheless, count as a fully explicit representation of a complex structure. It seems, then, that a little more must be said about the implicit/explicit distinction itself.

Functional Explicitness

It has often seemed obvious just when information should or should not count as explicitly represented. It seemed obvious whenever authors uncritically relied on the contrast between data structures (items represented using the resources of some internal code or formalism) and processes (computational operations applied to coded items). Thus, whatever was given as the content of a data structure was counted as explicitly tokened, whereas whatever was either emergent out of other data structures or part of the hard-wired processing characteristics of a machine was not explicit (see Fodor 1987, pp. 16–26). And whatever is known, but not explicit, is implicit. This is the image of explicitness as a property of a *syntactic formalism*.

Relative to such an image, connectionist systems appear anomalous, for it is a feature of at least some such systems that they blur the classical separation of data and processing (see chapter 2). This has led some commentators to hold that connectionist systems, insofar as they violate the code/process distinction, cannot be seen as tokening *anything* explicitly. Instead, these commentators suggest, the contrast between explicit and implicit itself dissolves, because "the distinction between what is explicitly represented and what is merely implicit . . . is a distinction that makes sense only in an orthodox programming context. Explicit contents are contents of data-structures; every thing else is implicit." (Cummins 1989, p. 154) This kind of conclusion reflects, I believe, a mistaken tendency to identify foundational computational ideas too closely with their particular incarnations in classical systems. It may be more productive to seek less restricted understandings of such concepts—understandings which can (at least in principle) cut across many types of computational device (connectionist, classicist, and types as yet undreamed of). Moreover, there is cause, quite independent of this general motivation, to be uneasy about the formal Syntactic Image of explicitness: It arguably places undue emphasis on ultimately irrelevant properties of familiar formalisms. Kirsh (1991) suggests that we are unduly bewitched by the image of "words in a text"—in particular, by the following properties (abstracted from Kirsh 1991, pp. 350–358):

> Locality: [Words] are visible structures with a definite spatial location.
> Movability: No matter where in a book a word is to be found, that word retains its meaning and its explicitness.
> Availability: The informational content of a word is directly available to the system reading it. No elaborate process of translation and interpretation is necessary to extract the information it represents.

Consider (still following Kirsh) the case of an encrypted content. Most of us seem to agree that information which is heavily encrypted (hidden away in a complex code requiring lots of further processing to retrieve the content) should not count as explicit. And yet it could easily meet the criteria of locality and movability. If it fails to count as explicit, it is the *availability* criterion which seems to be doing the work.

But now consider the case of a person who needs a specific item of information which is written out, in plain English, somewhere in an indexless book. Is that information explicit within the system (person and book)? The case violates the availability criterion *if* "the accessing process [is] viewed as part of the representation's usableness" (Kirsh 1991, p. 344). In short, we have a case (and there are many) in which "symbols which are *on the surface* in a structural [formal syntactic] sense may be below the surface in a process sense" (Kirsh 1991, p. 344).

This potential tension between structural and process immediacy is said to render our unanalyzed notion of explicitness dangerously unstable. Such instability is unavoidable if we grant, first, that part of the essence of the idea of *explicit* representation is that the content be available for use without much further effort (the intuition behind our rejection of encrypted information as explicit) and, second, that there is no relevant difference between the efforts involved in searching (as in the indexless-book case) and in decrypting. Kirsh (1991, p. 345) is in no doubt: "My own view is that there is not a relevant difference. Explicitness is tied to usability. And usability implies a match between the procedures available to the agent and the forms the content is encoded in. From a purely computational standpoint there is no fundamental difference between spending time and cycles in finding a datum in space (memory) and spending a similar measure of time and cycles computing that datum in time."

The claim, then, is that the theoretical core of the idea of explicitness should be the notion of easy usability of information (what Kirsh calls the "procedural notion"), but that we also have a *structural* image of explicitness (largely rooted in our experiences with one formalism) which often meets the procedural demands: words written out in a text, in a natural language in which we are fluent, and placed in front of us. And we therefore tend to hallucinate that something like the structural forms of natural language text is in fact essential to genuine explicitness. This structural illusion depicts a representation as explicit if it is "on the surface" of a data structure (as the word 'cat' is structurally explicit in the list {cat, dog, fly}). Kirsh, by contrast, wants an item to count as explicit in proportion to the ease with which it is recovered and put to use. Being the kind of processor we are (as human readers of text), we in fact find it easier to extract the cat information from a typed list than from a tangle of words. But if we were a different kind of processing "tool," we might have no difficulty with the "tangle"—hence, the cat information ought (relative to such a tool) to count as explicit, insofar as the information is ready for immediate use by an embedding system. Consider the idea of locality. Words of English occur as spatially isolated items, visibly separated from their neighbors. This feature certainly helps render the information they contain easily recoverable by the human reader.

(Compare the difficultyofreadinganon-spatially-isolatedstring.) But what this shows is just that, *relative to the human visual processor*, spatial isolation aids easy retrievability of meaning. Beyond that fact, there is no reason to suppose that spatial compactness and isolability matter. What really matters, Kirsh suggests, is not spatial isolability itself but isolability *by the system using the information*. As long as the system can find and use the information encoded in specific structures, it does not matter whether those structures are spatially distinct. A nice example (Kirsh 1991, p. 350) concerns the retrieval of color information. White light is composed of the spatial superposition of many wavelengths corresponding to distinct colors. Are these colors explicitly tokened in the white light? In line with our emphasis on a procedural notion of explicitness, we should reply that the question, thus posed, has no answer, for the real idea of explicitness involves tacit reference to a processing tool. Thus, the question should be: Relative to a processor p, is the information contained in structure s explicitly available? The correct answer will now vary according to the tool. Relative to the tool of unaided human vision, the answer in the white light case is No. Relative to a system deploying certain color filters, the answer will be Yes. Properly understood, the demand of locality is just a demand for easy (computationally inexpensive) separability of items with distinct contents by a host system. Similarly with movability. The intuition was that part of what is important about words on a page is that each word carries its meaning regardless of where it occurs in the text. But why (procedurally) should this matter? It matters only insofar as extreme context dependence of meaning increases the computational costs of retrieval of content, as lots of other local information needs to be decoded to allow access to the content in question. But some context dependence is clearly tolerable. An ambiguous word can carry a content which depends on its local surroundings. Likewise, the numeral 5 carries meaning in a context-dependent way—the notation 5 in 501 means 500, whereas the notation 5 in 51 means 50. To extract the significance of the 5 we need to survey the context, and that takes effort (and hence is a move away from total explicitness (easy usability)). But once we put the *processing* measure in the foreground, we can see that the extent to which context dependence defeats explicitness is relative to the ease with which context is taken into account by the processor. And some processors (e.g. connectionist ones) are very well adapted to the fluid processing of contextually nuanced data. Thus, the requirement of total movability (context invariance of meaning) as a constraint on explicitness is revealed as an artifact of lack of attention to the processing roots of the requirement and to the richness of the space of possible processors.

The Lost Dimension: Multiple Usability

The move toward a functional or ability-based model of explicitness (Kirsh) and structure (van Gelder) is sound and well motivated. But there is a further crucial (functional) dimension: the multiple usability of information. Suppose we take a LISP-style representation of sentence structure and write a conventional program to perform some complex task. In the usual case, such a program will involve a number of distinct subtasks which are dealt with by distinct subroutines. The final program then embodies knowledge about how to perform the task. But that knowledge is not fully task specific. If we then find ourselves faced with another task which is of a different yet related nature, we may well be able to use several of the subroutines developed for the original task in the new setting.

For instance, if we had a program which could recognize vowels for the purposes of pronunciation (i.e., could systematically distinguish vowels and consonants), it would often be possible to adapt it, using several of the original subroutines, so as to count the number of vowels in a sentence. This would not, however, be the case if we had used a single neural network to learn the task. The knowledge acquired by such a network tends, as we saw in chapter 4, to be unexploitable outside the context of the original task.

For a second example, take Chalmers' active → passive network, described above. This net learns to perform a task (word-order inversion) which is structurally similar to other tasks (such as *partial* word-order inversion—e.g., inverting only the third and the fourth word of a sentence). Yet, faced with such a task, we would have no way of exploiting the knowledge acquired by the Chalmers net. Instead, we would need to train a whole new net from scratch (using some of the same RAAM encodings, however).

The only case where network-encoded knowledge is usually portable is the case where a whole existing net can be used as part of some new, multi-network problem solution. In short, transfer of knowledge (and hence multiple usability of knowledge) is a clear weak spot of connectionist approaches. Karmiloff-Smith's work (discussed in chapter 4 above) suggests that human knowledge becomes progressively less and less task bound as development continues. When we say that someone commands an explicit representation of a structural body of problem-solving information, part of what we have in mind is, on this view, that she represents the knowledge in ways which allow its component parts (the subroutines) to be deployed in any of a variety of new problem domains. A full-blooded process-oriented account of structure and explicitness thus needs to address not only exploitability of informational elements (van Gelder) and ease of use (Kirsh) but also ease of *multiple* exploitability. Fully explicit and structural knowledge need not be coded in a quasi-linguistic form. But it must be coded in a multiply deployable fashion.

Fortunately, progress has been made even here. The key to a solution seems to be the development of networks which are, in a certain sense, self-modularizing. Jacobs, Jordan, and Barto (1991) present a network which begins life with an architecture already comprising a set of distinct modules but which does not know, at the outset, how to use those modules in a solution to a complex problem (i.e., it does not embody task-specific information—although of course it could if the modules were especially designed for a given task). The overall architecture then learns how to divide the problem up into subtasks and allocates separate modules to each such subtask. The process is akin to competitive learning: the modules compete to be allowed to perform subtasks. A beneficial result of this is that if the modules are in any way different from one another (e.g., one has more units and another less, or one computes a linear function and the other a nonlinear one) then the module best suited to that subtask will win out. Thus, if a problem has a linear component and a nonlinear component, these can be factored out accordingly.

Such a process of modularization has several advantages of special relevance to our overall discussion. An architecture which has assigned subtasks in this way allows useful transfer of learning, since, when faced with a new but related problem, the architecture will assign similar subtasks to the same module, which will learn faster as a result. It is also protected, to a degree, from the unwelcome effect of unlearning, since radically different functions will not be assigned to a single module (see Jacobs et al. 1991, p. 223). The biological advantages of the modularization regime also include reductions in the overall number of units and in the lengths of the connections needed—crucial factors in determining neural plausibility (ibid., pp. 225–226).

This notion of self-modularization (or, more accurate, of the self-determined exploitation of existing modules; a further step, and an important one, involves seeing whether the modules can be generated from scratch) may shed some light on potential mechanisms of representational redescription (see Karmiloff-Smith 1986 and chapter 4 above). Suppose that initial learning in a domain involved training a single net to perform the task. The solution would be efficient but task bound, incapable of having its elements exploited separately farther afield. Endogenous pressure could cause the brain to then use that single net as the source of a training signal to an architecture (as above) in which several modules compete and perform subtasks. The successful training of such an architecture would allow the wider and more flexible deployment of the knowledge, and the tendency to assign similar elements of future tasks to the appropriate existing module would encourage increasing informational integration over time, just as Karmiloff-Smith suggests.

Once again, we are witness to a subtle shift of emphasis from the text-like properties of an inner code to the development of a complex economy of inner processes which stand in no need of such a common concatenative code. What makes something a fully structured, explicit problem solution is just its embodiment as a bundle of distinct information-processing skills which can, in other circumstances, be exploited in pursuit of quite different ends. Such a bundle of skills can subsist just as well in a complex of connectionist subnetworks as in a classical symbol-processing economy.

In sum: We need to recast the notion of structure in terms of a multiple-usability criterion defined not across the syntactic parts of a quasi-sentential representational complex but across the several bodies of knowledge which a system is able to use to construct on-line problem solutions in a variety of contexts. The system's ability to draw on the *same* body of information in several problem-solving contexts is at the heart of this functional understanding of the idea of structure.

All the World's a Processor

Questions about structure and explicitness, I have argued, do not turn on properties of the occurrent representation itself, treated as a kind of disembodied text. Instead, they turn on the abilities of the overall system to cheaply retrieve and multiply exploit the various bodies of information to which it is privy. The reference in the previous sentence to the overall system suggests a question: once we have embraced such a processing-device-relative view of structure and of explicitness, it becomes necessary to ask what counts as a processing device. Kirsh (1991, p. 12) raises, but does not pursue, the claim that "information can be implicit in a system because that system is embedded in a particular environment." The case he seems to have in mind is one in which, in a certain sense, "a system well adapted to its environment contains information about that environment and about its momentary relations to that environment even though the information is built into the design of the system and so is in principle inaccessible" (ibid.). Thus (I suppose), someone might say that in a certain sense a fish's shape embodies information concerning the hydrodynamics of seawater, or that the visual system, since its processing uses heuristics which rely on certain properties of the distal environment, implicitly carries information about these properties. Consider, however, a somewhat different range of cases: cases in which a system can in fact access certain information (i.e., generate an internal representation of it), but only in virtue of some wider processing environment than that constituted by its onboard processing and storage apparatus. For example, I may be able to further exploit the individual parts of some problem solution only if I am augmented by some external memory (paper and pencil), or I may be able to retrieve and deploy some specific item of information only in a particular external setting (one in which it is cued by a written reminder). It seems to me that in those cases we have to allow that, relative to the broader processing tool of me + my environment, information which would otherwise count as unstructured and/or inexplicit should count as structured and/or explicit, for it is not clear why the skin should constitute the boundary of the processing environment relative to which such questions are to be decided.

To see this, consider the case where my brain is augmented by a mechanical processing device which increases my short-term memory span. There seems little doubt that the processing tool relative to which the internal representational states are to be judged (as structured, explicit, etc.) has been altered. But why is this different from taking the original processor (brain and body) and setting it in front of an external environmental device (paper and pencil) which likewise allows the augmentation of my short-term memory? I conclude that to take seriously our picture of structure and explicitness as processing-environment-relative properties of inner states is necessarily to allow that both the nature and ultimately the content (a structured content is different form an unstructured one, after all) of our inner states are always joint functions of their intrinsic natures and the broader environment in which they exist. In short, there is just no answer to the questions "What is the content of that state?" and "Is it explicit?" independent of considerations involving the processing capacities of the local system as currently embedded in some wider environment.

From Syntax to Process

A familiar image depicts mental processes as the logico-manipulative transformation of fixed symbol structures in a concatenative and recombinative inner code. Relative to such an image, we may define explicitness in terms of the presence of symbols, and structure in terms of their concatenation and recombination. Such definitions, however, appear clearly inadequate if we seek to consider structure and explicitness in fundamentally non-text-like systems, such as neural networks. To remedy this shortcoming, it is necessary to recast the ideas of structure and explicitness in a more functional (process-oriented) way. The suggested reading (building on proposals developed by Kirsh and van Gelder) treats knowledge as fully explicit if it is both easily and multiply deployable, and it treats a representation as fully structured if it is built up by drawing on several such bodies of (multiply deployable) knowledge. The notion of 'building-up' is functionally defined. Moreover, these functional definitions yield continuums of explicitness and structure. Knowledge can be more or less explicit according to how cheaply and how multiply deployable it is, and a representation can be more or less structured according to how flexible the system is in the use of the several bodies of knowledge implicated. Existing connectionist systems (such as Chalmers' active → passive net) lie toward the implicit, unstructured end of the continuum, insofar as the system's use of the stored information is characteristically quite special purpose and limited. What we need, it seems, is to model the kind of developmental progression (studied by, among others, Karmiloff-Smith; see chapter 4 above) in which knowledge which is initially limited in use becomes increasingly widely deployable. To do so is to model the progression from what I (following Cussins) have called nonconceptual content to conceptual content—a progression which is now revealed as identical with that from (relatively) unstructured to structured representation. Networks such as that of Jacobs et al. (1991) are a promising step in that direction.

Chapter 7

The Role of Representational Trajectories

A Developmental Journey

We have begun to see how recent connectionist approaches can make headway with the difficult problem of dealing with structure. The big question, however, remains: Will it prove possible for a complex yet recognizably connectionist learning device to acquire the same knowledge that humans acquire, and to deploy it in an equally flexible way? The question is, of course, currently unanswerable, not least because the extension and the boundaries of the label "connectionist learning device" are still being constructed (or discovered, depending on your metaphysical whims). One cause for optimism, however, is the increasing richness of connectionist thinking as a source of developmental models and insights. Regardless of whether the endpoint of the developmental journey is something more like a classical representational system or more like a connectionist one, it looks increasingly as if the way to understand how we get there (wherever it is) will involve conceiving of the brain as exploiting some kind of error-minimization—probably gradient-descent-style—learning. (See Churchland and Sejnowski 1992, pp. 130–137.) Moreover, it is not seriously to be doubted that the product of such learning is the setting of a very large number of physical parameters which together define a high-dimensional space (or spaces). The developmentalist must ultimately aim to understand the way nature's learning rules, inputs, and innate parameter settings combine to drive a system on a certain trajectory through that space. Connectionist modeling offers, at a minimum, the chance to develop intuitions about such matters by direct experience with a learning device which can indeed negotiate an error-minimizing path through such a space. Such is the developmental vein to be tapped in the present chapter, which displays the importance of the training sequence in determining the trajectory of a given network through a representational space.

Net Failures

Sometimes the failure of a system is more instructive than its success would have been. A case in point is Norris' (1990, 1991) attempt to use a multi-layer, feedforward connectionist network to model date calculation as performed by idiots savants (persons who, despite low general intelligence, are able to perform remarkable feats of specific problem solving). There are idiots savants who can tell you, for almost any date you care to name, what day of the week it falls on. The best such date calculators can successfully perform this task for dates in years which I can hardly pronounce, the top limit being about the year 123470. Norris (1991, p. 294) conjectured that, since idiot savant date calculators can solve such problems despite their low general intelligence, they may be using a "low-level learning algorithm" such as backpropagation of error in a connectionist net. The task, however, turned out to be surprisingly resistant to connectionist learning when Norris took a three-layer network and trained it on 10% of all the day-date combinations in a 50-year period. The network learned the training cases by rote, but failed to generalize to any other dates. Perhaps the fault lay with some simple aspect of the configuration? Norris tried permutations of numbers of layers and of hidden units, to no avail.

Here is a second example. Recall the kind of network detailed in Elman 1991c and described in chapter 2 above. This is a so-called simple recurrent architecture, comprising a standard three-layer feedforward network and a set of context units which constituted a kind of local memory (by copying the hidden-unit activation pattern and then feeding it back as input alongside the next input given to the system). We saw how the use of such an architecture enabled a network to learn about the classes and categories of words in a corpus of sentences. The same basic network structure was also used (see Elman 1991a,c) to study the ability of networks to learn representations of grammatical structure—e.g., to learn about verb agreement and clause embedding in sentences such as 'the girls whom the teacher has picked for the play which will be produced next practice every afternoon' (example from Elman 1991a). Elman's motivation in carrying out this work was, he tells us, to confront the challenge of modeling "complex, hierarchically organized information" in a connectionist manner. In particular, he sought to test the idea that the recursive nature of embedded relative clauses placed the grammars of natural languages out of reach of the learning and representational capacities of connectionist networks (a suspicion rooted in works (Chomsky 1957; Miller and Chomsky 1963) which seemed to place natural-language grammars outside the space of grammars learnable by statistical inference engines and finite-state machines and hence, it seemed, outside the space of structures learnable by familiar connectionist means). Elman thus attempted to get a recurrent network to learn, from exposure to a corpus of sentences, about grammatical structure in a simple artificial language. The language exhibited various target features, including verb-subject number agreement, multiple clause embedding, and long-distance dependencies. But, alas, the Elman net too failed at its task. It failed completely to generalize to new cases (i.e. to deal with inputs not given during training), and it got only a badly incomplete grip on the training cases themselves. The network had, it seems, failed to learn to use its resources (of units and weights) to encode knowledge of the deep organizing features of the domain—features such as whether or not an input was singular or plural.

This diagnosis can be supported by the use of principal-components analyses (see chapter 3 above), the results of which can be graphically illustrated by a state-space graph which plots the network's responses on a large corpus of trial sentences to two key domain properties: number (singular vs. plural) and depth of embedding. The network's response to these properties are plotted on a graph where X and Y coordinates correspond to depth of embedding and Z coordinates to number. The graph for the unsuccessful network is reproduced here as figure 7.1. Notice that the network's responses are relatively flat. The network is not using its resources to pay special attention (which would be evidenced in corresponding peaks of activation) to the properties plotted. Now compare figure 7.2, which illustrates a successful network's highly property-sensitive use of resources. The successful net uses its resources to respond dramatically and distinctively to properties which are, in fact, fundamental in the domain. As Elman (1991, p. 6) puts it, the unsuccessful

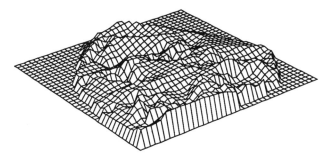

Figure 7.1
Graph of dimensions which encode embedding (x,y) and number (z) from an unsuccessful network. (From Elman 1991a, with permission.)

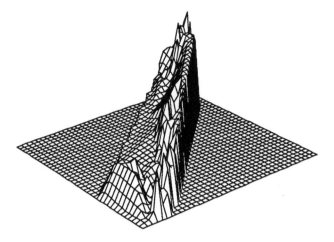

Figure 7.2
The same graph as in figure 7.1 but from a successful network. (From Elman 1991a, with permission.)

network has learned "a set of internal representations which do not reflect the true underlying sources of variance."

Thornton (1991a, p. 6) notes an interesting class of cases in which networks often fail to learn partitions which reflect the deep facts about the training cases. These are cases in which "the target mapping (of inputs to outputs) that is to be learned is based on the recognition (or exploitation) of a feature that is more than first-order, i.e. which cannot be defined directly in terms of the primitive attributes appearing in the training examples." Consider (Thornton's example) the network that Hinton (1989) trained to answer queries about family relationships among a certain set of named individuals. The network (when subjected to *post hoc* analysis) turned out to have learned partitions which traced certain features of the domain (e.g. nationality and age). These features were not given as training primitives; instead they were induced by the system as a means of performing the input-output mapping required. Thornton calls the initial primitives (the features directly present in the training inputs) *0th-order features*. Features which can be specified as sets of 0th-order features are then termed *1st-order features*. The interesting cases, then, concern 2nd-order and higher-order features. A 2nd-order feature is one which can only be defined over 1st-order (not 0th-order) features; for example, relative to the training primitives of the Hinton net, 'unusually-young-for-a-person-of-that-nationality-in-this-family-tree' is a 2nd-order feature, as it is a predicate which "can only be defined in terms of an age feature and a nationality feature, and these are themselves 1st-order features of the domain" (Thornton 1991a, p. 6).

The point is important, so let us look at one further example (Thornton 1989, p. 81). Consider a description language whose 0th-order primitives specify individual playing cards (Jack/Hearts, 3/Spades, etc.). First-order features relative to that language will include the set of all black cards, since this is definable directly as a subset of the initial primitives. But the set of all poker straights cannot be defined directly in terms of 0th-order primitives. Instead, the feature 'is-a-member-of-a-straight' picks out a given card only by reference to the role of that card in a sequence (e.g., 3/spades, 4/hearts, . . .). There is no 1-1 mapping between elements of the set of straights and individual instances picked out in the initial description language. (Contrast the above-mentioned case of black cards, where a stable 1-1 mapping between the feature 'black' and individual cards obtains.) Instead, to capture the feature 'is-a-straight' we need a description language which deals in whole hands—that is, in higher-order features which involve the combination of lower-order features. And the problem recurs. Suppose we now have a language which takes whole hands as primitive features and hence can define 'straight' as a subset of whole hands (i.e., now we have a 1-1 mapping using the higher-order primitives). Still there will be classes of hands which are not definable in this vocabulary—for example, the class of close hands (= a pair of hands X and Y where X (say) beats Y, but only just). This class is visible only once we attend to *relations* between whole hands, and hence it is not definable as a subset of the set of whole hands—again, there is no 1-1 mapping between primitives (in this case, whole hands) and membership of the class of close hands. More simply, the idea as I understand it is that to grasp the concept of *close sets* (e.g. KKK/QQQ as against KKK/444) you need to use the concept of a set of cards as a building block. If you lack the concept of a set, you will never (of course) grasp the concept of close sets.

What Thornton does is show in some detail (see especially Thornton 1989) that familiar connectionist learning algorithms, (and, incidentally, the major *classical* learning algorithms too) operate by constructing what he terms "neighborhood representations," and that these are, in effect, representations which define new features by seeking a 1-1 mapping between primitive items in an initial description language and members of the class about which it is inducing knowledge. All such learning devices are thus compromised in their abilities to learn features which are several levels of abstraction removed from the primitive features of whatever description language they began with.

Such a result may seem at odds with the well-established claim that a three-layer network, given sufficient units, can learn any input-output mapping whatsoever. The question, though, is not whether a given mapping can be learned but whether, in learning, the mechanism learns the kind of knowledge which will enable it to extend its success to *other cases* where the same kind of knowledge should bring success—that is, whether it has learned about regularities and features which will work in other (actual or counterfactual) cases. Thornton's claim is that, where such further success depends on the network's inducing knowledge of features which are of higher order (i.e. more than 1st order) with respect to the description language of the example cases, networks tend to fail, learning the required mapping only in some *nonextendable* manner (i.e., by means of a *kludge*). Consider the task of learning whether a given pair of numbers falls under an unspecified rule (Thornton 1991, pp. 10–11). A net is trained on pairs of numbers as input, and a supervised learning algorithm "tells" the network whether the correct diagnosis of that pair is positive (i.e., it fits the rule, or exemplifies the feature) or negative. Take as the training set, the following set of cases:

(0.4 0.4) +
(0.7 0.5) −
(0.18 0.9) +
(0.8 0.7) −
(0.4 0.4) +
(0.8 0.6) −
(0.1 0.4) +
(0.9 0.8) −
(0.07 0.7) +
(0.6 0.9) −
(0.2 0.6) +
(0.7 0.3) −
(0.2 0.2) +
(0.4 1.0) −
(0.3 0.9) +
(0.1 0.9) −
(0.4 0.8) +
(0.05 0.4) +

The underlying rule here is that an input pair counts as falling under the rule just in case the first number cleanly divides the second. Thornton trained a network on this body of data (using backpropagation) and found that a network with 10 hidden units would learn the target mapping very well. However, *post hoc* analysis showed that none of the partitions the net was making was dealing with the property of *being divisible*. Instead, they encoded other, locally indicative features of the particular instances (e.g., Respond Yes if the two numbers are equal).

Thornton (1991a, p. 11) comments that "the target mapping was based on the concept of division, but none of the mathematical concepts that one might expect to be utilized in a representation of division was evidenced in (the network's) configuration of boundaries. Putting it another way, there is nothing about the arrangement of boundaries . . . that would be much use in dealing with a *different, division-related problem* (e.g. deciding whether one number divides another number a certain number of times)." (The emphasis here is mine.)

Thornton ignores the possibility that a network might learn an *unexpected* but powerful and extendable way of partitioning the space— one which does not use familiar mathematical concepts but which nonetheless constitutes the kind of knowledge required to deal with other related cases. It is clear enough, however, that this is not what has happened in the case at hand.

The reason the net fails to learn a powerful, extendable problem solution, if we accept Thornton's claim, must be that divisibility is in some sense a higher-order property relative to the training primitives (pairs of numbers). Although this is intuitively the case, it would be nice to see this implicit claim made precise. Thornton's discussion is elusive in this respect, but he is certainly asking the right question: Under what conditions will a net learn the deep features which organize a batch of training data? And he is gesturing at the central problem which Elman (1991a) shows prevents networks from learning such features. This problem can be summarized as follows:

> (Representational-Trajectory Hypothesis)[1]
> In domains organized around basic rules and features which interact to yield complex rules and features, it can be fatal to connectionist learning to allow the net to deal with the complex cases early in its training. In such circumstances, the net tries to account for the regularities governed by the complex ("second-order") features without yet knowing the basic ("first-order") ones. Under these conditions, the second-order features are effectively unlearnable and the first-order ones are obscured by the wild hypothesis thrown up in the attempt to cover the second-order cases.

Thornton lays all the blame at the foot of the initial description language, and obviously a description language which explicitly fed the network the basic features (the right "building blocks") would ensure successful learning. But the description language of the inputs is only one factor in connectionist learning, and what you lose on the swings of initial primitives you may make up on the roundabouts of configuration and training, as we shall now see.

How to Learn the Right Thing

What can be done to remedy the kinds of failure chronicled in the preceding section? One way of solving a learning problem is, in effect, to give up on it. Thus, it could be argued that certain features simply cannot be learned, by connectionist means, on the basis of certain bodies of training data, and hence that the "answer" is either to give up on connectionist learning (for that task) or to build more of the target knowledge *into* the training data in net-accessible ways. Very often the solution to a learning failure will be to alter the input description language. Nonetheless, the input description language, although it no doubt could be manipulated to solve many instances of network failure, need not always be tampered with. In the present section I examine a variety of ways of dealing with the kinds of failure described above by keeping the training corpus (and hence the input description language) fixed and instead manipulating one of a variety of parameters that are often neglected.

Recall Norris' unsuccessful attempt to model date calculation. To generate a successful model, Norris reflected on the logical form of a particular date-calculation algorithm. The algorithm involves three steps. First, day/date pairings are specified (by rote) for a base month (say, November 1957). Second, offsets are learned to allow the generalization of the base-month knowledge to all other months in the base year. Finally, offsets between years are learned (i.e., a one-day offset between consecutive years, modulo leap years). With this algorithm in mind, Norris chose a global configuration comprising three distinct subtasks: base-month modeling, base-year transformations, and cross-year transformations). Each subnet was trained to perform its own specific part of the task (in logical sequence), and learning in it was stopped before the training of the next subnet was begun. Thus, learning was stopped in subnet 1 before the training of subnet 2 was started, and so on. Subnet 2 would take output from subnet 1 and transform it as needed, and subnet 3 would take output from subnet 2 and do the same.

The upshot of this preconfiguration and training management was, perhaps unsurprisingly, a system capable of solving the problem in a fully generalizable manner. The final system was about 90% accurate, failing mainly on leap-year cases of the kind that cause difficulty for human date calculators (see Norris 1991, p. 295). This result is, at best, only mildly encouraging. True, it shows that the problem can be solved by connectionist learning. And true, the solution does not require amending the input description language. But the solution depends on a task-specific configuration (and training regime) which is bought only by drastic human intervention. If the goal is to develop good psychological models of human problem solving, such intervention is, as far as I can see, legitimate only if we can reasonably suppose that the long-term processes of biological evolution in our species have preconfigured our own neural resources in analogous ways or if we are assuming that the configuring can be automatically achieved, in individual cognitive development, by processes as yet unmodeled. Thus, the question that faces us is whether there exist fixes which do not depend on *unacceptable* kinds of human intervention. Recent work by Jeffrey Elman (1991a) suggests that the answer is a tentative Yes and that the key lies in what I shall label the *scaffolding of a representational trajectory.* Hence we move to our second fix: manipulating the training.

Recall Elman's failed attempt to get a recurrent network to learn the key features of a simple grammar. One way of solving the problem is, it turns out (see Elman 1991a), to divide the training corpus into graded batches and to train the network by exposure to a sequence of such batches, beginning with a batch containing only the simplest sentence structures and culminating with one containing the most complex structures. Thus, the net is first trained on 10,000 sentences exhibiting (e.g.) verb-subject number agreement but not containing any relative clauses, long-distance embeddings, etc.; then it is gradually introduced to more and more complex cases. The introduction of the progressively more complex cases is gradual insofar as it is accomplished by grading the sentences into five levels of complexity and exposing the net to example batches at each level in turn and insofar as the network is "reminded," at each subsequent stage of training, of the kinds of sentence structure it has seen in the earlier stages. For example, stage 1 consists of exposure to 10,000 very simple sentences, and stage 2 consists of exposure to 2,500 sentences of a more complex kind plus 7,500 (new) very simple cases.

This "phased training" regime enables the network to solve the problem—i.e., to learn the key features of the artificial language. And it does so without amending the basic architecture of the system and without changing the content of the corpus or the form of the input code. What makes the difference, it seems, is solely the sequential order of the training cases. Why should this be so effective? The answer, according to Elman, is that phasing the training allows the network to spot, in the early stages, the most basic domain rules and features (e.g. the idea of singular and plural and the idea of verb-subject number agreement). Knowing these basic rules and features, the net has a much smaller logical space to search when faced with the more complex cases. It is thus able to "constrain the solution space to just that region which contains the true solution" (Elman 1991a, p. 8). In contrast, the original net (which did not have the benefit of phased training) saw some very complex cases right at the start. These cases forced it to search wildly for solutions to problems which in fact depended on the solutions to simpler problems. As a result, it generated lots of *"ad hoc"* small hypotheses, which then obscured the grammatical structure of the simple cases. Such a net is, in effect, trying to run before it can walk, with the usual consequences.

At this point we begin to see a common thread uniting the grammar case and the date-calculation case. Both domains require, in a very broad sense, *hierarchical* problem solving. In each case there is a problem domain which requires, for its successful negotiation, that a system decompose the overall problem into an *ordered series* of subproblems. In the grammar case, this involves first solving (e.g.) the verb-subject number-agreement problem and only later attacking the problem of relative clauses. In the date-calculation case, it involves (e.g.) first solving the problem for the base year and only later attacking the problem of other years. The general moral is that there is a class of domains in which certain problem solutions act as the "building blocks" for the solutions to more complex problems. In such domains, connectionist learning is efficient only if the overall problem domain can somehow be decomposed and presented to the net in an ordered sequence. In the absence of such decomposition, the basic regularities (the "building blocks") are obscured by the net's wild attempts to solve the more complex problems, and the more complex problems are, practically speaking, insoluble.

The key to success, as we have seen, is to somehow sculpt the network's representational trajectory—to force it to solve the "building block" problems first. This can be achieved either by direct manipulation of the architecture and training (Norris) or by "scaffolding" a network by the careful manipulation of the training data alone (Elman). The Norris solution, however, was seen to involve undesirable amounts of problem-specific human intervention. The phased-training solution is a little better, insofar as it does not require problem-specific preconfiguration of the architecture. The third and final fix I want to consider is one which involves neither phasing the training nor preconfiguring the architecture to suit the problem. It is what Elman calls "phasing the memory," and it represents one approximation to the ideal of an *automatic* means of sculpting the representational trajectory of a network.

Recall that short-term memory, in the Elman network, is given by a set of so-called context units whose task is to copy back, alongside the next input to the net, a replica of the hidden-unit activation pattern from the previous cycle. The "phased memory" fix involves beginning by depriving the network of much of this feedback, and then slowly (as training continues) allowing it more and more until finally the net has the full feedback resources of the original. The feedback deprivation worked by setting the context units to 0.5 (i.e., eliminating informative feedback) after a set number of words had been given as input. Once again, there were five phases involved. But this time the training data were not sorted into simple and complex batches. Instead, a fully mixed batch was presented every time. The phases were as follows.

Phase 1: feedback eliminated after every third or fourth word (randomly)

Phase 2: feedback eliminated after every fourth or fifth word (randomly)

Phase 3: feedback eliminated after every fifth or sixth word (randomly)

Phase 4: feedback eliminated after every sixth or seventh word (randomly)

Phase 5: full feedback allowed (i.e., the same as the original net used in the earlier studies)

In short, we have a net which, as Elman puts it, "starts small" and develops, over time, until it reaches the effective configuration of the original recurrent net. This "growing" network, although exposed to fully mixed sentence types at all stages, is nonetheless able to learn the artificial grammar just as well as did the "phased training" net. Why should this be so? The reason seems to be that the early memory limitations block the net's initial access to the full complexities of the input data, and hence it cannot be tempted to thrash around seeking the principles which explain the complex sentences. Instead, the early learning can target only those sentences and sentence fragments whose grammatical structure is visible in a four-or-five-word window. Unsurprisingly, these are mostly the simple sentences (i.e., those which exhibit such properties as verb-subject number agreement but not long-distance dependencies, embeddings, etc.). The "phased memory" solution thus has the same functional effect as the phased learning: it automatically decomposes the net's task into a well-ordered series of subtasks (first agreement, then embeddings, and so on). The key to success, we saw, is to somehow achieve task decomposition. The great attraction of the "phased memory" strategy is that the decomposition is automatic—it does not require task-specific human intervention (as the Norris solution or the phased-training solution does).

What the findings show, according to Elman, is that the combination of early limitations and subsequent maturational growth may in fact be a crucial and positive factor in determining the ability of finite-state, statistically driven gradient-descent learning machines to penetrate certain theoretical spaces. As Elman (1991a, p. 8) eloquently puts it: "Seen in this light the early limitations on memory capacity assume a more positive character. It is natural to believe that the more powerful a network, the greater its ability to learn a complex domain. However this appears not always to be the case. If the domain is of sufficient complexity, and if there are abundant 'false solutions,' then the opportunities for failure are great. What is required is some way to artificially constraint the solution space to just that region which contains the true solution. The initial memory limitations fill this role; they act as a filter on the input, and focus learning on just that subset of facts which lay the foundation for future success."

It is always reassuring to learn that the use of limited resources (as in the net's early memory limitations) can bring positive benefits. In suggesting a precise way in which early cognitive limitations may play a crucial role in enabling a system to learn about certain kinds of domain, Elman's work is clearly of great interest to developmental cognitive psychology. In the next section I will try to extend and to clarify the developmental dimensions while questioning the generality of the specific "phased memory" solution.

The Bigger Picture: Scaffolding and Development

Networks faced with a hierarchically structured problem domain have, we saw, a distressing tendency to get "lost in space(s)." They try to solve for all the observed regularities at once, and hence solve for none of them. The remedy is to sculpt the network's representational trajectory so as to force it to focus on the "building block" regularities first. The ways of achieving this are remarkably various, as was demonstrated in the preceding section. It can be achieved by direct configuration of the architecture into task-specific subnets, or by redesigning the input code, or by fixing the training sequence, or by phasing the memory. In fact, the variety of parameters whose setting could make all the difference is, I believe, even larger than it already appears. To see this, notice first that the mechanism by which both the Elman solutions work is *undersampling*. The network begins by looking at only a subset of the training corpus. But actual physical growth (as in the incremental expansion of the memory) is not necessary in order to achieve such initial undersampling, even if no interference with the training corpus (e.g. sorting into batches) is allowed. The heart of the phased-memory solution is not physical growth so much as *progressive resource allocation*. And this could be achieved even in a system which had already developed its full, mature resources. All that is required is that, when the system first attends to the problem, it not allocate all these resources to its solution. In the Elman net, the memory feedback was initially reduced by setting the context units to 0.5 after every four or five words. A similar effect would be obtained by adding noise after every four or five words. Even switching attention to a different problem would do this, since, relative to the grammar problem, the new inputs (and hence the subsequent state of the context units) would be mere noise. A limited attention span in early infancy might thus be a positive factor in learning, as might the deliberate curtailing of early efforts at problem solving in adult cognition. In general, it seems possible that one functional role of salience and selective attention may be to provide precisely the kind of input filter on which the phased-memory result rests. (In the case of learning a grammar, it is worth wondering whether the fact that a young child cares most about the kinds of content *in fact* carried by the simple sentences may play just such a functional role (i.e., whether the child's interests yield a selective filter which results in a beneficial undersampling of the data). There is a kind of "virtuous circle" here, since what the child *can* care about will, to an extent, be determined by what she can already understand.)

Less speculatively, Elman himself has noted (in a personal communication) that there are mechanisms besides actual synaptic growth which might provide a physical basis for early undersampling—for example, delays in cortical myelinization resulting in high noise levels along poorly myelinated pathways.

A further developmental factor capable of yielding early undersampling is the gradual development of physical motor skills. This provides us with a staged series of experiences of manipulating our environment, with complex manipulations coming after simple ones. Once again, it may be that this automatic phasing of our learning is crucial to our eventual appreciation of the nature of the behavior of objects (that is, to the development of a "naive physics"—see Hayes 1985).

Going deeper still, it is worth recalling the functional role of undersampling. The role is to enable the system to fix on an initial set of weights (i.e. some initial domain knowledge) which serves to constrain the search space explored later when it is faced with more complex regularities. As Elman (1991, p. 7) puts it, "the effect of early learning . . . is to constrain the solution space to a much smaller region"—i.e., to a region containing fewer local minima. Given this reading, however, we can see that a variety of other factors could play the same role. One is the presence in the initial system of any kinds of useful innate knowledge—that is (in connectionist terms), any presetting of weights and/or preconfiguration of networks which paves the way for a solution in a given domain. (See chapter 9 below.) A second source of constraint might be the basic domain divisions embodied in public language. (This is the idea of public language as a "semantic scaffold," developed in Plunkett and Sinha 1991.) The child's representational trajectory is surely heavily sculpted by the groupings of objects dignified by the provision of a public-language label. Indeed, we already saw (in chapter 5) how the provision of such labels speeds up the process of category learning. More mundanely, the whole process of teaching a child about the world already embodies the ideal of a staged series of understandings. All these various methods and factors make sense as different ways of encouraging the initial formation of simple but powerful ways of partitioning a problem space and (hence) of constraining later learning in a beneficial way. Grasping the nature of a learning mechanism may thus help us to unify a variety of factors studied by developmental psychologists. Seen through the lens of Elman's work, all the above are ways of staging knowledge acquisition so as to promote the understanding of high-level theoretical spaces. Studies by Keil (1987), Carey (1985), Bruner (1970), Piaget (1955), and others may usefully be understood in these terms. In the context of some of these studies (e.g., Carey 1985), it is worth noticing that the early partitionings of a space may usefully (i.e. beneficially) constrain later learning even if they are, in fact, ultimately inadequate. There is no reason yet to suppose that the only initial partitions which can prompt the later negotiation of deep theoretical spaces are those which will form part of the final picture! For instance, in individual learning of physics or philosophy, it is common to teach students false but simple divisions and theories so as to prepare them for more sophisticated learning. One reason for this may be that the false theories constrain the stu-

dents' future thinking in ways which actively enable the later acquisition of the true ones. The fact that so much changes between (e.g.)
a child's early ideas about death and the adult concept in no way
implies that the early way of partitioning cases does not fulfil the kind
of constraining function I have been discussing.

The catalogue of speculations could be continued, but the effective
moral is already clear. It is that attention to the basic mechanisms
highlighted by the Elman experiments reveals a unifying thread for a
superficially disparate bag of factors which have occupied cognitive
developmental psychology since time immemorial (well, since 1934
at least). What we need to understand, before we venture to pronounce on what connectionist networks will or won't be able to learn,
is nothing less than how cognitive development is "scaffolded" by
innate knowledge, culture, and public language, and how broadly
maturational processes and processes of individual learning interre-
late. Connectionism and developmental psychology are headed, it
seems, for a forced union, to the benefit of both parties.

That is the good news. I want to close this section by looking at the
downside and highlighting two limitations on Elman-style solutions.

The first limitation, which afflicts any "phased memory" approach,
is that phasing the memory can be effective only in cases where, as a
matter of fact (i.e., "as luck would have it"), merely statistically
driven undersampling of a training corpus is equivalent to task decomposition. It happens, in the domain of artificial grammar, that an
initial four-or-five-word window isolates the set of training data necessary to induce the basic "building block" rules of the domain. But
it ain't necessarily so.

The second limitation is more fundamental, and it constitutes an
increasingly prominent stumbling block for the connectionist approach. It is the problem of unlearning or "catastrophic forgetting"
(French 1991). Very briefly, the problem is that the basic power of
connectionist learning lies in its ability to buy generalization by storing distributed representations of training instances *superpositionally*—that is, using overlapping resources of units and weights to
store traces of semantically similar items. (See chapter 2 above.) One
upshot of this is that it is always possible, when one is storing new
knowledge, that the amended weights will in effect blank out the old
knowledge. Vulnerability of old knowledge to new knowledge sets
such networks up for a truly Pythonesque fate: exposure to one
"deadly" input could effectively wipe out all the knowledge stored in
a careful and hard-won orchestration of weights. The phenomenon
is akin to the idea of a deadly joke on the hearing of which the human
cognitive apparatus would be paralyzed or destroyed! For a connec-

tionist network, such a scenario is not altogether fanciful. As French (1991, p. 4) comments, "even when a network is nowhere near its theoretical storage capacity, learning a *single new input* can completely disrupt all of the previously learned information." The potential disruption is a direct result of the superpositional storage technique. It is thus of a piece with the capacity of "free generalization," which makes such nets attractive. (It is *not* caused by any saturation of the net's resources such that there is no room to store new knowledge without deleting the old.) Current networks are protected from the unlearning by a very artificial device: the complete interweaving of the training set. The full set of training cases is cycled past the net again and again, so it is forced to find an orchestration of weights which can fit *all* the inputs. Thus, in a corpus of three facts, A, B, and C, training will proceed by the successive repetition of the triple ⟨A, B, C⟩ and not by training to success on A, then passing to B and finally to C. Yet this, on the face of it, is exactly what the phased-training and phased-memory solutions involve! The specter of unlearning was directly and artificially controlled in the Norris experiment by stopping all learning in a successful subnet. As Norris (1991, p. 295) commented: "When subsequent stages start to learn they naturally begin by performing very badly. The learning algorithm responds by adjusting the weights in the network. . . . If learning had been left enabled in the early nets then their weights would also have been changed and they would have unlearned their part of the task before the final stage had learned its part." What magic protects the Elman nets from this dire effect? The answer, I suspect, is that Elman protects the initial "building block" knowledge by allowing the complex cases in *gradually*, alongside some rather heavy-duty reminders of the basics. Thus, in the phased-training case, at phase 2 the net sees a corpus comprising 25% complex sentences alongside 75% new simple sentences. Similarly, in the phased-memory case, the net at phase 2 sees a random mix of four-word and five-word fragments and thus *gradually* allows in more complex cases alongside reminders of the basics. The current vulnerability of nets to unlearning requires us to somehow insulate the vital representational products of early learning from destabilization by the net's own first attempts to deal with more complex cases. Such insulation does not seem altogether psychologically realistic, and marks at least one respect in which such networks may be even more sensitive to representational trajectory than their human counterparts.

The bigger picture, then, is a mixed bag of pros and cons. On the plus side, we have seen how the broad picture of the vital role of representational trajectories in connectionist learning makes unified sense of a superficially disparate set of developmental factors. On the minus side, we have seen that the phased-memory solution is limited to domains in which merely statistically driven undersampling is luckily equivalent to task decomposition, and that the endemic vulnerability of networks to unlearning[2] makes the stepwise acquisition of knowledge an especially (and perhaps psychologically unrealistically) delicate operation. In the next section I shall argue that, despite these real and pressing problems, the issues that have been raised suggest a new angle on at least one famous "anti-connectionist" argument: Fodor and Pylyshyn's (1988) story about the systematicity of cognition.

Systematicity and Cognitive Architecture

We have seen just how complex is the question "What knowledge can be acquired by a connectionist network?" Even if we are considering a fixed, mature network configuration and a fixed, training corpus and input code, what the net learns can still be heavily dependent on additional parameters, such as the course of training and the progressive development (if any) of the net's resources (or use of resources) during training. With this in mind, recall the basic form of the so-called systematicity argument presented in Fodor and Pylyshyn (1988). The argument begins (see chapter 1 above) by defining a notion of systematic cognition such that a thinker counts as a systematic cognizer just in case her potential thoughts form a fully interanimated web. More precisely, a thinker is systematic if her potential thoughts form a kind of closed set—i.e., if, being capable of (say) the thoughts "A has property F" and "B has property G," she is also capable of having the thoughts "A has property G" and "B has property F." A similar closure of relational thoughts is required, as is illustrated by the overused pair "John loves Mary" and "Mary loves John." The notion of systematicity, then, is really a notion of closure of a set of potential thoughts under processes of logical combination and recombination of their component "parts."

There are many pressing issues here—not least the extent to which daily concepts and ideas such as 'loves' and 'John' can be properly supposed to isolate component parts of thoughts (see chapter 10 below). For present purposes, however, it will be sufficient to highlight a much more basic defect. To do so, we must look at the argument in which the notion of systematicity operates:

(1) Human thought is systematic.

(2) Such systematicity comes naturally to systems that use classical structured representations and logical processes of symbol manipulation.

(3) It does not come naturally to systems that use connectionist representations and vector to vector transformations.
(4) Hence, classicism offers a better model (at the cognitive psychological level) than connectionism.

Of course, the above argument is put forward only as an inference to the best explanation; hence, it would be unfair to demand that it be logically valid. But even as inference to the best explanation it is surely very shaky. Consider a parallel argument which might easily have seemed convincing (say, at the close of the second section of the present chapter):

(1) Human cognition regularly penetrates hierarchically organized problem domains.
(2) Classical methods of learning and representation are well suited to such highly and sequentially structured domains.
(3) Connectionist methods of learning and representation are not.
(4) Hence, classicism offers a better model (at the cognitive psychological level) than connectionism.

The flaw is now apparent. It is a mistake to suppose that the question of what kind of thing a connectionist network will learn is to be settled by reference to the generic form of the architecture and/or the learning rules. Many other parameters (such as the system's development over time) may be equal determinants of the kind of knowledge it acquires. Even the observation of a pervasive feature of mature human cognition (e.g., systematicity) need not demand explanation in terms of the basic cognitive architecture. It could instead be a reliable effect of the regular *combination* of a basic connectionist architecture with one or more of a variety of specific developmental factors (including, surely, the effects of learning a systematic public language). (See Dennett 1991b for an argument that *language* learning is the root of such systematicity as human thought actually displays.) The contrast is between systematicity as something *forced* onto a creature by the basic form of its cognitive architecture and systematicity as a *feature* of a domain or domains (i.e., as something to be *learned about* by the creature as it tries to make sense of a body of training data).

What I am recommending is, in short, a kind of gestalt flip in our thinking about systematicity. Instead of treating it as a property to be directly induced by a canny choice of basic architecture, it may be fruitful to try treating it as intrinsic to the knowledge we want a system to acquire. For example, we want the system to learn that an open-ended set of individuals and animals, and not just Fred, can fall under the public-language concept 'happy', and that the concept of loving is not the concept of an exclusively one-way relation. We thus treat the space of public-language concepts as just another complex space and ask what we must do to enable a learning system to negotiate it. We end up treating the space of systematically interanimated concepts as just another theoretical space—a space which may one day be negotiated by a (no doubt highly scaffolded) connectionist learning device. The mature knowledge of such a system will be expressible in terms of a (largely) systematically interwoven set of concepts. But the systematicity will be learned as a feature of the *meanings* of the concepts involved. It will flow not from the shallow closure of a logical system under recombinative rules, but from hard-won knowledge of the nature of the domain. Why settle for anything less?

Escaping the Developmental Vacuum

Consider an impossible question: What comes naturally to a connectionist system? Understood as a question about what kinds of theoretical space may be amenable to the connectionist treatment, this question is dangerously underspecified. It becomes tractable only once a variety of parameters are fixed. These include such obvious items as the large-scale configuration of the system (into subnets, etc.), and also such less obvious ones as whether training is phased and whether the mature state is reached by a process of incremental "growth." The effects of these less obvious and superficially more peripheral factors are functionally equivalent to those involving the large-scale configuration. The key to success, in all cases, is to somehow help the network decompose a task into an ordered series of subtasks. In the absence of such decomposition, networks have a tendency to get "lost in space(s)." They try to account for all the regularities in the data at once, but some of the regularities involve others as "building blocks." The result is a kind of snowblindness in which the net cannot see the higher-order regularities (because it lacks the building blocks), nor can it isolate these (as it is constantly led off track by its doomed efforts to capture the higher-order regularities).

Learning about complex theoretical spaces, then, is a delicate matter. Connectionist learning needs, in such cases, to be *scaffolded*. As we saw above, the functional role of the kinds of scaffolding investigated by Elman could be mimicked by a wide variety of superficially distinct developmental factors. This intimacy between connectionist learning and much wider developmental factors reveals a flaw in the systematicity argument against connectionism as cognitive theory. Although systematicity (in mature, adult human thought) is indeed pervasive, it need not be traced directly to the nature of the underlying cognitive architecture. Instead it may be fruitful to try thinking of systematicity as a knowledge-driven achievement, and hence as one which may depend on the setting of any of the multitude of parameters which determine what kind of thing a connectionist network will learn. To say this is not, alas, to prove it. What is really needed is a demonstration of how a well-scaffolded connectionist engine might in practice come to learn a fully interanimated set of concepts. But the gap between the observation that systematicity is rife and the conclusion that it must be directly traced to the basic form of the underlying architecture is real enough. If something cheaper than an innate symbol system will do, nature probably found it.

We have also encountered our first example of an important distinction—viz., that between the *gross inputs* to a network (such as the sentences fed to the phased-memory Elman net) and the *effective* inputs (the structures in the input data which actually power learning). The phased-memory case shows that these two factors may come apart where a lack of short-term memory acts as a filter on the usable inputs. Other ways in which the gross and effective data may come apart, and the potential significance of this for ideas about innate knowledge, will be pursued in chapter 9.

Chapter 8

The Cascade of Significant Virtual Machines

Transition Machines

Human cognitive development is marked, at least at times, by rather sudden shifts. It is initially tempting to suppose that such shifts cannot be explained by reference to the essentially gradual and continuous processes of weight adjustment that characterize connectionist (gradient-descent) learning algorithms. Instead, such shifts might seem to be best explained by the sudden switch from one kind of computational device to another, or by the triggering of some latent and fundamentally more powerful knowledge schema, or whatever. Surprisingly, it turns out that one of the most attractive features of connectionist approaches to the modeling of developmental phenomena lies precisely in the ability of such approaches to generate powerful new accounts of such apparent discontinuities in human knowledge acquisition. The reason is that small changes in the weights can, at times, lead to dramatic changes in surface behavior. Where such a change in surface behavior occurs, we may still conceptualize it (I shall argue) as the result of a transition between virtual machines. But the relevant notion of a virtual machine is defined here by the surface behavior—it is the way the system looks to an external user. Conceiving development as a cascade of such virtual machines is a useful heuristic device, but we ought not to blindly assume that the surface discontinuities which warrant such talk are echoed by fundamental discontinuities in the form of knowledge storage, retrieval, or subsequent learning.

Hybrid Models

One possible explanation of any qualitative shift in the nature of surface performance is to assume that some fundamentally different kind of representational resource has come on line—a resource which thereafter exists alongside the distributed connectionist representation, each being used when most appropriate. This kind of story, in which distributed connectionist representations are augmented by those of some other style, constitutes the "hybrid systems" approach to cognitive modeling.

Two basic types of augmentation are standardly considered: to add a device which manipulates symbolic expressions in the familiar classical manner (connectionist-classicist hybrids), and to add a second connectionist device which manipulates (e.g.) local connectionist representations (distributed-localist hybrids). The first option seems initially attractive (Clark 1989a), and there are several promising models in the recent literature.[1] One such model is Shavlik and Towell's (1989) combination of classical explanation-based learning with learning in a neural network. Explanation-based learning (EBL) is an approach deeply rooted in a classical, symbol-using paradigm. An EBL system takes a solution to a "sample" problem and then (often using specialist domain knowledge) generalizes that answer into a more widely applicable form. Such a system might be required to learn a concept by exposure to a small number of examples. Its task is to fix on the relevant features of the examples and ignore the rest. (Contrast this with standard connectionist learning techniques, which may use very little prior knowledge but which require many examples and tend to reflect all the statistical properties of the training set.) Shavlik and Towell noticed a trouble with EBL systems: We don't always have a correct domain theory to apply to the examples. But a trouble with connectionist learning is that the knowledge is not available in a form which makes it easily applicable to different but systematically related cases. The strength of the EBL approach (Dejong and Mooney 1986) is precisely that "in this type of learning the solution to a sample problem is generalized into a form that can later be used to solve conceptually similar problems. The generalization process is driven by the explanation of why the solution worked." (Shavlik and Towell 1989, p. 232)

Shavlik and Towell's idea is to get the best of both worlds by exploiting a hybrid system which acts as follows.

Step 1: The EBL component is given a rough domain theory.

Step 2: It is given some example cases and allowed to build an explanation of why an item belongs to a given category.

Step 3: This explanation is used to preconfigure a neural network (e.g., to suggest a network topology) and to preweight the features isolated as significant.

Step 4: The network thus created is exposed to more examples.

Step 5: After a period, the net is analyzed and the weights which were most altered by the new training are isolated.

Step 6: The features associated with the altered weights are used to help build a new and better explanation in the EBL component.

And so the cycle continues. A worked example from Shavlik and Towell involves learning what to classify as a cup. The EBL system learns a rough domain theory in which something will count as a cup if it is stable, liftable, and open, and in which something is liftable if it has a handle. This theory captured 70% of the cases. A neural network was then preconfigured to stress the properties thus isolated and trained on the corpus of examples.

The preconfigured network was found, after training, to get 100% of the cases right *and* to generalize well to new cases. By contrast, a control network which was trained on the same data but without the pre-weighting of features learned the training cases properly (albeit more slowly) but failed to generalize successfully. In fact, the unaided net learned an overly general concept which, although it captured 90% of all cupcases in the subsequent test set, also wrongly classified many noncups as cups. (It identified only 68% of the noncup cases as noncups.) This is of special interest to us insofar as it supports the suggestion that learning in first-generation networks is too lazy. The nets learn the simplest way of correctly classifying the training set, but that way is often shallow and nongeneralizable. The learning must be constrained, and this is just what EBL-based preconfiguration does.

Nonetheless, the bad news is close at hand. Only steps 1–4 of the algorithms have been implemented. There is no passage back, as yet, from the neural-network solution to an improved explanation in the EBL component. Such a passage requires the isolation and interpretation of the weights which have been most altered by training. It is easy to imagine the automatic isolation of such weights, but the process of interpretation is much harder. The more localist are the learned network representations, the easier such interpretation will be. But the whole point of having a network component is to allow the device to capture subtle dimensions of the task. Such subtleties may resist easy symbolic interpretation.

A second way of augmenting the representations developed by a first-generation network is to combine highly distributed and localist connectionist representations.[2] This is attractive because the problem of communication between the two components is eased by the similar kinds of computational operation which we can perform on each. A characteristic early example of such a model is Hinton's (1988) proposal to equip connectionist systems with two kinds of representation, one of which is a compressed manipulable version of a larger (expanded, microfeatural, distributed) representation. The compressed representation (the "reduced description") could then be used to facilitate inter-network communication and as a kind of stand-in where the fully expanded version is uneconomical or difficult to use. In a similar vein, Legendre, Miyata, and Smolensky (1990a,b) detail a two-level connectionist model of linguistic well-formedness called "harmonic grammar." The core idea here is to deploy "a low-level connectionist network using a particular kind of distributed representation, and a second, higher level network that uses local representations and which approximately and incompletely describes the aggregate computational behavior of the lower network" (Legendre et al. 1990a, p. 2). The benefits of such a package include fluent on-line processing by the lower net, with judgments of grammaticality (linguistic well-formedness) being mediated by the higher-level (rule-and-symbol-encoding) net. Most important, however, the higher net's rule and symbol knowledge is still of the characteristic connectionist kind, in which rules are soft and are not subject to the law of the excluded middle (i.e., they need not unambiguously apply or fail to apply). The upshot is that the higher network's grammaticality judgments are *graded*—e.g., of two unaccusative verbs, one can be more unaccusative than the other. Whereas reliance on hard rules would yield a system in which violation of some condition resulted simply in the judgment that the sentence was ill formed, it is more natural in the connectionist version to have violations diminish well formedness by degree. Such quantitative judgments of well formedness are psychologically realistic and reflect our general ability (see chapter 5 above) to make graded judgments of category membership. Holyoak's (1991) notion of "symbolic connectionism" is similarly inspired. As he puts it, "symbolic (i.e. localist) connectionist models can make inferences that standard symbolic systems are often too brittle to derive, using knowledge that diffuse (i.e. fully distributed) connectionism systems cannot readily represent" (ibid., p. 317).

The main drawback of the Legendre-Miyata-Smolensky net is, once again, that it seems to involve an unhealthy amount of human orchestration. The human theorist is actively involved in constructing the higher-level network, changing variables in the harmony equations for the lower net, "pruning" the number of such variables by appeal to a set of independently motivated linguistic constraints (Holyoak 1990, p. 8), and so on. Although these advanced hybrid models exhibit a laudable representational multiplicity, they provide little indication of how such a multiplicity might automatically be developed by a system merely on the basis of a set of training inputs and connectionist learning rules. In short, existing hybrid models seem to duck the hard developmental questions. Yet the plausibility of such models depends precisely on filling this lacuna. A more promising avenue of research, I shall now argue, posits a single underlying computational and representational style and attributes surface discontinuities to the attempts of standard learning algorithms to deal with a complex body of data and mappings.

The Past Remembered

Recall the original (Rumelhart and McClelland 1986b) connectionist model of the acquisition of the English past tense. In barest outline (for detailed treatments see Rumelhart and McClelland 1986b; Pinker and Prince 1988; Clark 1989a), the model aimed to reproduce a distinctive pattern of changing performance over time—a pattern which was once supposed to be exhibited by children and to be evidence of a transition (over developmental time) between reliance on rote learning techniques and the use of a computationally distinct, rule-based mechanism. The pattern in question is the so-called U-shaped curve (see, e.g., Bever 1982) in which early performance is marked by the successful production of a small set of mixed (regular and irregular) past tenses. This early success, however, is supposed to give way to a period in which characteristic errors occur. The child may now fail to produce the correct past tense forms of irregular verbs (e.g., go → went) and instead produce overregularization errors (go → goed). This kind of mistake (the "dip" in performance between the successful production of a few mixed verbs and the mature ability to deal correctly with a large number of verbs of both types) was once treated as persuasive evidence of the emergence of a fully rule-based system which, though initially overapplied, would ultimately be devoted solely to dealing with the regular cases, leaving a distinct rote-memory system to encode knowledge of the irregular exceptions.

Rumelhart and McClelland (1986b) set out to challenge this received wisdom by showing how both types of knowledge (and the distinctive developmental pattern just described) could be catered for within the confines of a single computational approach. To that end, they used a simple two-layer[3] pattern associator to learn a variety of mappings of (phonological representations of) present-tense forms to (phonological representations of) past-tense forms.[4] The training set comprised 420 English verbs. Training involved an initial stage in which the net was trained on 10 high-frequency verbs (8 of which were irregular) and a subsequent stage in which the rest of the corpus (including now a much higher proportion of regular verbs) was introduced. The net produced some interesting performances. It reproduced the basic U-shaped developmental profile described above. It also reproduced some finer-grained developmental details observed in children, such as the temporal succession of two types of overregularization: the overregularization of the present form (go → goed) and then the misapplication of the regular ending to the correct past-tense form (go → wented).

These results were presented as a subsequent challenge to the idea that knowledge of the regular form is subserved by a separate and distinct computational mechanism. Instead, the model depicts the U-curve performance as the product of the continued application of a *single* storage-and-retrieval technique to a growing and changing body of training data. And therein, of course, lies the problem. It has seemed to many (see especially Pinker and Prince 1988) that the model's reproduction of the U-curve data is a direct effect of the statistical transition, during training, between a stage in which a high proportion of the data consists of irregular verbs to a subsequent stage in which the majority of the data consists of regulars. No wonder, it is claimed, the device then overregularizes. But this is not (the critics argue) psychologically interesting, since human overregularization errors occur without the benefit of such convenient manipulations of the input data, and reflect not the changing statistics of a training set but the attempt to impose rule-involving order on a body of stored knowledge.

Changing the Past

In an important series of recent publications, Kim Plunkett and Virginia Marchman have reopened the past-tense debate in an especially revealing way. They have shown that the production of essentially stage-like behavior is a fundamental property of networks which use superpositional techniques (see chapter 2 above) to store data involving multiple types of mapping, and that such behaviors need not depend on ecologically unrealistic manipulations of the input data (*pacé* the standard criticisms rehearsed above). Cast in the terminology of the present treatment, the moral is that techniques of superpositional storage can be responsible for the development over time of a succession of different types of Significant Virtual Machines (SVMs), and that such successions will be observed even in the absence of gross manipulations of the statistics of the input data.

Plunkett and Marchman's (1989, 1991) steady rehabilitation of the past-tense debate involves two distinct moves. The first is to challenge the received understanding of the performance pattern itself;

the second is to show that the actual performance patterns of human children can be closely approximated by networks which make only ecologically realistic assumptions about the input data.

Concerning the performance pattern itself, the key point is that there is not, in fact, a single gross U-curve which characterizes children's performance. Instead, "overregularizations are not class-wide and . . . micro U-shape profiles recur for the same and different verbs over a wide developmental span" (Plunkett and Sinha 1991, p. 29). That is, it is not, after all, the case that children's performance undergoes a single period of overregularization. Instead (see Bybee and Slobin 1982 and Marcus et al. 1990), the U-curve profile appears for different individual verbs at different times, and a U curve for a given verb may be repeated in subsequent development.

Apart from this fragmentation of the overregularization phenomena, there is also, it transpires, evidence of distinctive irregularization errors in which certain regular verbs are treated on the model of subclasses of irregulars. In such cases (see Marchman 1988), the best explanation of the errors seems to be that the knowledge about irregulars is stored not as a rote list (as in the classical model) but rather in "some kind of associative network in which recurring similarities are recorded and superimposed" (Marcus et al. 1990, p. 54).

Bearing this revised understanding of the actual performance data in mind, we can now return to the question of network models and the statistics of input data. Plunkett and Marchman (1991) show that with a static input vocabulary (in which the same training set is used throughout) the actual performance data (the micro U-curves and the irregularization errors) can be nicely reproduced. The reason is that the net must seek an overall assignment of weights (a "position in weight space") which respects all the various types of mapping represented in the training set. But in so doing it must exploit a gradient-descent procedure in which changes are made (either after each pattern (stem-past pair) is presented or after each full sweep through the training data, depending on which update routine (pattern or batch) is in use) to the weights most responsible for the current error. As a result, performance on individual verbs will often change and oscillate as the net searches first this way and then that for an acceptable position in the space of possible weight assignments. And it is here, according to Plunkett and Marchman, that we find the deep root of network's abilities to display U-shaped learning. Gross manipulations of the training set provide especially marked opportunities for a net to suddenly focus on a different set of mappings. But the tendency to increment performance on one type of mapping at the expense of a temporary decrement in performance on another is built into the use of connectionist learning techniques with distributed representations and superpositional encoding from the start.

The static input vocabulary network of Plunkett and Marchman (1991) bears this out. As Plunkett and Sinha (1991, p. 29) observe, despite a static input set, "micro U-curves are observed in which individual verbs may undergo repeated decrements and recovery in performance (and) error types are *not* restricted to overregularizations. Errors are also observed in which regular verbs are mapped as if they are irregular verbs." Plunkett and Sinha point out that the presence of this last class of irregularization errors in humans seems to provide strong evidence in favor of a single mechanisms' being used to encode knowledge of both the regular and the irregular classes.

There is some debate as to whether what Plunkett and Marchman term "micro-U-curves" should properly be said to be U-curves at all. The classical depiction of a U-curve stresses that the performance decrement follows a period of highly accurate output, but these "micro U-curves" can occur even before highly accurate performance is achieved. Thus, Marcus et al. (1990, p. 30) complain that "in Plunkett and Marchman . . . the learning curves all start out at levels of performance far *less* than 100% and then increase; the authors misleadingly term the small downward wiggles in this overall increasing curve as 'U-shaped development.'" Since, however, decrements can also occur after full success (on a single given verb) has been achieved, it seems that the closest actual parallel to the classical idea of a U-curve is preserved, albeit in a slightly more general form. I shall therefore continue to speak of these effects as U-shaped developmental episodes.

Moreover, it is incorrect to complain that the U-curve behaviors found in such nets are merely artifacts of a careful choice of design parameters whose overall effect is to recapitulate the classical explanation. In this vein, Marcus et al. (1991, p. 59) argue that "someone might find design parameters (input coding, network topology, learning rate, training schedule, etc. etc.) that allow some connectionist model to simulate children by displaying the right rote and regularization modes at different points in development using a unitary network. But in such a case the explanation of why children overregularize is not that they are connectionist networks but that the mechanism they possess, connectionist or otherwise, is designed to display (those) rote and rule behavior patterns."

We have seen, by contrast, that the general tendency to display (micro) overregularization errors is a deep feature of connectionist models—one that flows directly from the use of superpositional storage in the context of a connectionist learning algorithm. It is of course true that to mimic the precise details of a child's learning trajectory we would have to engage in some detailed and pointed tailoring of such factors as the initial weights and the training schedule. In view of the wide variety of individual developmental profiles in children, this should be no surprise. What happens in detail does depend on the precise setting of a huge variety of design parameters. This very fact, as we shall see in chapter 9, imbues the connectionist approach with a great potential for modeling innate knowledge in a biologically plausible and neurally implementable way.

Plunkett and Marchman's static input vocabulary net is thus revealed as a useful demonstration that U-shaped performance in nets need not rely on manipulations of the input data. But it is of course true that children's vocabulary sizes do increase over time, and it is also true that even a fixed input set may exhibit significant internal statistical structure. Further aspects of stage-like development may be attributable to either or both of these factors, and I will end my discussion of the "new past tense" by briefly examining each, again following work reported in Plunkett and Sinha 1991.

The point about internal statistical structure is just that, even within a fixed training corpus (a fixed set of verbs), we must allow for the influence of *token frequency.* Thus, even if the proportion of a given type of irregular verb is low, a child may see more instances of specific such irregulars (specific irregular tokens) than, say, instances of a specific regular. High token frequency is needed if a "strange" verb is to be properly learned, whereas a less strange verb (one which belongs to a large subtype) can be learned despite low token frequency. It is thus perhaps no accident that highly irregular verbs (e.g., go → went) have high token frequencies. If they didn't, they would not be learnable, and they would disappear from the language (or be regularized). Within a given simulation, "the type and token frequency parameters associated with . . . verbs in different mapping classes . . . cannot be manipulated arbitrarily if the network is to master the training set" (Plunkett and Sinha 1991, p. 32, reporting work by Plunkett and Marchman (1990)).

The following four types of mapping class were represented in the work of Plunkett and Marchman:

(1) arbitrary mappings, such as go → went
(2) identity mappings, in which the stem and the past are the same, such as hit → hit
(3) various vowel change mappings
(4) regular mappings, in which a suffix is added to the stem.

For a wide range of simulation configurations (roughly, any which had the minimum resources of hidden units and layers needed to do

the job), it transpired that, for example, the arbitrary mappings required high token frequencies (15, as against 5 for the identity mapping) to ensure that a net would master these alongside the other
verbs. Irregulars which fall into robust subclasses can tolerate somewhat lower token frequencies. Fully regular verbs can (but need not)
have very low token frequencies. The fascinating final result of the
Plunkett-Marchman simulation is that "the type of token frequency
parameters . . . required for the successful learning closely resemble
the observed type and token frequency parameters of spoken English" (Plunkett and Sinha 1991, p. 32).

The assumption that the brain uses a single, superpositional, gradient-descent learning, pattern-associating device to learn the past
tense thus allows us to explain a variety of facts concerning type and
token distributions in English. Moreover, it is possible to use the
same approach to try to *predict* what the distributions must be if languages containing given mappings are to be learnable (Plunkett and
Marchman 1991). Such cases suggest that we are only now beginning
to scratch the surface of the explanatory projects opened up by the
connectionist approach to linguistic phenomena.

We move, finally, to the remaining issue of the potential role of
incremental vocabulary growth in models of the past tense. Plunkett,
Marchman, and Knudsen (1990) show a *critical mass* effect in a net
which is trained in two stages:

(1) The net is trained on a set of 20 stem/past tense pairs.

(2) Once success on the original 20 is achieved, new verbs are
introduced (as stem/past tense pairs) *one at a time*; i.e., the training set is repeatedly incremented by one pair, and training is
repeated.

Two types of incremental learning at stage 2 were investigated. In
one ("criterial expansion"), the net was trained to success on each
newly expanded training set (i.e. the previous set plus one) before
the next increment was allowed; in the other ("epoch expansion"),
increments occurred after a fixed training regime regardless of the
net's level of success. Interestingly, criterial expansion was not a success. It seems as if the criterial regime encouraged the network to
create unnecessarily dramatic weight distributions (e.g. very large
weights feeding into a given unit) and that these overplayed solutions
then prevented[5] the net from finding the correct solution to subsequent problems. In incremental learning, it seems, it does not pay to
concentrate for too long on each new training set. As Plunkett et al.
(1990, p. 19) put it: "In order for networks to avoid entrenchment in
specific areas of weight space, training must ensure that a variety of

weight changes occur. If the network is repeatedly trained on a limited and fixed number of patterns, where a series of similar weight changes occur, further training may fail to promote necessary reorganizations or may even enhance the network's entrenchment in a particular region in weight space." The solution is to use epoch expansion in which a new verb is introduced after every five epochs of training until a vocabulary of 100 verbs is reached, and then after each single epoch of training up until an "adult" vocabulary of 500 verbs is achieved.[6] The presence of this kind of incremental learning has two interesting effects. First, overall (final, "adult") performance is better here than in a net which is trained on the final corpus from the outset. This result is already familiar to us from chapter 7. But second, there is a sudden transition from a state of rote-style representation to some more systematic encoding which takes place when the vocabulary reaches a specific amount (40–50 verbs). It is obvious when such systematic representations have been created, as they enable the network to deal with novel cases in a way which no amount of rote knowledge can support. The ability of networks to exhibit these sudden transitions (the "jump" between Significant Virtual Machines) is still not fully understood, but there are three clear possibilities:

(1) The network is finally forced (once it reaches some saturation level for rote learning) to seek a whole new encoding and, in simple cases, can discover one quite rapidly once it has to.

(2) The error surface exhibits a gradual slope followed by a sudden cliff.

(3) The presence of nonlinear activation functions allows a small change to some early weights to make a very large difference to the network's overall performance, and can result in sudden dramatic falls in the TSS (total sum squared error) for a given training set.

In the case of sudden transitions occurring within the context of incremental learning, one may suspect the first explanation; a probable case of the second is discussed later in this chapter. In any case, the interesting fact is that, despite the inherent gradualness of gradient-descent learning, there are various ways in which a network may exhibit sudden transitions between different types of overall performance profile. It is in this sense that connectionist learning (using superpositional storage, distributed representation, and nonlinear activation functions) can model the developmental succession of different virtual machines (supporting qualitatively different abilities, as in the case of rote and systematic knowledge) while nonetheless employing a single kind of underlying architecture, and a fixed, gradual, gradient-descent learning algorithm.

The moral, then, is that networks can exhibit sudden changes in general performance (as evidenced in a sudden shift from rote to generalizable knowledge) which are not due to the "coming on line" of some computationally distinct rule-encoding device. Instead, they are due to a reorganisation of the original network prompted by changes in the nature or in the mere quantity of training data. The explanatory emphasis for understanding such sudden transitions is thus shifted from the nature of a special inner device to the nature and quantity of the training data. Such cases augur a deep methodological sea change. Understanding the mind will, I believe, come to be conceived in an increasingly less disembodied (Cartesian?) way. The nature and the temporal sequence of presentation of the training data will be seen as perhaps the most profound determinants of the shape of performance profiles over developmental time.

In sum: The debate about past tense is far from over. New models and new data combine to open up a range of new explanatory possibilities. At the heart of these possibilities lie two facts of much more general interest. First, we are beginning to see the deep and illuminating interplay between connectionist learning algorithms and the shape of the training data. Second, we are beginning to see the potential of such models to explain sudden qualitative shifts in performance profile (the succession of Significant Virtual Machines). It would be tragic indeed if the early criticisms of a specific example (the model of Rumelhart and McClelland 1986b) were to blind us to these wider horizons.

Gross Architecture and Stage-like Behavior

We saw in the previous section how stage-like behavior can emerge from a relatively unstructured network as a result of the complex interplay of training data (and sequence of training) and gradient-descent learning. We should not think, however, that the gross architectural structure of the learning device is now wholly unimportant as a source of stage-like transitions. In the present section we will review a demonstration (McClelland 1989; Plunkett and Sinha 1991) in which significant architectural prestructuring interacts with the statistical nature of the training set to yield marked behavioral stages.

There is a famous problem in which children must judge how a beam, balanced on a fulcrum, will move when weights are added on one or both of the sides. The weights are of varying sizes, and they can be placed closer to or farther from the fulcrum. The classic picture of performance on this task depicts the child as moving through three stages (and sometimes a fourth):

(1) The child judges that the beam will go down on the side on which the largest weight is placed.

(2) The child learns the role of distance from the fulcrum, but only as a "decider" in the case where both weights are equal.

(3) The child learns that weights and distance are both potent parameters, but is not sure how to trade them off against one another.

(4) Some children learn or discover how the tradeoff works— i.e., they acquire the idea of torque. Most children (and adults) remain at stage 3, however.

McClelland (1989) trained a three-layer network to perform the judgment task. The net was prestructured to have two distinct input channels: one for a weight coding and one for a distance coding. It had two output units: one whose activity was designated to correspond to the beam falling to the left, the other to the right. Equal activity in both indicated a state of balance. Each input channel comprised two banks of input units, with activity patterns representing the weights and distances of two objects (hence, there were four input patterns each time). Each bank of input units was connected to a separate set of two hidden units (hence, there were four hidden units in total), and the four hidden units were connected in fully feedforward fashion to the two output units. One bank of input units coded for distance for each of the two objects, the other for weight. Thus, weight and distance were catered for by *architecturally distinguished* early processing channels, with integration occurring only *after* the hidden-unit layer. The net began with random weights and was trained on a sample of good input/output patterns. The sample, however, contained more variations in the weight parameters than in the distance ones; this distortion was supposed to reflect children's greater general experience with the weight parameter.

The McClelland net, like a child, learned first to rely on weight and then, in a sudden transition, to allow distance to count also. In a way, this is unsurprising. The training data, by incorporating more variations on the weight parameter, provided the weight channel with more information relevant to solving the problem. Weight changes occurred in the distance channel, but more slowly. Eventually, however, a point was reached where the distance-channel weights had sufficient magnitude to make a decisive contribution just in case the two weights were equal—here we see the transition to stage 2. Further training reinforced the net's "view" that distance information constituted a useful predictor, until eventually it could be relied on even in cases of unequal weights (the transition to stage 3). The point to notice is just that the combination of gradual weight changes with two distinct channels of early processing and some statistical bias in the training data yielded a system whose external behavioral profile displayed sudden shifts despite the continuous nature of the weight changes determined by the learning algorithm (see Plunkett and Sinha 1991, p. 66). Cast in our terms, the early training created a Significant Virtual Machine which was 100% weight oriented. But alongside it, there developed a distance-oriented virtual machine. The integrated activity beyond the hidden-unit layer allowed this second machine to be gradually incorporated and exploited. Thus, a new virtual machine, in which information from each channel was weighed and utilized, was created. The cascade of such machines is determined in part by the gross original architecture and in part by the statistics of the training data.[7]

The external appearance of a simple succession reflected in our talk of a cascade of virtual machines must not be taken seriously as a picture of the inner computational story. The system's surface abilities *do* change dramatically over time, and via a series of reasonably clear stages, and it is in terms of this cognitive surface (or user illusion; see Dennett 1991c) that the sequence of virtual machines is defined. But as far as the underlying machinery is concerned, there are no sudden transitions or changes of computational device. Both channels are active all along, and from the outset influence from both is integrated beyond the hidden-unit layer. It is just that the distance-dependent data take longer (courtesy of the nature of the training set) to achieve *significant influence* over the output (or "judgments") of the net.

Generalization Revisited

To round off the discussion of the connectionist treatment of developmental transitions, let me re-address three questions which have loomed quite large:

> Can connectionist approaches adequately address the need to achieve increasing informational integration over developmental time?
> Can connectionist learning techniques support structure-transforming generalizations?

Must all transitions between Significant Virtual Machines be failure driven within the connectionist paradigm?

In short, let me return to some of the issues raised by my discussion
of the apparent limitations of connectionist learning (chapter 4) and
by my discussion of the distinctive nature of knowledge of concepts
(chapter 5).

Consider first an intriguing demonstration[8] in which a simple recurrent network seems to make a sudden, non-failure-driven transition between a state of knowledge which supports widespread local
success (very low total sum squared error on the training set) and a
subsequent state of knowledge which supports much wider success.
This is a recurrent network devised by Jeff Elman which is trained to
judge whether the current sum of a temporally extended (and continuing) series of inputs is odd or even. Given as inputs the sequence
1 1 0 1, it should give as outputs the sequence 1 0 0 1. That is, given
the first input, 1, it must judge that the total is odd and hence output
1. Next it gets another 1, which gives an overall total of 2, which is
even; hence, it must output 0. The next input is a 0, so the total stays
at 2 and hence the output remains at 0. Finally a further 1 is input,
making the total 3 (odd); thus, a 1 should be output. The net is trained
on several such sequences, the boundaries between sequences being
marked by a resetting of the context units to 0. The network used was
a simple recurrent net with one input unit, three hidden units, one
output unit, and the three context units already mentioned. The
training data for the network consisted of 1000 sequences of 1's and
0's, with a maximum sequence length of six consecutive inputs. The
net was initially trained for 20 epochs, i.e. 20 complete passes
through the training set. To test the network, we used (as suggested
by Elman and Plunkett) a file containing a running sequence of 100
1's. (This sequence is much, much bigger than any sequence seen in
training, when the maximum sequence length was 6.) Obviously, the
correct output response to the test set of 100 1's is a sequence of al-
ternate 1's and 0's (1 0 1 0 1 . . .). After testing, we continued training
the net for a further 5 epochs, tested it again, and then trained to a
total of 50 epochs.[9]

The results were surprising. At 20 epochs we had a net which was
able to perform the task for sequences about as long as the maximum
length seen in training, but not for much longer ones. (In fact, the 20-
epoch net succeeded up to about eight successive inputs; however,
its performance then decreased, and it failed totally after about 18
inputs.) Remember that if the desired output is (say) 1 0 1 0 the net
can produce increasingly poor approximations to this, ranging from

(e.g.) 0.9 0.1 0.9. 0.1 (very good) down to 0.6 0.5 0.6 0.5 (bad) and on down to 0.5 0.5 0.5 0.5 (failure). Hence our judgment that the performance "tails off."

At this point it would be natural to judge that the network's generalization is simply limited (forever) by the maximum length of the training sequences. True, it does reach just beyond this length. But we may understand this as the network's having learned a solution for six-bit strings which allows interpolation *between* the training items. The success just beyond the six-bit limit can then be seen as a limiting case of an interpolation effect. In short, the net has achieved local success—it has a very low total sum squared error on the training data. But its solution is not fully generalizable to novel situations, such as those involving much longer sequences. After 25 epochs of training, however, it is able to succeed for the entire 100-bit sequence, albeit with only moderate "confidence" (Elman's term)—it outputs 0.70 for odd and 0.48 for even by the end of the sequence. By 50 epochs the confidence level is high (0.9 for odd, 0.4 for even).

What is most surprising, however, is that (as subsequent analysis showed) the jump between a local (limited-length sequence) solution and (what looks to be) a fully general one was in fact achieved over the space of a single epoch of learning. In our simulation, epoch 21 was crucial. At epoch 20, as reported above, the net failed beyond eight-bit sequences. At epoch 21, it succeeded (barely, alternating 0.47 and 0.48 in the end) for the sequence of 100 inputs. The net thus exhibits a sudden, dramatic leap in its generalization performance over the space of a single epoch of training. Moreover, the network seems here to be achieving just the kind of transition highlighted by developmentalists such as Annette Karmiloff-Smith (recall chapter 4 above)—viz. the transition between local mastery of a principle or concept (such as judging odd or even in cases resembling, though not necessarily identical to, cases seen in training) and more flexible and globally applicable mastery (judging odd or even for strings of any length whatsoever). Only at this second stage, according to Elman, does the net have knowledge of the principle or concept which is independent of the examples used in training.

Concerning the "sudden leap" in generalization capacities, we may observe that this is another clear case in which the gradualness of the weight-adjustment algorithm is accompanied by rather dramatic stages in gross performance. Once again, the problem (as posed to the net) constitutes an error surface with an interesting shape. At 20 epochs, the "local" problem solution has reduced the total sum squared error to quite a small amount. But in ironing out the remaining tiny error on the training, the net is forced to reorganize its knowledge in an especially powerful way[10]—a way which, as it happens, involves solving the problem for sequences of unbounded length.

If this *is* the correct explanation of the network's behavior, however, then there is a clear sense in which it is not exhibiting quite the kind of *non-failure-driven* transition which Karmiloff-Smith imagined. Part of Karmiloff-Smith's idea (see chapter 4 above) was that the child's transition from local to more global and flexible solutions need not be prompted by failure—instead it could be the result of endogenous pressure to work on (reorganize, integrate) our own stored knowledge even when that knowledge is already perfectly adequate to solve existing problems.

However, we now see (and this is a point of some import for developmental theorizing) that the notion of being driven by failure is profoundly ambiguous. Like so many terms in common use in cognitive science, it is ambiguous between an internal computational sense and an external gross-behavioral sense. Thus, the network just described is capable, at 20 epochs, of reasonable gross-behavioral success relative to the local task demands (i.e., the six-bit-maximum training sequences, and novel sequences up to about eight bits). But despite that surface success, it is still generating internal error signals. These may be caused by gross failure on a few residual training cases or (more subtle) by the presence of error signals due to low confidence judgments. Thus, it may correctly judge a sequence to be odd, but do so with low confidence (e.g., outputting only 0.6). Since the target output is 1.0, an error signal will be generated even when there is gross-behavior success. The essential point is thus that change may be failure driven relative to some inner computational criterion even if it is *not* driven by any failures to achieve goals or make correct judgments in the external world.

There are two further senses in which the net just described is not (despite initial appearances) a paradigm case of the kind of developmental transition highlighted by Karmiloff-Smith.

> The mature (50-epoch) generalization abilities of the network do not obviously involve what we termed *structure-transforming* generalizations (i.e. ones in which we exploit knowledge which was acquired to solve some problem P to solve a different but structurally related problem).
>
> There is no sense in which the transition modeled involves the increasing *integration* of knowledge acquired in different domains—a key feature of our treatment of concepts.

In the next section I will develop a speculative account which draws these threads together.

Going Beyond Success

How might a network achieve true non-failure-driven learning? At first sight, the question seems silly. In networks which learn using gradient-descent procedures, all change is driven by the internal error signal. Non-failure-driven change (in this inner, computational sense) is, hence, impossible. Or is it? Recall the techniques of skeletonization. The idea here (see Mozer and Smolensky 1989 and chapter 5 above) is to compute a measure of relevance for each unit in (say) the hidden layer of a trained system and then delete the units least critical to performance. This is achieved by having an automatic procedure compare how well the system does with a given unit to how well it would do without it, and deleting the losers. What is attractive about the skeletonization procedure is that it provides a possible mechanism for endogenously driven developmental change of the kind which enables a system to go "beyond success" in something like the way envisaged by Karmiloff-Smith. Thus, whereas a standard first-order connectionist system will cease to alter its weights once it is fully successful in its target domain, a system with a built-in skeletonization procedure could take such on-line success as the signal to engage in a further process of self-analysis and reorganization. Moreover, this process helps to loosen the system's ties to the total statistical profile of the training set, and to move the network in the direction of real knowledge of a rule for a domain. Thus, Mozer and Smolensky (1989, p. 9) comment that "while the weights merely reflect the statistics of the training set, [the measure of relevance] indicates the functionality of the units."

But rather than prune an existing net, it may sometimes be more beneficial to use the existing net to train a new one which tries to solve the same problem but with different (reduced) resources. Imagine a net, with 100 hidden units, which has learned a lookup-table-style solution to a given problem. Such a net could be used to generate the training data for a different net which attempts to solve the problem using fewer hidden units (and which, hence, is more likely to learn a powerful, generalizable problem solution). Such a technique could be applied even when the error on the training set is effectively zero, and hence represents another possible way of incorporating endogenous pressure to go "beyond success."

Expanding on the same theme,[11] we might consider the case where several separate nets encode local, efficient solutions to specific kinds of problems. In such a case, these nets could be used to train one further net to solve all the problems. In trying to find a single set of weights able to support all the behaviors required, the new net may be forced to find new and more powerful ways of solving the problems. This would correspond to the idea (see chapters 4 and 5 above) that representational redescription is closely tied to informational integration. A different approach, mooted in chapter 6 above, would be to use the original nets to train a single architecture comprising several modules, much like the net of Jacobs, Jordan, and Barto (1991). Such a process would induce a set of modules in which similar parts of the various problems tackled by the original nets are dealt with by specific modules (e.g., if nets a and b both solved problems with a linear component, a single module, using a linear function, would be allocated to compute a solution to both). Such a scenario holds out the greatest promise so far of catering for structure-transforming generalizations (chapter 4) in which the transfer of part of one original problem solution is able to facilitate success on a different but partially structurally similar problem. These speculations (which are currently under empirical investigation—see note 11) reflect the need, powerfully canvassed in Karmiloff-Smith 1992b, for connectionists to begin to think not just in terms of individual tasks but also in terms of the development of multiple problem-solving abilities within a single system.

Some Interesting Features

A number of interesting features of a connectionist approach to the modeling of representational change and development have now been discerned. They include the following:

1. The natural production of (micro) U-curve phenomena resulting from the attempt to encode multiple types of mapping in a single set of weights.
2. The ability to exhibit clear stages in gross output behavior (sometimes marked by rather sudden transitions) despite the inherent gradualness of the standard weight-adjustment algorithms. The roots of such stage-like behavior include
    2.1 the effect of the nonlinear activation function,
    2.2 the gross initial structure of the net, and
    2.3 the statistical structure and sheer quantity of the training data.
3. (Following on from 2.3 above) the heavy dependence of much of the developmental profile on the nature and amount of the training data rather than on the details (number of units, layers, etc.) of the connectionist processing device.
4. The importance of the order of presentation of the training data in determining both mature competence and the stages of knowledge acquisition.

5. The methodological possibility of using our knowledge of associative learning to predict the necessary token frequencies of items within a training set.

6. The depiction of gross behavior in terms of a succession of Significant Virtual Machines without any additional commitment to correspondingly dramatic changes in the internal computational story.

7. The distinction between two ways of being failure driven: a gross way, in which failure involves an incorrect act or judgment, and an internal way, in which failure just involves the presence of an error signal associated with what might nonetheless be a perfectly effective and adequate output in its environmental context.

8. The distinction (more on which in chapter 9) between gross and effective training data.

9. The speculative depiction of nets' actually going "beyond success" by acting as teachers for other nets using reduced resources or performing multiple other tasks.

I have deliberately labored this rehearsal to stress the unexpected richness of connectionism as a tool for studying development and representational change. This facet of connectionism—its ability to generate rich and testable stories about processes of representational change—may well prove to be its most enduring contribution. By placing change and process at the heart of a computational approach to cognition, and by conceiving of developmental transitions as heavily determined by the training set to which the system was exposed, it enables us to reconcile the existence of general developmental principles and large scale individual variations (Bates and Elman 1991), and it enables us to think of representational change in terms which go far beyond the syntactic paradigm (see chapter 1 above) in which change is either innately specified or assimilated to processes of logical derivation and the generation and testing of hypotheses.

Chapter 9
Associative Learning in a Hostile World

Statistical Minds?

The rich developmental promise of connectionism lies, we have now seen, in its depiction of minds as transition machines—associative engines[1] whose temporally unfolding cognitive profiles depend most heavily on the statistics and sequential flow of the data, the passing show of sensory stimulation. But this promise hides a cost: the price of this sensitivity is an apparent vulnerability to the whims of a potentially hostile environment. More concretely, associative learning, heavily dependent as it is on statistical distributions in the input data, seems to be uncomfortably hostage to environmental fortune on two counts. First, it looks unable to account for the acquisition of (knowledge of) any principle or concept which lacks an appropriate statistical presence in the training data. Second, such successful learning as occurs always does so only thanks to the benevolence (as Jerry Fodor likes to put it) of the training environment; that is, learning is never robust against the vagaries of the input environment. In a sense these are really two angles on the single problem of achieving successful learning in cases where the gross inputs are statistically inappropriate for training an associative engine to some target performance. This problem is widely perceived to be the fatal flaw in connectionisms's aspirations as a source of cognitive models. Much human learning, it is argued, is simply *not* hostage to environmental fortune in anything like the same degree. We learn to solve problems (such as the understanding and the production of language) in a fantastically wide range of environmental conditions.

The problem is real, but the solution (or so I shall argue) is not to abandon the insights gained by attempting to understand mind as, at root, a sophisticated kind of associative engine. Instead, the solution is to begin to take seriously the project of understanding the mind as an *evolved* associative engine, i.e. one which brings a large amount of initial structure to the problems it tackles. Correlatively, it will be important to see mind as an embedded evolved associative engine, i.e. one capable of actively creating some of the environments from which it will receive teaching inputs.[2] As a side benefit, this chapter will show that the connectionist paradigm we have been exploring allows us to imagine a variety of rather subtle types and degrees of innate knowledge, the understanding of which may prove crucial for the future development of more biologically realistic connectionist (and other) models.

The Hostage Problem

The moral of our investigation (chapter 7) of the use of associative learning techniques in hierarchically structured problem domains was, roughly, that—despite some initial failures—associative learning techniques can lead to success in such complex and highly structured task domains. But the nets were seen to be highly sensitive to the order of presentation of training data, for successful learning depends on achieving the right temporal sequence for the learning of subsolutions (i.e., the right representational trajectory over time). In a related vein, many of the interesting developmental phenomena reported in chapter 8 were seen to depend crucially on the statistical distributions in the input data. Change the distributions and you will change the developmental profile. This vulnerability to the input statistics has led Jerry Fodor to conclude that connectionists are forced to assume that the training environment is (to use Fodor's term) hyperbenevolent. The trouble, he claims, is that *"it's just not true* that learning depends on the strict regimentation of experience. You learn most of what you know (including, notably, as Chomsky has often emphasized, most of what you know about how to talk) under the most haphazard environmental conditions. . . . Here's the methodological moral: if your model of the mind doesn't work because the environment isn't hyperbenevolent, *blame the model, not the environment."* (Fodor (forthcoming), p. 3)

Fodor's objection helps us to cast the systematicity argument in its proper role. The point of that argument is, as we already observed, decidedly *not* to suggest that no connectionist net can learn a systematically interpenetrating body of knowledge. Fodor is quite happy to accept that they can. Rather, the point is that, *insofar as* any net does so, its doing so will be a result of the particular training regime. Nothing about the underlying architecture positively encourages the development of systematic cognitive competencies. The great thing about so-called classical architectures for Fodor (and Pylyshyn) is that they make systematicity virtually compulsory, whereas for the connectionist it seems to depend on environmental luck. Yet if the latter really were the case, Fodor claims, we would surely find many more asystematic minds in nature than we in fact do. Conclusion: Associative learning does not afford an acceptable (environmentally robust) explanation of the fact of pervasive systematicity. Once again, the vulnerability of the computational device to the ebb and flow of training data is making Fodor uneasy.

In sum, the single worry underlying a variety of criticisms of connectionism is just this:

> (The Hostage Problem)
> Associative learning is unacceptably hostage to environmental fortune. Its success depends crucially on the continued presence of a friendly training environment in which appropriate data are presented in an appropriate order.

To defuse the Hostage Problem, we need first to highlight an unwarranted assumption which is implicit in the objection as just rehearsed: that it must be the case either that the mind is so organized that learning is *not*, after all, driven by the statistical properties of the training data, or that successful learning is a *total* hostage to environmental fortune. Such a polarization of the options is, I shall argue, unnecessary and unhelpful. There are lots of ways in which a fundamentally connectionist learning device may be partially shielded from direct susceptibility to the full statistical profile of the gross inputs to the system, yet remain fundamentally an associative engine. These ways are, however, obscured by the tendency (endemic to classical cognitive science—see Clark 1987) to think of the mind in isolation from its embedding in an active, environmentally located organism. And they are further obscured by the tendency to equate connectionist models of learning with *tabula rasa* models in which no significant evolved structure is brought to bear. Neither of these convenient blind spots can be tolerated if connectionist approaches are to achieve their true potential. Once we go beyond these blind spots, two interrelated responses to the hostage problem become visible. They involve (1) the potential for evolution to exploit (where necessary) the gap between the gross environmental input to an organism and the input to a specific internal neural network and (2) the potential for an active being to create some of its own training environments. In the next section I will expand on each of these responses.

Embedded Evolved Associative Engines

I touched on the point about embedded agents in chapter 7 when I conjectured that the gradual acquisition of sensorimotor skills, and the consequent gradual expansion of our capacities to actively explore an environment (creating more and more complex self-training data as we do so), might be one source of a kind of natural "staged training"—one obviously less hostage to environmental fortune, since we are creating our own training data as we go along. More generally, a large and respectable body of work in cognitive developmental psychology (see the review in Rutkowska 1992) depicts the child as engaging in a series of *problem constructions*. Specific developmental sequences are thus depicted not as derived directly from the child's continued attempts to solve a single problem, but as driven by the sequence of discoveries determined by the creation of a sequence of *different* problems. As Rutkowska puts it (1992, p. 30): "At the scale of developmental change, naturally intelligent systems do not construct a problem space and then select a path to the predetermined goal; rather, they appear to construct the goal and the problem space through coming to 'solve' the problem." Thus, an infant may, early on, deploy an action program which enables her to manipulate objects, but such manipulation later leads to new *goals* in virtue of the child's finding that it can lead to the discovery of new (out-of-sight) objects. The earlier abilities to act thus lead to the child's constructing new problem spaces for herself, as part of a complex interplay between the cognitive system and the environment in which it operates. It is essential to this perspective—which Rutkowska (1992, p. 30) associates with Varela's (1989) "enaction" framework and with Piaget's epigenetic, action-based view of knowledge—that the mind be treated in its proper role as part of an embedded system which creates new problem spaces as part of its ongoing activity in the world. (See also Rutkowska 1991.)

In drawing attention to the embedded, active agent's ability to be a partial determinant of her own sequence of problem spaces, we thus make a little progress with our Hostage Problem. Perhaps a well-chosen sequence of problem constructions can smooth out some of the vagaries of "raw" environmental inputs, and perhaps we may construct our problems *in the light* of our inputs. Hence, it is less likely that we shall fail to solve a given problem because the inputs are inappropriate. Instead, we should simply find ourselves addressing a different problem. Such a solution does not go nearly far enough, however, for the obvious reason that what we require is that certain *specific* (important) problems be solvable in a way which is reasonably robust against environmental fluctuations. Never getting things wrong is small consolation if you achieve it by never addressing the important problems! Thus, it is time to introduce the evolutionary dimension. Eventually we shall see how embeddedness and evolution may work together to support an even richer response.

The evolutionary response to the Hostage Problem consists, we said, in exploiting the gap between gross inputs to the system and actual training inputs to a specific network. We saw one way of exploiting such a gap in chapter 7, where we considered how the gradual expansion of short-term memory in a recurrent network could lead to an incremental increase in the complexity of the *effective* training data. Thus, although the *actual* (gross) input to the net remained fixed, the *effective* input (the data the net was able to actually address) was subject to progressive change and growth. In the case described in chapter 7, however, it seemed clear enough that there was something depressingly *fortuitous* about the network's data filtration. It seemed to be mere luck that the slow growth of short-term memory achieved the required task decomposition. Perhaps, however, the gap between gross and effective inputs can be exploited in much more powerful and nonfortuitous ways, for evolution may have created structures within us whose specific task is to "massage" gross environmental inputs in ways designed to facilitate the success of associative learning in the actual environment. This idea is best introduced by means of a fairly detailed example.

The example, drawn from the artificial life literature, concerns a neural net (Nolfi and Parisi 1991) whose task is to guide the behavior of a virtual "organism" in a virtual world.[3] The organism receives input specifying the angle and the distance of the nearest "food" element among a random distribution of such elements in the virtual environment (a square grid comprising a number of cells, each of which corresponds to a location in the environment). Its task is then to issue a motor command which facilitates subsequent ingestion. The motor parameters involve turning (any angle between 90° left and 90° right) and moving forward (any number of cells between 0 and 5). Arrival in a cell containing a food element constitutes ingestion, and the food element disappears.

Nolfi and Parisi used a standard three-layer feedforward network with two input units (coding angle and distance of subsequent motion) and seven hidden data units. All initial weights were random. The usual connectionist strategy at this point would be to go on to train the network to compute the desired function by presenting it with a large set of good input-output pairs and letting the backpropagation algorithm find a set of weights which exploits the sensory information in a way leading to successful "activity" (ingesting food). But there are, as Nolfi and Parisi note, several obvious drawbacks to such a strategy. The biggest drawback is the heavily *supervised* nature of the learning operation. The net has to be provided with what is, in effect, an external teacher which already knows what the correct performance would be for each training case. It is unlikely, however, that such a teaching function is always available to a real biological organism. Moreover, it often seems more realistic to picture an organism's *goals* as being to some extent, constructed by the organism as it goes along. As Nolfi and Parisi (1991, p. 1) comment, "One would like to have organisms develop their own goals without being told from outside what these goals should be." Such self-developed goals would be capable of changing and developing as learning continues, thus enabling us to model the development of a sequence of *problem constructions* (and not just problem solutions) much as Rutkowska suggests.

Standard work with genetic algorithms[4] does away with the supervised teaching regime by specifying general adaptive behaviors (e.g. ingestion of food as a prerequisite of survival and reproduction) and then allowing competition among multiple organisms (different random weights, in the first instance); the more successful organisms are allowed to reproduce (e.g., to copy initial weights, with small mutations, to a new generation). This regime achieves, over evolutionary time, a kind of gradient-descent learning in which error (failure to ingest) is reduced generation by generation without the need to explicitly specify correct behaviors.

Such purely evolutionary approaches, however, do not address the important issue of individual learning. One clear (and important) possibility is to combine evolutionary approaches and unsupervised individual learning strategies of various kinds. A second, less obvious possibility is to retain the idea of supervised learning but to evolve networks which generate the teaching signal (the specification of desired behavior) *for themselves*. Nolfi and Parisi term such networks *auto-teaching networks*.

An auto-teaching network has two parts. In this case, one part takes sensory input and produces a motor command. This is the standard $2 \times 7 \times 2$ network described above. But tacked onto this is a further (partial) subnet (called the *teaching network*) whose task is to generate the desired outputs for use in a self-supervised teaching mode. Thus, the overall architecture is as shown in figure 9.1. The teaching network shares the input units with the standard network, but it has a proprietary set of hidden units which then connect to a sequence of so-called teaching units. The activation pattern on these units will function as the target output on which the backpropagation learning (in the standard net) will operate.

Initially, the weights in both subnets are random. Hence, it would be a miracle if useful food-seeking behaviors were learned. Instead, the teaching net sees the sensory input, devises (given the random

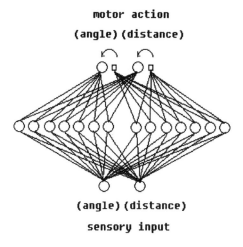

motor action

(angle) (distance)

(angle) (distance)

sensory input

Figure 9.1
Nolfi and Parisi's Artificial Organism. Boxes indicate teaching-signal outputs from
teacher subnet (right) to standard subnet (left). (From Nolfi and Parisi 1991, with
permission.)

weights) a no doubt wholly inappropriate target output, and uses it
to train the standard network to mimic it—a wonderful case of the
blind leading the blind!

The next step, however, lets in some light, for the system is then
allowed to *evolve* by the method described above. A variety of organisms (teaching net–standard net pairings) are generated, with varying
(random) initial weights, and the most successful are allowed to reproduce (i.e., to copy, with some small random variations, their initial weights to a new "baby" organism). It is the *initial* weights of the
standard net which get copied, and not its weights after learning; the
latter would constitute an unacceptably Lamarckian form of evolution. In addition, only the weights in the standard net are subject to
adjustment (learning) during an individual organism's lifetime. The
weights in the teaching net are static during its individual lifetime.

After 200 generations, each of which (except, of course, the first)
comprised slightly mutated copies of the 20 most successful organisms of the previous generations,[5] the organisms had evolved teaching nets capable of passing good teaching input (target outputs) to
the standard net. Otherwise put: ". . . evolution selects progressively
better teaching weights . . . the networks of the later generations[6]
internally generate teaching input that can be used by the networks
themselves to learn during their life how to search for food efficiently" (Nolfi and Parisi 1991, p. 8).

A reasonable fear, at this point, might be that nothing much has been achieved by the evolutionary detour involved in the selection of an auto-teaching capacity. Perhaps all that has happened is that the teaching net has evolved so as to solve the "ingestion maximization" problem, and the standard net then copies this evolved solution; in that case there is no real gain over the straightforward method of general evolution.

Two results, however, suggest that the actual situation is much more complex and interesting. First, the final degree of success achieved by the complex auto-teaching organisms is markedly greater than that achieved, over the same period of evolutionary time, by a control simulation in which only the standard net is used and no individual learning ever occurs. When selective pressure is applied directly and solely to the standard net (and no individual learning ever occurs), the evolution of some degree of successful ingestion is quicker, with worthwhile improvements showing after just five generations (compared to 20 for the complex net). But the final result (after 200 generations) is worse; that is, the complex nets at 200 generations consistently outperform those from the control group. Second, it turns out that the problem solution finally learned by the standard net is actually better than the one evolved in its associated teaching net! To show this, Nolfi and Parisi allowed successful organisms to move directly in accord with the target outputs generated by the teaching net instead of with the outputs produced by the standard net. They found that the eating behavior coded for by the teaching net alone was less successful, by a margin of about 150 items per lifetime, than that achieved by the standard net if the teaching net is allowed to train it. The explanation of this seems to be that there is some difference between what constitutes a good teaching input at a given moment and what would actually constitute the best action (i.e., the best target for teaching purposes is not always the best *action*). This observation hints at how the findings of Nolfi and Parisi dovetail with the observations in chapter 7 above concerning the importance of representational trajectories in connectionist learning.

But before the full picture can emerge, one more piece of the puzzle must be laid out. The piece in question concerns the role of the initial weights of the standard network in promoting successful learning. One clear possibility was that evolution might have selected the right weights directly in the standard net, despite the teaching net's presence in the setup. But this was easily seen not to be the case, as the standard net of a 200th-generation organism, frozen at birth and allowed to generate the usual lifetime of actions, performed abysmally: it clearly did *not* encode any solution to the ingestion problem at birth. It might seem, then, that the initial weights of the standard net played no special role. If so, then the randomization of those weights at birth ought not to matter just so long as the resulting standard net is then trained using teaching inputs from the evolved teach-net. Probably the single most striking and revealing of Nolfi and Parisi's findings was that this was not so. Far, far from it. In fact, the randomization of the standard weights at birth completely wiped out the ability of the complex organism to learn to approach food. The conclusion follows that "the standard weights are not selected for directly incorporating good eating behaviors . . . but they are accurately selected for their ability to let such a behavior emerge by life learning" (Nolfi and Parisi 1991, p. 10).

Now things fall into place. The initial weights of an evolved standard net are important in two ways. First, they matter in the way that initial weights always matter: bad random weight assignments can block successful learning by quickly leading the net into local minima. But second, they matter insofar as the teaching net has coevolved, in the succession of individual organisms, with a fixed (subject to minor mutation) initial standard net. The teaching net will thus have learned to give training inputs appropriate to *that* initial position in weight space. This would go some way toward explaining the discrepancy between the success achieved by the teaching nets alone and the successes achieved by the correct pairings of teaching net and standard net, for some of the teaching net's outputs may be geared not (directly) to coding the best immediate behavior but instead to pushing a specific standard net (one whose initial position in weight space is "known"[7] to the teacher) toward a good solution to the problem. In this way the initial weights on the standard net, though they encode no useful knowledge about the domain, are still essential to the overall system's ability to learn about that specific domain. The two subnets will have coevolved so as to encode between them a solution to the problem of how to learn about a given domain *given* the usual types of input and *given* an initial location in weight space.

A final twist to Nolfi and Parisi's investigations concerned the introduction of individual learning for the teaching network as well. In the simulation just described, the teaching net was amended only by genetic evolution. As a result, its behavior was static within each individual lifetime, in the sense that if sensory input PQ caused it to issue a teaching signal RT at time T then the same input would have the same effect at all other times were it to be received again. However, as we saw in chapter 7, it is often beneficial for networks to receive different *kinds* of training at different temporal stages of learning. Differences in the effective training data (in this case, the output of the teaching net) produced by the same sensory input received at different times might also be a source of stage-like transitions, as was discussed in chapter 8, for some such transitions might then be traced to changes in the kind of auto-teaching being produced and hence to the construction, given sensory input PQ, of different *problems* at different developmental moments. In an attempt to begin to model such further complexities, Nolfi and Parisi studied a population of organisms (teaching net–standard net pairings) in which each subnet passed target outputs to the other and the backpropagation algorithm was allowed to work on each. A channel was thus opened up between the standard net and its "teacher" such that the teacher could change its output (for a given input) as a result of weight changes determined by the output of the standard net. The output of each subnet contributes to changes in the weights within the other during the lifetime of the organism.[8] Thus, there is space for the teaching outputs of the teaching net to change during the organisms's lifetime.

The performance of the "reciprocal teaching" net was, perhaps, disappointing. It did not exceed (and did not even quite match) that of its predecessor. It is of interest, however, that in this case *neither* subnet, when tested at birth, encoded anything like an acceptable solution to the problem (whereas in the previous case the evolved teaching net constituted a good solution, though not as good a solution as the one its attendant standard net would come to learn). Yet working together the two subnets achieved a good degree of success. Here, then, we find an even subtler kind of innate knowledge, in which what has evolved in the two subnets is the capacity to *cooperate* so as to learn (and to learn to teach) useful food-approaching strategies. But neither net is now clearly marked as the student or the teacher in this endeavor. Instead, the two nets, in the context of the training environment, present a delicately harmonized overall system selected to facilitate just the kind and sequence of learning necessary to meet the specified evolutionary pressures.

The Space of Innate Knowledge

The crucial moral of the above discussion is that the space of possible ways in which knowledge might be innate in a system is very large and includes some very subtle cases. It is worth dwelling on this a little. Recall Fodor's depiction of mind as a locus of a fixed set of innate representational elements, and of concept learning as the process of trying out combinations of those elements. This view (the Syntactic Image rehearsed in chapter 1 above) depicts the use of a structured, concatenative symbol system as an innately specified part of our basic cognitive apparatus. And it is this fact which Fodor cites as the chief explanatory advantage of classicism over connectionism, insofar as it predicts the *pervasiveness* of systematic cognitive competencies. Associative minds, Fodor argues, are in no way compelled to develop such systematic competencies but are instead painfully hostage to environmental fortune. We are now in a position, however, to sketch some other possibilities.

The key to these possibilities is the simple idea that the training data seen by various subnetworks engaged in forms of associative learning need not correspond to the gross environmental inputs to the system. There is plenty of room for a *transformation factor* of some kind (or kinds) to intervene. Once we see that the way such a transformation factor (the teaching net in Nolfi and Parisi's simulations) works can *itself* be the product of evolutionary pressure, we begin to see how nature might contrive to insulate its associative engines from some of the vagaries of the environment. In so doing, we need not (and typically will not) return to a position in which the actual environmental inputs are barely relevant (as in a triggering scenario). Instead we face a rich continuum of possible degrees of innate specification corresponding to the extent to which a transformation factor molds the actual inputs in a certain direction. In addition to this, it is clearly possible that the initial weights in the learning network (the standard net, in the terminology of Nolfi and Parisi) may themselves have been selected so as to facilitate the acquisition of knowledge in a given domain. And more subtle still, they may have been selected so as to facilitate the acquisition of that knowledge *given* a coevolving transformation function (such as the teaching net), and vice versa (that is, the transformation function may be geared to the specific position on an error surface occupied by the standard net to which it is attached). Thus, the overall picture of ways in which various tendencies to acquire knowledge may be innately specified is already enormously complex. It gets more complex still once we notice that evolution could select a transformation function which itself changes over time, and even more complex if that "temporally loaded" transformation function is evolved to respond to feedback from the net it is serving. And the space of possible *kinds* of transformation function is itself large. Nolfi and Parisi investigate one kind in the auto-teaching paradigm, but it includes any case where the training input to one net is the output of another rather than direct environmental stimulation (i.e., it applies to all cases in which we confront a cascade of networks passing signals to one another). In all such cases, we are still depicting the mind (*pacé* Fodor) as fundamentally an associative engine, and we may stop far short of providing it with any set of innate representational elements. Nonetheless, we depict it as a highly structured system, bearing significant innate biases and delicately coupled to the environment in which learning will take place. Between Fodorian innateness and the *tabula rasa* there extends a vast space, maneuvers in which reduce the extent to which even fundamentally associative minds need be fully hostage to environmental fortune.

These observations bear on several of our earlier concerns.

First, the common complaint (chapter 5) that connectionist learning is unacceptably bound to the statistical profile of the training data can again be seen to be misleading: Although it is true that the statistics of the effective training data are crucial, it is also true that the effective training data need not always correspond to the gross training data (environmental inputs). This is yet another case where we need to distinguish carefully between an external and an internal sense of a key term (this time, 'training data'). Given that it is the internal, effective training data which count, we must beware of concluding too quickly (from some examination of the actual gross inputs) that a given solution would not be found by a connectionist mind.

Second, we see that a degree of insulation against the vagaries of the gross external environment is entirely consistent with our being fundamentally associative engines. It is even possible that the development of systematic cognitive competencies is being encouraged by some subtle internal massaging of the training data!

Finally, we can now describe yet another way in which something like representational redescription may occur but which (like the cases described in chapter 8) is less rationalistic than the original description of the process suggests. Instead of depicting all redescription as involving a direct change in the nature of the internal representation of a *solution*, we may see it as a cognitive change caused by an endogenously determined change in the way a network sets up a *problem*. This could occur in the presence of any temporally loaded transformation factor which determined a change in the way gross external inputs are taken as training data by some deeper system. Such a change in the effective data would induce a new solution even if the gross inputs remained unchanged. In this way, we may conceptualize at least some phase-like transitions as flowing from a change in the way the child constructs the *problem space* for herself.

Minimal Nativism[9]

We have seen over the last two chapters some of the many ways to enrich the original connectionist approach. The most crucial step in this process is to recognize the important role which innate knowledge and gross initial structure must play in the development of realistic and powerful connectionist models. The discussion in the second and third sections of this chapter shows how surprisingly subtle parts of this innate specification might be. Instead of encoding knowledge about a domain X, a net might, for instance, start with knowledge about *how to learn about* domain X given the kinds of input nature will provide. This possibility (of innate knowledge one step removed, as it were) extends also to the question of initial gross structure.

Thus, consider once again the question of modularization. It has become increasingly clear that, for certain complex problem domains, connectionist learning algorithms will prove efficient only if they operate on a highly prestructured system. The balance-beam architecture (chapter 8) is a relatively weak example of this, as is Norris' solution to the problem of date calculation by idiots savants (chapter 7). The most persuasive case I know of concerns the use of backpropagation learning to train a net to recognize handwritten zip codes for the U.S. Postal Service. The problem is clearly highly complex, and seems to be soluble only because the initial network is a multilayer structure in which learning is heavily *constrained* in *domain-appropriate* ways. In particular, a technique called "weight sharing" (in which the weight changes made to several connections are constrained to be identical) was used to induce a set of feature detectors—banks of units which (because they share the same set of weights) will detect a single feature in a variety of locations. The network has three hidden layers (H1, H2, and H3 in figure 9.2), the connections into H1 and H2 being both local and heavily constrained. H1 is itself composed of 12 groups of 64 units, which are configured as 12 separate 8 × 8 feature maps. Similar heavy prestructuring occurs at subsequent layers (e.g., H2 involves 12 feature maps, each of which comprises 16 units in a 4 × 4 plane). All the units in each map are constrained to have identical weights; among the 1,256 units and 64,660 connections in the net, there are, as a result of such constraints, only 9,760 independent parameters.

Full details for the net are given in Lecun et al. 1989. The point, for our purposes, is just that the highly structured net succeeds in efficiently learning the task—it is described as "state of the art in digit recognition" (ibid., p. 549)—only because the learning is so highly and appropriately constrained. The architecture builds in geometric knowledge about the task. Several less highly constrained networks were tried and found severely wanting (ibid., pp. 548–549).

But such heavy prestructuring, as was argued in chapter 7 above, is not always an acceptable solution if we seek to explain how *natural* systems learn to negotiate such domains. It will be plausible only in

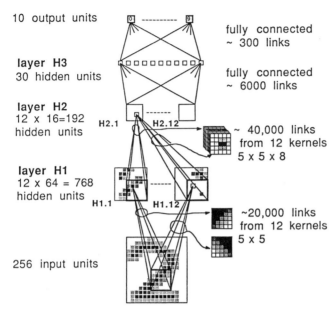

10 output units

fully connected
~ 300 links

layer H3
30 hidden units

fully connected
~ 6000 links

layer H2
12 x 16=192
hidden units

H2.1   H2.12

~ 40,000 links
from 12 kernels
5 x 5 x 8

layer H1
12 x 64 = 768
hidden units

H1.1   H1.12

~20,000 links
from 12 kernels
5 x 5

256 input units

Figure 9.2
Network architecture. (From LeCun et al. 1989, with permission.)

cases where the problem is biologically basic enough to drive natural selection to build special structures into the brain for that very purpose. Nonetheless, as our earlier discussion shows, there may be interesting kinds of innate endowment which fall short of total prestructuring yet facilitate learning in the domain. For instance, it may be that evolution has bequeathed us an ability to *learn to modularize* our cognitive resources in ways which foster success in complex domains.

It may seem at this point that the distinctive role of the *data* for connectionist theorizing about cognitive development (chapter 8 above) is diminished. In fact, however, it is just that we are seeing how very complicated the true story must be. We must struggle to understand a system whose subtle innate resources have been selected precisely to facilitate the success of associative learning devices embedded in a specific kind of organism and a specific environment. Exclusive focus on either data or innate structure is thus bound to mislead. In a prestructured net (or one which has deployed an innate tendency to amend its own gross structure), cognitive development is still driven by the statistics of the gross data set. But those statistics are systematically distorted as if through a kind of squashing function. Some effects are amplified, others diminished. The pre-structuring thus adds a further kind of nonlinearity to the net's responses to the *gross* training data!

A nice example combining the ideas of subtle innateness, data sensitivity, and self-modularization is given by Annette Karmiloff-Smith. It concerns the well-established, presumably innate tendency of the neonate to attend to face-like stimuli (Johnson and Morton 1991). In what might such an innate tendency consist? Do we need to imagine that the details of the human face are already encoded in the weights of some subnetwork at birth? No. Karmiloff-Smith (1992b, p. 256), following Johnson and Morton, notes that "all that is required is something like the specification of the face contour, with three high-contrast blobs inside an arrangement similar to the face." Once provided with an innate mechanism which preferentially attends to (i.e., is a feature detector for) visual inputs exhibiting that rough pattern, evolution can step back and let the data carry the rest of the burden, for it will have succeeded in setting the scene for the later data-driven development of a species-specific face-recognition module. The innate tendency to attend to three-blob stimuli will cause the cortical circuits downstream from this (subcortical) mechanism to receive training inputs which are heavily dominated by actual human faces. Those circuits will then *learn to become* specialized for human face recognition. As Karmiloff-Smith puts it (ibid.), "the infant's human face recognition *becomes* domain specific and progressively modularized as development proceeds."

Thus, rather quite small initial biases, of a wide variety of kinds (see also the range of cases described in chapter 8), can have profound implications for the way a network develops in a given environment. This "magnifying-glass" effect provides an opportunity which evolution, being the laziest of designers (Clark 1989a, chapter 4; Jacob 1977), could not be expected to ignore. Evolution will surely favor a *minimal nativism* as depicted in the following principle:

Minimal Nativism
Instead of building in large amounts of innate knowledge and structure, build in whatever minimal set of biases and structure will ensure the emergence, under realistic environmental conditions, of the basic cognitive modules and structures necessary for early success and for subsequent learning.

For examples of Minimal Nativist outlooks, see Karmiloff-Smith 1992a,b. In a similar vein, Carey (1990) notes that one alternative to the suggestion that (e.g.) the concept of a person is innate is that what is innate may actually be something more minimal which, in the child's real environment, is bound to lead to the rapid development of such a concept. Thus, it could be that what is innate is not the idea of a person as a potential social partner but rather a special interest in events which involve contingent responses to the child's own actions. This more minimal innate sensitivity would quickly lead to knowledge of persons, since "people are the main source of contingent reactions" (Carey 1990, p. 166).

Ramsey and Stich (1991) use the term 'minimal nativism' but their usage differs from mine in a crucial respect. For them (p. 292), Minimal Nativism is the claim that in the domain of language learning, "the child approaches the task of language acquisition with an innate learning mechanism that is strongly biased in favour of certain grammars and against others." But (and this is the crucial point) the bias in question is *not* conceived of as *specific* to the task of language learning. Instead, it is the kind of bias involved in being able to learn at all (as against being a tape recorder) and in learning grammar X instead of grammar Y (given that both are in some sense compatible with the data). Thus, any random weighted connectionist net which learns using backpropagation (say) will count as having a Minimal Nativist endowment on the Ramsey-Stich usage.

By contrast, I am using the term 'Minimal Nativism' to refer to cases in which a network brings task-specific biases to bear on the learning. In this respect, the imagined innate endowment I am imagining actually fits the *strongest* model of innate knowledge countenanced by Ramsey and Stich (1991, p. 307)—a rationalism in which "the innate . . . mechanism embodies biases or constraints that are specific to the task."

Minimal Nativism, in my usage, does not signify any lack of task specificity in the biases. Rather, it signifies something about the *way* such task-specific biasing may be achieved. In particular, such biasing need not involve anything very rich, or complex, or rule-like. Small details concerning initial configurations and connection weights can, we saw, make all the difference to the ability of a net to learn to solve a given problem. What I am calling Minimal Nativism is thus what Ramsey and Stich might well have called *Minimal Rationalism.* It is rationalism insofar as it countenances quite task-specific biases, but it is minimal insofar as these may fall fantastically short of anything like innate knowledge about linguistic universals, persons, naive physics, or whatever. Indeed, the kind of innate endowment imagined is not happily described as knowledge at all. It is more like the laziest possible fixing of a few assorted parameters so as to facilitate the *subsequent* attainment (by learning) of states properly described as involving knowledge.

In sum: One of the most exciting aspects of connectionist approaches is that they provide a perfect computational arena for "magnifying-glass" effects of a variety of different kinds. Such effects can be induced by facts about gross initial structure or by subtle variations in initial weight assignments. In either case, the acquisition of the target knowledge will be driven by the use of associative learning techniques applied to a rich body of data. It is just that evolution will, in the laziest way possible, have slightly loaded the dice. The upshot is that we can now begin to explore a variety of ways in which knowledge may be *partially* innate. As Bates and Elman (1992) point out, we can think quite seriously in terms of "90% or 10% of any innate idea." We can also think in terms of innate tendencies to construct the problem space in specific ways, to auto-teach, and to learn to auto-teach! The new space is amazingly rich, and we are only just beginning to skim its surface.

Nature's Problem

Evolution, we may be sure, did not make higher cognizers by loading their skulls with neurons and synapses and leaving it at that. Instead, much of our power must derive from the initial structuring of those resources and from the initial setting of various parameters (such as weights, in the connectionist idealization). The sum of such initial structure and settings determines the extent of our innate knowledge. But how should we conceive of such knowledge? Fodor depicts it as consisting crucially in a set of innate representational atoms; however, as we have seen, many other possibilities exist. Thus, suppose we accept as evolutionarily basic (see Clark 1989a) some kind of very broadly connectionist, associative learning device. Nature's problem is then how to promote successful learning *given these basic resources* in organisms *embedded in a specific type of environment*. Once the problem is set up in that way, however, a very different range of solutions seem appropriate, for it is then taken as given that learning will be at root the data-driven development of increasingly fit behaviors and representations. Thus, one way to introduce innate knowledge is to evolve ways of transforming the kinds of gross input data presented by a specific environment so as to present the problem to the associative engine in the most beneficial way (a way which may need to change over time, as we saw). At the same time, the initial weights of the learning device are subject to selection, and a delicate coupling between these weights and the kind of training regime selected may emerge. The upshot is that innate information is not located "in" the organism, but neither is the organism a *tabula rasa* vulnerable to every statistical quirk of its sensory experience. Moreover, the *kind* of innate prestructuring that is necessary to induce specific developmental patterns (such as the development of specific kinds of module) may be surprisingly minimal, courtesy of the magnifying-glass effects described in the preceding section. Therefore, this chapter ends on an optimistic note. The solution to the hostage problem is not to give up on associative learning; it is to begin to explore the rich space of ways in which associative learning may be sculpted by the complex interplay between gross data and a variety of significant endogenous forces.

Chapter 10

The Fate of the Folk

Two Dogmas of Super-Fodorian Realism

Call any learning device which is fundamentally driven by the statistics of patterns in the input data an associative engine. A broadly connectionist associative engine may then be defined as one whose basic mode of operation involves

some kind of statistically driven learning,
the development of distributed representations,[1]
superpositional storage techniques,

and

context-sensitive representation and retrieval.

If the conjectures of previous chapters are at all plausible, then the human mind may very well turn out to be a broadly connectionist associative engine (albeit a highly evolved one which exploits various kinds of minimal nativist bias). This possibility has recently been argued to have serious consequences for the folk-psychological image of mind as a locus of causally active propositional attitudes.[2] I have argued elsewhere (Clark 1989a) against this general kind of inference. However, recent attempts to link connectionist approaches to worries about the folk-psychological framework have introduced new arguments, and my own position has mutated slightly into something a little more radical. It seems germane, then, to consider (one last time) the fate of the folk.

The direct impetus for this treatment lies with two different (but related) recent attempts to forge a link between the putative goodness of connectionism as a model of mind and the failure of the folk framework: that of Ramsey, Stich, and Garon (1991) and that of Davies (1991). These authors focus on the discrete causal efficacy of folk-individuated contents and on the conditions of the ascription of grasp of a concept, respectively, and both of the works cited are instances of what I (in chapter 1) termed Super-Fodorian Realism—that is, the insistence (which goes beyond Fodor's own stated commitments) that, unless something like a Fodorian vision of mind is correct, we humans (on philosophical grounds) are not properly treated as loci of beliefs, desires, and other propositional attitudes. Fodor's view, by contrast, seems to be that the link between our status as believers and the presence of a classical concatenative combinatorial inner code is an empirical one. The classical story is then depicted as the best *explanation* of (what is taken as given) our being true believers. The failure of the classical story would not, as far as I can tell, force Fodor to reject the image of us as true believers on conceptual grounds. This exegesis is, however, rather a delicate matter, and I record it only tentatively.

The Super-Fodorian position is, however, crystal clear. It is that the image of mind as a broadly connectionist associative engine is incompatible, on conceptual grounds, with its folk-psychological image. This alleged incompatibility turns on two claims which I shall shortly dispute and which together constitute the two dogmas of the section title:

> *First dogma*   Beliefs etc. must show up as causally active and scientifically respectable inner states.
> *Second dogma*   Ascription of grasp of a concept is ascription of a unitary inner state.

Both dogmas are false. Once we reject them, we see why the folk can keep a considerable distance from the details of the believers' innards.

Causal Efficacy and Propositional Modularity

A cluster of arguments linking the fates of folk psychology and connectionist representation is to be found in the work of Ramsey, Stich, and Garon (1991), who depict the commonsense understanding of mind as involving a crucial commitment to what they call *propositional modularity*.[3] The thesis of propositional modularity claims that propositional attitudes are *"functionally discrete, semantically interpretable* states that play a *causal role* in the production of other propositional attitudes, and ultimately in the production of behavior" (Ramsey et al. 1991, p. 204).

Propositional attitudes are functionally discrete insofar as we are happy to speak of agents' gaining or losing individual beliefs (ibid., p. 205). They are semantically interpretable insofar as folk psychology condones generalizations based on the semantic properties of beliefs. We group people together as all believing that so-and-so, and we expect lawful regularities in their behavior to be captured as a result. The predicate 'believes that p' is thus meant to be *projectable* in the sense of Goodman (1965). And, finally, these functionally discrete, semantically interpretable states are said to play a causal role in the production of behavior. An individual belief can be cited as the cause of a particular action.

Traditional AI models, according to Ramsey, Stich, and Garon, are visibly compatible with the demands of propositional modularity. They are compatible because they recognize a distinct syntactic state corresponding to each gross semantic state as picked out by the use of propositional-attitude talk. Semantic network models (Quillian 1968), production systems (Newell and Simon 1972), and straightforwardly sentential models (McCarthy 1968) all allow the *functional localization* of the information relating to some particular belief or memory. (Functional localization is not the same thing as physical localization. Many models which are functionally classical are physically nonlocal in their storage of information.) In a system with functional localization we can always ask "Did a particular piece of knowledge (such as the belief that cats have fur) play a role in the production of such and such behavior (e.g., in the inference to a given conclusion)?," and the question will have a definite answer visible once we know what inner syntactic state corresponds to that information. A standard semantic network (to give Ramsey, Stich, and Garon's example) may derive a conclusion by a process of spreading activation which never activates the 'cats have fur' node—in such a case, the system can be seen to have reached its conclusion without calling on that information. It is this kind of "semantic transparency" which Ramsey, Stich, and Garon fail to find in our chosen class of connectionist models, and it is this failure which, they believe, underwrites the eliminativist conditional—viz., that if such models are good models of human cognition, then the belief/desire framework of folk psychology is shown to be fundamentally mistaken.

Ramsey, Stich, and Garon offer two main arguments whose purpose is to highlight an alleged incompatibility between connectionist storage and representation and the assumptions of propositional modularity: an argument concerning superpositional storage and causal efficacy and an argument concerning natural kinds. Let us rehearse these in turn.

Superpositional Storage
We are asked to consider a network (called Network A) whose task is to answer Yes or No to each of 16 questions. The questions are posed by giving the network a coding for a proposition as input (e.g., 'dogs

have fur') and reading off an answer by consulting a single output unit which is interpreted to mean Yes if it comes on and No if it stays off. It is a simple matter to deploy a standard connectionist learning algorithm to train a network to succeed in this task. The trained network will take a vector of values across input units to code the proposition and will learn a set of weights leading to and from the hidden units which will mediate just the input/output profile we desire. Suppose that we have 16 input units, and that we code 'dogs' as the pattern 11000011 across the first eight and we code 'have fur' as the pattern 00001111 across the last eight. The system learns to take the input

1100001100001111

and give 1 (i.e., Yes) at the sole output unit. The learned weights connect the 16 input units to a layer of four hidden units and on to the output unit. The important fact is that this single array of weights must be subtly adjusted (via an automatic learning algorithm) so as to work not just for one proposition but for all 16. The knowledge is thus stored superpositionally in one subtly orchestrated set of weights.

At this point we are already, according to Ramsey, Stich, and Garon, starting to cross swords with folk psychology, for the folk would like to say that it is the belief that dogs have fur which causes them to answer Yes to the question "Do dogs have fur?" But if our memory was organized in the superpositional connectionist style, it seems unclear that it would make sense to say that it was that particular piece of stored information (rather than the rest) which caused the output. As Ramsey et al. (1991, p. 212) put it: "The information encoded in Network A is stored holistically and distributed throughout the network. Whenever information is extracted . . . *many* connection strengths, *many* biases, and *many* hidden units play a role in the computation. And any particular weight or unit or bias will help to encode information about *many* different propositions. It simply makes no sense to ask whether or not the representation of a particular proposition plays a causal role in the network's computation." In other words: It is meant to be no more the case that it was the network's knowledge that dogs have paws that caused the Yes output than it was the case that its knowledge that cats have fur caused it, for it is all stored in a single set of weights.

What is worrying Ramsey, Stich, and Garon here is the threat of what Stich, in a later piece (1991, p. 181), calls *total causal holism*. Such holism implies that, in any cognitive episode involving our stored beliefs, it is not the case that just one belief is causally implicated, or even that many beliefs are causally implicated. Instead, *every* belief which the system stores (in a single set of weights) counts as causally implicated! But such total causal holism, Stich suggests, is surely incompatible with the folk-psychological practice of citing specific clusters of beliefs in explanations of specific actions.

In fact, as we shall see, the worry that connectionism leads to such a radical causal holism is largely unfounded. Ramsey, Stich, and Garon go on, however, to make a more subtle claim, which is also grounded in the facts about superpositional storage. The claim is best introduced by citing some examples given in the original paper.

Consider Alice. Alice wishes to send some e-mail and believes she can do it from her office. She also wishes to speak to her research assistant and believes she can do this at her office. But—and here is the crux—she might (according to the folk-psychological views about belief) go to the office as a result of just one of these two belief-desire complexes, both of which she possesses and either (or both) of which would be sufficient to yield the behavior (Ramsey et al. 1991, p. 205).

The second example concerns Inspector Clouseau. Suppose Clouseau believes that the butler said he spent the evening at the village hotel, and that he took the morning train home. And suppose Clouseau also believes that the hotel is closed and that the morning train is not running. Then Clouseau could infer (from his knowledge of what the butler said) that the butler is lying. And he could do so either by spotting the inconsistency over the hotel or by spotting the inconsistency over the train, or by spotting both. But it at least makes sense, on the folk-psychological conception, to imagine that he in fact draws the conclusion solely by reflecting on one of the two pieces of evidence. In short: "We see commonsense psychology invoking a pair of distinct propositional attitudes, one of which is causally active on a given occasion while the other is causally inert." (Ramsey et al. 1991, p. 206)

In what follows I shall use a different example—one which I find clearer and which preserves all the essential structure of the cases used by Ramsey et al. Consider Christine. Christine has the following two desires: She desires a pint of Coopers and she desires to sit near an open fire. She also has the following long-standing beliefs: that the Dingo and Whistle serves draught Coopers and that the Dingo and Whistle has an open fire. One night, while out walking, she reads and understands the pub sign 'Dingo and Whistle'. She goes in. And yet, it makes sense to suppose that she went in *solely* because of her desire for an open fire, even though the desire for Coopers, on its own, would have been sufficiently potent to cause her to enter.

The general form of the claim, then, is that someone might believe all
of

$$P, P \rightarrow Q, Q \rightarrow S, P \rightarrow R, R \rightarrow S$$

but might, on a given occasion, happen to use only the Q information
in coming to the conclusion that S.

The upshot of this is that certain connectionist models flout the
folks' apparent commitment to what I shall call the *equipotency claim*:

> Equipotency Claim
> An agent may have two long-standing beliefs which are both
> equipotent (both apt to cause the same piece of behavior on a
> given occasion), AND YET the agent may *as a matter of fact* act on
> the basis of only one of the two beliefs.

The worry is that, in view of the facts about superpositional storage
chronicled above, it seems to make no sense to suppose that one of
the beliefs rather than the other is active at a given moment.

Natural Kinds
The second kind of argument I dub "the argument from natural
kinds." It goes like this: Suppose you train a second network, called
Network B, on 17 propositions (the same 16 as in Network A, plus
an extra one). Network B will learn a set of weights which are *globally*
different from those of Network A. This is because the use of superpositional storage means that the way you encode a proposition is
crucially dependent on what other knowledge the network has to
store.[4] The result is that a 17-proposition network must store all 17
propositions in a way subtly different from the way the 16-proposi-
tion network stores its 16, even if the 16 are a subset of the 17.
Contrast this with the more conventional procedure of adding a dec-
larative representation (e.g., a sentence) to a list structure. The list

> dogs have fur
> cats have fleas

and the list

> dogs have fur
> cats have fleas
> cats have fur

have a common typographic subset. Such commonality can be preserved in traditional symbolic models, but it seems to disappear in
superpositional connectionist storage. The conclusion this is meant to
force on us is that where folk psychology finds a natural psychologi-

cal kind (all the believers that dogs have fur), connectionist psychology does not, for the units-and-weights description of all the various networks which might encode such knowledge have no common subpart. As Ramsey, Stich, and Garon put it (1991, p. 213): "The moral here is that though there are *indefinitely* many connectionist networks that represent the information that dogs have fur just as well as Network A does, these networks have no projectable features in common that are describable in the language of connectionist theory (thus) the class of networks that might model a cognitive agent who believes that dogs have fur is not a genuine kind at all but simply a chaotically disjunctive set."

I think we can capture the spirit of these eliminativist arguments in a simple picture. Imagine the following two ways of storing sentences. In the first way, you keep a discrete token of each sentence on a slip of paper in a drawer. It is then easy to see how to use the tokens one at a time. In the second way, you token each sentence as a pot of colored ink. You then take a vat of water and throw in all the pots. It is now not easy to see how to use the colors separately; worse still, the resultant overall color will vary according to the global set of pots of ink put in. The commonality among various vats which token the same sentence is now lost to view. The question then is: How could a vat-and-inks (read superpositional connectionist) style of storage be compatible with the assumption of propositional modularity? The root of the Ramsey-Stich-Garon-style worries is thus the apparent incompatibility of connectionist storage and retrieval with the folk image of beliefs as individually causally efficacious items.

Conceptual Modularity: The Bottleneck of Content

Ramsey, Stich, and Garon (1991) predicate their eliminativist conditional on considerations relating to the functional localization of *propositional* contents in a connectionist system. It is thus an argument from *propositional modularity*. It is possible, however, to argue for the same conditional on the basis of considerations relating to the functional localization of *concepts*. Such arguments are arguments from *conceptual modularity*.

Conceptual-modularity arguments have their roots in the thought (Strawson 1959; Evans 1982) that a distinctive feature of propositional-attitude states is that to be in such a state *requires* that you be master of the individual concepts involved in its specification. Such mastery reveals itself in an ability to have an indefinite number of other thoughts which involve the exercise of the concept. To take a very simple case: "Any thought that we can interpret as having the content that a if f involves the exercise of an ability—knowledge of what it is for something to be f—which can be exercised in indefinitely many distinct thoughts, and would be exercised in, for instance, the thought that b is f." (Evans 1982, p. 103)

To have the thought that polo players never wear green hats, you must be master of each of the various concepts involved. To be master of the concept of 'green,' you must be able to apply the concept in any case in which the use of color concepts does not commit a category mistake.[5] Likewise for the concept of a hat and the concept of a polo player. What this means is that (ruling out category mistakes) you must be able to use the concept in relation to an arbitrary object. In short: If you can think about an object b, and you are truly able to think, of an object a, that a is f, and if thinking that b is f would not commit a category mistake, then (to satisfy the constraint) you must be able to think that b is f. Following Evans (1982), this has become known as the *generality constraint*.

As Davies (1990a) points out, the generality constraint is a constraint only on conceptualized content. Nonconceptualized (or subdoxastic) content is not subject to such a constraint, since to be in a subdoxastic state does not imply that you are master of the concepts involved in describing it. Thus, my visual system may be in a state properly characterized as involving the subdoxastic content that there is a steep texture gradient at a certain point in my visual field; however, for this to be true I do not need to be master of (or even to have heard of) the concept of a texture gradient.

To parley the generality constraint into an *a priori* demand for functionally localized inner states or processes corresponding to familiar contents, Davies proceeds via two stages.

In the first stage, he defines a notion of *causal systematicity* as follows: Relative to some pattern in the inputs to a device, the device's processing is causally systematic if and only if all the input-output transitions which conform to that pattern implicate a common mechanism. Such a mechanism must be sensitive to some property of the inputs which engages the mechanism in question and which correlates with the common factor fixed on when we described the pattern.

Here is a nonsemantic example (from Davies 1991). A drinks machine might take four types of token: square red ones, square blue ones, round red ones, and round blue ones. Watching it in action, we may discern a certain pattern—for example, all square tokens result in coffee being dispensed, and all round ones in tea; and all red tokens (square or round) result in the adding of milk, while blue ones do not. Is the device causally systematic relative to these generalizations? It would not be if the device were fully modular (that is, built of four completely separate drink dispensers, each activated by one of the four types of token). To be systematic instead requires (e.g.) that a *common* processor or mechanism is engaged by (e.g.) all square tokens and is, on each occasion, the source of the coffee. In sum: Relative to some pattern G, the requirement of causal systematicity is the requirement that "there should be a mechanism whose presence in the system explains all the input-output transitions that conform to the pattern described by G" (Davies 1991, p. 235).

The general notion of causal systematicity applies to semantic patterns quite directly. If a being is given a series of inputs like 'John is a bachelor', 'Fred is a bachelor', and 'Peter is a bachelor' and gives as outputs 'So John is unmarried', 'So Fred is unmarried', and 'So Peter is unmarried', respectively, we can discern a pattern: Wherever the input concerns a bachelor, the output is that the person is unmarried. It can then be asked whether this semantic pattern has as its basis some real causal systematicity in the system producing the responses.

In the second stage, Davies needs to persuade us that folk psychology is *committed* to the proposition that genuine casual systematicity underpins such semantic patterns. This commitment follows, he claims, from the generality constraint itself. To see why, we are to reflect that what the constraint demands is not merely that anyone who can think A is F and B is G must be capable of thinking B is F, etc. Rather, it demands that the *set* of abilities (to think A is F, B is F, etc.) be grounded in a unitary mastery of the concept ". . . is F." But, Davies argues, the mere fact of an input-output pattern cannot make this so, any more than the mere fact of an input-output pattern in the fully modular drinks machine *made* it the case that it deployed a common mechanism in all the coffee-dispensing episodes.

To accept the generality constraint, Davies concludes, is to accept a demand for causal systematicity relative to a description of ourselves as concept graspers. It is to accept that if a set of inferences is to be explained by reference to a common piece of concept mastery (e.g. mastery of the concept 'bachelor') then there must be some internal factor which is critical in each of the inferential transitions concerned and which is common to all of them. The demand is thus for a single inner state which is active whenever a cognitive episode involving a given concept occurs and which can be uniquely associated with the concept concerned.

I shall call this the demand for *conceptual modularity*, since it asks for a processing-level commonality between inner states which share (according to folk psychology) a conceptual component. The demand of conceptual modularity seems to be more fundamental than the demand for propositional modularity, for it is grounded in the independently plausible requirements of the generality constraint. Like the demand of propositional modularity, however, it is not obviously met by a certain class of connectionist systems. To see why, recall the characteristic feature (made much of in chapter 2) of *soft, context-sensitive representation*. One upshot of this feature (as exemplified in the coffee example of chapter 2) was that no single pattern of hidden-unit activation corresponds to a single conceptual-level content. Instead, we expect a variety of patterns of hidden-unit activation, the differences being attributable to the semantic context (e.g. coffee in the context of a cup). Such patterns may overlap to form a family-resemblance-style grouping, but there need be no simple syntactic pattern which is common to every inference involving a concept.[6] Instead, the internal states involved in mediating the inference from 'Nigel is a bachelor' to 'Nigel is unmarried' may show only a family resemblance to those mediating between 'Bruce is a bachelor' and 'Bruce is unmarried', and so on (see Davies 1991, pp. 248–249). Whereas a classical system can filter all such inferences through a single logical bottleneck, a distributed connectionist system will use one of several routes, depending on the details of surrounding context. This is, in fact, just the property celebrated by Smolensky in the following passage (1988, p. 12): "In the symbolic paradigm, the context of a symbol is manifest around it and consists of other symbols. In the subsymbolic paradigm the context of a symbol is manifest inside it and consists of subsymbols."

Once again, what Smolensky is praising is the lack of context-independent abstractions standing for everyday semantic elements, such as 'coffee' and 'dog'. And what Davies fears is the inability of a system which (*prima facie*) lacks such recurrent abstractions to meet the demand of strict causal systematicity of inferential transitions. The upshot of it all, according to Davies (1991, p. 250), is "a tension between the connectionist program for modeling cognition and our commonsense conception of ourselves as thinkers."

Connectionism, it seems, extends an "invitation to Eliminativism" (Davies 1991, p. 250). Or does it?

Concepts as Skills

The demand for conceptual modularity, as just presented, is the demand for a *causal* common factor uniting the inner states which correspond to the deployment of a *single* concept in an individual on different occasions. It is the demand, in short, for a causal bottleneck (a processing-level commonality) in cases where the folk discern the repeated deployment of a given concept. The lack of any such commonality is meant to fragment the competence underlying our behavior so that it will not satisfy the generality constraint.

One immediate problem with such an approach is that it leaves the notion of a causal commonality underspecified, and with it the very idea of functional localization. Thus, we need to distinguish at least the following possible unpackings of the idea of a causal common factor.

> *Ultra-strong commonality*   There is a physical brain state p such that whenever a given subject makes an inference (according to folk psychology) involving a concept F, P occurs.
>
> *Strong commonality*   There is some scientific level of description of the subject's brain states such that there exists a principled (perhaps mathematical or statistical) means of grouping together all those states or processes involved in inferences depending on a concept F.
>
> *Weak commonality*   There is commonality, but it is visible only if one uses the ontology and the ascriptive apparatus proper to the folk level of description.

On the face of it, there seems to be a tension between the idea of a genuine cause and the idea of weak commonality. At the other end of the spectrum, ultra-strong commonality seems too harsh a demand. Even a conventional computing system may not always use the same physical resources to process a particular inference. Yet the information contained in a production rule such as

If X > 3, then output 'cup'

is surely capable of acting as a causal common factor in a series of state transitions. That leaves only strong commonality. Davies himself (1990a) seemed at first to think that context-sensitive distributed representations would *contravene* the demand of strong commonality, since they would not provide processing states which consistently appeared whenever a given concept was (putatively) implicated in some internal state transition. But this (as Davies recognizes in his 1990b and 1991 papers) is not necessarily so. Strong commonality is satisfied if we can motivate a higher level of description which (e.g.) groups together a variety of patterns of hidden-unit activation as embodying the system's grasp of the concept of 'bachelor', and it is quite possible that a cluster analysis (see chapter 3 above) of a network should provide just such a grouping. Such an analysis discerns a mathematical unity among a wide variety of occurrent states.

Appeal to such a higher level unity allows the theorist to discern a genuine syntactic (i.e., nonsemantic) commonality between cases which are very various at the lower (units and weights) level. Davies' requirement could be met by the discovery of a high-level unity just as well as it would be met by the discovery of a low-level one. In fact, he acknowledges such a possibility explicitly in the 1991b paper when he allows (p. 112) that beyond the level of the "formal description of a network in terms of units and connections, activations, and weights" there may be "some other scientifically vindicated level of description of connectionist networks at which there are the right kinds of . . . causal commonalities in processing."

The key words here are "scientifically vindicated." Davies can allow that if some independent scientific procedure (e.g. a cluster analysis) unearths unobvious but scientifically respectable notions of causal common factors, and if these factors are plausibly linked to the folk contents, *then* folk psychology turns out to be compatible with our being connectionist engines.[7] In such a case we are using connectionist resources to support an inner story which (viewed at the higher level) vindicates the folk ontology. Such a situation still falls short of one in which the connectionist resources are used simply to implement a classical symbol *system*. Not every system which has states properly regarded as symbolic is a classical symbol system. There are two reasons for this, one positive and one negative. The positive reason is that the system whose "symbols" are groupings of distributed activation patterns will have abilities to generalize, interpolate, and even make mistakes (such as crosstalk errors resulting from overlapping subsymbolic constituents) in ways which are quite alien to a classical framework. The negative reason is that even if a network (say, via cluster analysis) turns out to merit symbolic labels for some of its states, that does not yet make it a real symbol system. It may still lack any straightforward atom-and-molecule structuring of its inner states, and its processing may (*a fortiori*) fail to be sensitive to such structure. (See chapter 4 above.)

What, though, if there is no higher level of scientific or mathematical description at which recurrent analogues for the folk-individuated items (concepts) can be found? We need to face this question since, although our theoretical understanding of connectionist systems will surely involve the use of *post hoc*, higher-level analyses to assign more abstract tasks and contents to basic (units and weights) system states, it remains an open question to what extent they will map neatly onto the contents cited in ordinary mentalistic discourse. It is certainly *possible* that the unity perceived by the folk (when they cite the same concept in two thought ascriptions) may find no echo in more scientific depictions of the inner economies in question. This could be true both across species (were we to discover, say, concept-using Martians), across individuals of the same species, and even of the same individual at different times. The philosophical question I want to pose (and here we are especially close to issues dear to Daniel Dennett (1987)) is, therefore, this: How fragmented (relative to folk talk) can our inner representations turn out to be without compromising the folk-psychological discernment of unities and commonalities? The answer, I think, is simple: They can be almost arbitrarily fragmented, for the folk unities are properly grounded in folk interests and in folk individuative resources.

Stich clearly disagrees with such a tolerant view in his 1983 book, where we find an especially clear case of the demand that folk unities have a microstructural echo. He argues that if it were to turn out that the brain deployed two quite distinct systems, one producing verbal outputs and one producing nonverbal behaviors, folk psychology would be badly compromised. The reason given is that the folk depict a single state (the belief that P) as capable of causing either a verbal output (e.g., an avowal of P) or a P-appropriate action. But this picture of a single state cannot, Stich claims, be correct if the microstructural story reveals two distinct and independent subsystems. Much the same kind of issue must surely be raised by the increasingly strange and unexpected range of dissociations of cognitive abilities studied by cognitive neuropsychologists and experimental psychologists such as Ellis and Young (1988), Warrington and McCarthy (1987), Shallice (1988), and Humphreys and Riddoch (1987). In the inner realm, folk-psychological items fragment. Things fall apart. The combined fluidity and fractionability of the inner economy (relative to the folk ontology) is nothing short of astonishing. But it can be astonishing, confounding all our natural expectations, without compromising the folks' explanations of actions or the ontology of folk solids. To see how, let us return (somewhat ironically) to the works of Gareth Evans.

Evans, recall, is the source of the requirement known as the generality constraint: that to have the structured thought that P is F (i.e., to have a thought involving distinct concepts of P and of F) you must be master of the general concept of P and that of F (i.e., you must know how to predicate F of other objects and how to attach other predicates to P). Davies invoked this very requirement to oil his version of the eliminativist conditional. If we look at Evans' own discussion of the generality constraint, however, we find an interesting variety of claims, some of which are indeed suggestive of an inner "modularity" demand and others of which seem explicitly to reject any such interpretation. The inner modularity idea appears to be supported by the reference to the selective disappearance of grasp of a particular concept. Thus, we read in Evans 1982 (p. 102) that ascription to a subject of the concept F, as evinced in her ability to think Fa, Fb, Fc, etc., is to be understood as the ascription of "a state—the subject's understanding of . . . 'F'—which originated in a definite way and is capable of disappearing (an occurrence which would selectively affect [the] ability to understand all sentences containing . . . 'F'."

In the contemporary reader, such a passage is bound to evoke thoughts of deficit data and cognitive neuropsychology—of patients whose grasp of some concepts is fully impaired yet whose grasp of others remains intact. Nonetheless, there is a way of taking Evans' comments which divorces them from commitments to particular kinds of internal story. It involves taking very seriously the notion of grasp of a concept as possession of a skill. Consider the following passage, which occurs just before the "disappearance" claim: "[the generality constraint] might seem to lead immediately to the idea of a language of thought, and it may be that some of the proponents of that idea intend no more by it than I do here. However, I certainly do not wish to be committed to the idea that having thoughts involves the subject's using, manipulating, or apprehending *symbols*—which would be entities with nonsemantic as well as semantic properties, so that the idea I am trying to explain would amount to the idea that different episodes of thinking can involve the same symbols. . . . I should prefer to explain the sense in which thoughts are structured, not in terms of their being composed of several distinct *elements*, but in terms of their being a complex of the exercise of several distinct conceptual *abilities*." (Evans 1982, p. 101) Or consider this: "It is a feature of the thought-content that John is happy that to grasp it requires distinguishable skills." (ibid., p. 102)

We are thus invited to think of grasp of a concept (e.g. 'being happy') as possession of a skill—a skill which involves knowing that being happy is a multiply instantiable state (knowing that it is not just John who could be happy; it could be Fred, or Sally, or the cat, and so on).

Here, then, is a proposal. Let us agree with Evans that the generality constraint requires that a being who is to have the thought that John is happy must be exercising two distinct skills: the ability to think about John (and hence to have *other* John thoughts, such as 'John is sad') and the ability to think of happiness (and hence to have other happiness thoughts, e.g. 'I am happy'). The thought that John is happy is thus "a joint exercise of two distinguishable abilities"

(Evans 1982, p. 104). But let us further insist that each of these abilities or skills may be sustained by a very loosely knit set of inner computational states. What welds the states into a single skill is not the fact that they can be seen to share some common property visible in the vocabulary of physics, or that of neuroscience, or even that of computational psychology. Instead, these several scientifically disunified inner states combine to constitute a single skill because their combined presence enables an agent to successfully negotiate some macro-level domain which interests us in virtue of the form of our daily human life. The claim is, thus, that to ascribe grasp of a concept is to ascribe an overall skill (in some domain of folk-psychological interest) which may (consistent with the validity of the folk ontology and explanations) depend on one of a variety of computationally disunified subskills. By "disunified" I mean that the subskills need display no unity visible without the lens of folk-psychological interests. Instead they amount to a bag of tools, some of which may be verbal, some imagistic, some sensorimotor, and so on. Taken together, the tools make you an expert negotiator of the domain in question (e.g. dealing with dogs). As an "expert" you can talk about dogs, interact with them in a variety of contexts, spot cartoon dogs, understand metaphors involving dogs, and so on. The point to bear in mind is just that there need be no non-folk-psychologically-identifiable state which is implicated in *all* of these cognitive episodes. A somewhat parallel case would be the idea of a skill at golf. We can say that someone has a skill at golf, and this may involve the ability to drive, to make short iron shots, and to putt. But we need not assume that any science of the mind will reveal a common factor which constitutes the person's skill at golf and which is active on the occasion of a good drive *and* on the occasion of a good iron shot *and* on the occasion of a good putt. Instead, these subskills may appear fully disunified as soon as we remove the lens of the folk-psychological interest. It is the existence of a folk domain ('golf') which legitimates our gathering together of this particular set of subskills under the label of 'skill at golf'. Likewise, I claim, it is the existence of the folk domain ('dogs') which legitimates the gathering together of an otherwise disunified set of skills as what is needed to 'grasp the concept of dog'.

Exactly *what* set of subskills is required if a being is to be credited with grasp of a given concept is, obviously, a genuinely vague question. The bag of skills varies from individual to individual in some respects, and (although certain skills may be necessary in the case of some concepts) it will often be a vague question just where to draw the line between those who possess concepts and those who do not. This is, I think, vagueness in just the right place. If we consider, say, young infants, nonverbal animals, and brain-damaged adult humans, we can find each class exhibiting subsets of the set of subskills we normally associate with grasp of the concept. Do they "have the concept," or not? It is a vague matter. The only true answer is that they share some of the usual subskills and lack others. The old chestnut of verbal skills (must you, as Geach (1957) claimed, know when to apply a word if you are to count as grasping a concept?) goes the same way. These are just more subskills, on a par with the rest. In the absence of specific arguments about particular concepts, we should assume that possession of such subskills has no privileged role to play in concept ascription. The upshot of all this is that in most cases the question "Does X *really* have 'the concept' of such and such?" will be spurious. It will be like asking whether someone whose short iron work was patchy could have a skill at golf. There is no God-given answer to such questions; and (as a rule of thumb) where God fails, philosophy had better not succeed.

The model of concepts as (potentially scientifically disunified) bags of skills gives us, I believe, all that we asked for. It shows us that the requirement of inner scientific unity is misplaced for the simple reason that ascribing a concept does not commit us to the presence of any associated unitary and recurring inner state. Instead, ascribing a concept is more like ascribing a skill. It is making a comment on a person's state of knowledge and on the person's ability to engage in a variety of semantically related cognitive tasks.

This understanding of the nature of a concept allows us to moderate some of the more radical-sounding claims made by theorists such as Barsalou (recall chapter 5 above). When Barsalou claims that we may never construct the same concept twice, he is being needlessly paradoxical. There is surely a perfectly good sense in which we can speak of the same concepts being deployed in a variety of cognitive episodes involving quite distinct contexts. The root of the more radical-sounding claim is just the tendency to uncritically identify the idea of a concept with the idea of an *occurrent state*. It is this idea which we now give up. Occurrent states will indeed be context dependent, various, and altogether unstable (in Barsalou's sense). But what we are doing when we ascribe to someone grasp of a concept is better divorced from considerations of particular occurrent states. Instead, we are crediting the person with a body of knowledge (stored, e.g., in the long-term weights of a number of subnetworks) which can power a variety (perhaps an open-ended one) of occurrent states according to local factors. In short: In ascribing a concept we are really ascribing a body of knowledge and skills whose manifestations may be both internally disparate (in terms of occurrent representational states) and externally disparate (in terms of, e.g., abilities and verbal and nonverbal skills).

Such a view of concepts is not new; a recognizable version of it can be found in Ryle 1949. Ryle comments, for example, that "when we characterize people by mental predicates, we are not making untestable inferences to any ghostly processes . . .; we are describing the ways in which those people conduct parts of their predominantly public behavior" (p. 50). Of course, Ryle insists, we are not merely describing their *actual* performances. Instead, we are describing "the powers and propensities of which their actions are exercises" (ibid.). Or, as I would say, we are describing the mixed bag of cognitive skills which determine the space of the agent's possible and likely actions.

How are such bags of skills selected? That is, why do we group together any particular bag of skills, given that there may be no particular internally motivated reason to draw the line in one place rather than another? The answer, as best I can see, must be that the groupings emerge only against the biological and cultural background of human needs and institutions. Consider the golf example again. Why are the various subskills (putting, driving, etc.) grouped together to support what we talk of as a single skill (at golf)? Just because, as it happens, we have created contexts which demand that particular complex of abilities. Likewise, we have created contexts in which certain bags of subskills are required if we are to flourish and succeed. That context is, to some degree, the province of public language. The space of words is doubtless one determinant of the particular constellations of cognitive skills we choose to focus on. We care about whatever it takes to come to know enough about (say) dogs to count as understanding the word 'dog'. What determines the individuation of concepts (given that we cannot relate it to inner facts) is, however, a hard question and I am aware that I have no fully adequate answer. Schiffer (1991, p. 14) also raises the question of "what determines the kinds of properties in which one is interested in the explanatory context" and is likewise led to offer an account in which it is (at least in part) our pragmatic concerns which determine the answer. Dennett, too, in discussing the explanatory virtues of folk psychology, is led to stress the pragmatic utility, in view of our daily concerns, of a vocabulary in which we can discern patterns which, in a real sense, are simply not there at lower levels—see, for example, his discussion of the practice of predicting whether someone will get a particular joke (1987, pp. 76–77). Much more must be done to make the story complete, but I hope the general pragmatic flavor of the proposal is at least clear. Talk of concepts elevates mixed bags of inner subskills into folk-psychological unities. It does so only against a background of human needs and institutions (just as in more mundane cases, like that of skill at golf). Thus, to possess one such skill may positively require you to embody a varied and shifting panoply of inner states whose unity is not displayed at any further, inner level of description. Thus is the trap of conceptual modularity sprung.

Cognitive Science without Concepts

Much of cognitive science, it is true, seems to assume a notion of concept according to which concepts enjoy one life as entities which figure in folk discourse and another life as well-formed inner computational structures apt for analysis and simulation. Paul Thagard (1990, p. 266), pursuing a computational theory of concepts and of conceptual change, writes:

> My proposal . . . is to think of concepts as complex structures akin to frames. . . . Schematically, a concept can be thought of as a frame-like structure of the following sort:

> Concept.
>   A kind of:
>   Subkinds:
>   A part of:
>   Parts:
>   Synonyms:
>   Antonyms:
>   Rules:
>   Instances:

A concept, on this view, is deeply analogous to a data structure in a computer (ibid., p. 255). Such approaches take our commonsense mentalistic ontology as specifying a set of cognitive items which have to be recapitulated in the computational simulation of human cognition.

By contrast, the view I have been developing is deliberately sympathetic to work in cognitive science and cognitive psychology which depicts our inner resources as unlikely to correspond in any interesting way to the vocabulary of mental states and processes deployed by folk psychology. Thus, my view is consistent with that of those cognitive psychologists who reject the idea of "concepts . . . as the building blocks of thought . . . (and) formal deductive inference . . . as the process which operates on these building blocks" (Oaksford and Chater (in preparation), p. 105).

Instead, we should treat concepts as *products* of human cognition—products whose integrity is dependent on macro-level folk practices.

Concepts need not show up as atoms or as molecules of the inner cognitive economy. Unlike Oaksford and Chater, however, we do not go on to conclude that the commonsense ontology is (as they put it) "incoherent" and that the folk explanations are false. Quite the contrary. The folk explanations simply occupy a different arena.

Skepticism about the folk solids' role in guiding computational modeling is also increasingly common among researchers working on real robotic systems (i.e., on so-called autonomous systems). A complaint heard from such researchers is that the mentalistic vocabulary of daily talk is simply inadequate and misleading as a design specification for a robot system. Smithers (1991, p. 1) describes a classical approach as follows: ". . . folk theoretic descriptions have . . . been used to inform and specify the design of artificial systems. For example, we will typically say that some robot needs to *know K* so that it can believe B which, given its desire D, will lead it to adopt goal G, to achieve task T. This *knowledge level* description (Newell 1982) is used as a specification for a *symbol level* design that identifies what symbolic representation structures and computational operations and processes are required." Such an approach, Smithers claims, has led to very little success in actual robot building. He ascribes much of the blame for this failure to the "tacit (and often unappreciated) use of folk psychology to provide the methodological framework" (ibid., p. 2). Smithers is not alone in this view. A new generation of roboticists (and some simulation workers too) are actively seeking to bypass the kind of heavily symbolic approach to real-world problem solving which is the legacy of the classical knowledge-level perspective (see Brooks 1987, 1991; Malcolm, Smithers, and Hallam 1989; Steels 1991; and a variety of papers in Meyer and Wilson 1991).

It is important, however, to distinguish two options. A researcher could reject the very idea of a representational level intervening between input and action. This is how I read Brooks. He attacks the whole idea of what he calls an "abstraction barrier," viz. the idea of a stage in a system's information processing where an activity (e.g. planning) is performed using a symbolic code. Consider (Brooks' example) a mobile robot that must negotiate some small area of physical terrain. One way of achieving this is to have a cognitive module which plans a route in explicit, symbolic form and then passes commands to a lower-level program which (let's say) moves the wheels. In Brooks' terms, the lower-level program then simply "does the right thing": it responds directly to the action specification by controlling the requisite motors. Surely it would be crazy to insert another symbolic planner into the system between the lower-level program and the wheels, to plan how to vary the currents and the voltages! Brooks' claim is that by pondering such absurdity we can begin to see that the whole idea of an abstraction barrier is, in effect, an artifact of an overly rationalistic model of intelligence. At every point, he believes, we have a choice between inserting a symbolic planner and inserting a program which just "does the right thing." In practice this means short-circuiting the classical sense-think-act cycle (see Malcolm et al. 1989) by setting up tight, sensitive feedback loops between sensing and action. Some quite impressive results in simple robotics have been achieved by entirely eschewing the notion of internal manipulation of symbolic models—see the various examples of work in the "new robotics paradigms" surveyed in Malcolm et al. 1989.

An alternative is that (in advanced, flexible systems, at least) there are plenty of inner states worth calling representations, but that the kinds of content they carry and the kinds of processing they participate in will be radically alien to the folk picture. Such representations will not correspond in any interesting way to familiar concepts, and they will not take part in anything like formal proof-theoretic operations. Such a view is, I think, more optimistic than the previous one insofar as it predicts that we will (in virtue of, e.g., the analysis of neural networks after learning) come to understand the workings of the mind at levels of abstraction well above those deployed by biological neuroscience. It simply denies that such understanding will involve the familiar abstractions and posits of the folk-theoretic level.

Explaining Behavior[8]

Since the folk constituents of thought (concepts) need not have robust inner analogues, it would be surprising indeed if the larger-scale folk structures (the propositions embedded in propositional-attitude talk) required (on pain of eliminativist conclusions) such inner vehicles. In the absence of such identifiable vehicles, however, how are we to respect the above-mentioned demands of propositional modularity?

A conservative response, mooted in Clark 1990b, involves accepting the basic requirements of propositional modularity laid out by Ramsey, Stich, and Garon and attempting to show how such requirements may in fact be met even by superpositional, distributed connectionist nets. I shall rehearse the conservative response once again, as it is important to see that the level of description at which Ramsey et al. describe networks may be a source of some distortions in the arguments. But I shall then go on (following Clark 1991b) to pursue a more radical response which rejects part of the characterization of propositional modularity itself.

The conservative response is basically just to note that connectionist nets may be described, in theoretically valid ways, by means of constructs much coarser than the units-and-weights specifications favored by Ramsey et al. and then to argue that the demands of propositional modularity may be met by rediscovering the folk solids (propositions, in this case) using such coarser analyses. Recall the cluster analysis of NETtalk in chapter 3, which resulted in a tree structure displaying the way in which the network had learned to structure the space of weights so as successfully to solve the problem. What that revealed was, in the words of Churchland (1989), the "similarity metric" which the weight space embodies—that is to say, which inputs, and which groups of inputs, are treated most similarly to other inputs and other groups of inputs. The results were striking: At the bottom level, NETtalk grouped together items such as p and b inputs. A little higher up, it grouped all the various soundings of 'o'. At the very top, the system has divided the space into two large sectors, one corresponding to vowels and the other to consonants.

Now, NETtalk, in common with most such systems, began its training sequence with a random pattern of weights which were slowly corrected by the learning algorithm. The authors of NETtalk, Sejnowski and Rosenberg (1986), gave an identical training sequence to a number of networks which began with different assignments of random weights. Since these in effect amounted to "knowledge already stored" (even though the "knowledge" is nonsense relative to the task), the difference in random initial weights affected how the networks stored the learned material. This is the same effect that Ramsey, Stich, and Garon mentioned in their discussion of network A's and network B's storage of a particular proposition. Like network A and network B, the various trained versions of NETtalk had very different descriptions at the units-and-weights level of analysis. Nonetheless, it turned out that all the versions of NETtalk yielded pretty much the same clustering profile when subjected to statistical cluster analysis. In short, it was possible to discover a scientifically respectable higher level of description which unified what had seemed, at the level of units and weights, to be a chaotic disjunction of networks.

The moral is that there may be higher-level descriptions which are scientifically well grounded and which reveal commonalities between networks which are invisible at the units-and-weights level of analysis. Suppose we performed such an analysis on a complex, action-determining net and found that clustered patterns of activity were usefully labeled with familiar propositions (e.g., cluster X looks like a 'dogs have fur' grouping, cluster Y like a 'cats have tails' one, and so on). Then propositional modularity would be satisfied[9]; actions determined by any pattern of activity falling into a given cluster could be said to be discretely caused by the associated, propositionally specified "belief."

Or consider the argument from natural kinds. The pivotal fact was the lack of any units-and-weights kind uniting nets A, B, and so on. But we can now see that this argument is brutally reductionist about well-motivated kinds. The fact that networks which are quite various at the units-and-connectivity level of description are still to be treated as instances of a psychological kind need occasion no more surprise than the fact that an Amstrad and an Atari may, subject to running the right software, be treated as instances of a computational kind (e.g., as instantiations of a certain word-processing package). All that the variety-of-networks point establishes is that connectionist *psychology* may need at times to avail itself of higher-level descriptions than units, connections, and weight descriptions. But the example of cluster analysis shows that it is possible to reveal that a whole set of networks fall into an equivalence class defined by the way their various assignments of weights partition the possible input patterns into significant subspaces. Thus, it would be perfectly legitimate (given the common clustering profile) to assign all the instances of NETtalk to a psychological kind even though they look very different at the units-and-weights level. Such a grouping might help us explain some shared error patterns and the relative difficulty of processing various inputs. Of course, as Churchland (1989, p. 178) points out, for certain explanatory purposes (such as predicting how future learning will affect weight distributions) the differences will make a difference. My point is only that there may be some legitimate psychological-explanatory interests which call for the higher-level grouping provided by the cluster analysis.

The conservative response is, thus, to hope to untangle the web of superpositional storage by means of some higher level of scientific description of the network—a level at which the familiar folk solids (concepts and propositions) pop back into view. While I still believe strongly that multiple higher-level analyses of networks will be needed to satisfy our explanatory purposes (see chapter 3 above), I think we concede too much to the eliminativist camp by allowing that some such descriptions must recapitulate the folk solids if they (the folk solids) are to be tolerated as elements of true explanations of behavior. Instead, it may well be the case that such higher level descriptions lead us not to the folk solids but to a whole new geometric, process-oriented vocabulary for understanding the inner workings of the mind. Talk of error surfaces, hyperspaces, principal components, representational trajectories, and attractors may well come to dominate the psychological study of mind. Such talk must explain the rich behaviors on which our folk ascriptions are predicated, but it need not (and I increasingly suspect that it will not) correspond to the specific items (concepts) and structures (propositions) beloved of the folk. In short, the folk talk would only specify some of the *targets* of the cognitive scientific endeavor; it would not specify the inner system involved (see Clark 1989a and chapter 1 above).

What, on such a scenario, are we to make of the demand for propositional modularity? The correct and more radical response is to reject outright the idea that folk psychology is necessarily committed to beliefs and desires as being straightforwardly causally potent. Such straightforward potency does indeed seem to require the existence of scientifically isolable inner items which *realize* the propositionally described states and do the causing. But there are other ways (see also Jackson and Pettit 1988 and forthcoming) in which a construct can have explanatory value—ways which do not require that it be identified with any specific underlying scientific essence.

In developing this idea, I take as my starting point some ideas due to David Ruben.[10] In an unpublished manuscript titled "Folk Physics and Explanatory Relevance," Ruben focuses not on folk-psychological explanation but rather on folk-*physical* explanation—that is to say, on explanations of macroscopic events where the explanation is itself cast in the daily vocabulary of physical talk (e.g., "The match lit because it was struck."). Such explanations look to be folk theoretic, useful and true, yet not every folk-theoretic description of the event of the match's being struck seems explanatory of its lighting. To use Ruben's example, we can imagine that the match is yellow and that the striking involves a downward motion. We could then offer the following (non)explanation: The match lit because a yellow object was lowered. This story depicts a true fact concerning the token striking, but it is a fact which, as Ruben says, seems "simply *irrelevant* to the explanation of the match's lighting." The first question before us is, thus, how to distinguish explanatorily relevant from explanatorily irrelevant folk (or commonsense) properties of the event. Ruben describes two general strategies for making such a distinction. The first, which he calls the *microstrategy*, holds that "in order to distinguish explanatory and non-explanatory folk properties, it is necessary to connect the former, but not the latter, in some way with underlying scientific properties which appear in the strict laws of a (more) basic science." An alternative strategy (the *macrostrategy*) holds that "it is possible to draw the distinction between explanatory and non-explanatory folk properties using only the resources available at the folk level itself." As Ruben notes, the macrostrategy can allow that the distinction may also be drawn at some micro level, but it insists that descent to the micro level is not necessary in order to unpack the distinction. Ruben cites Peter Menzies (1988) and Stephen Schiffer (1991) as adherents of the macrostrategy.

What does the macrostrategy involve? The basic move is very straightforward. It is to replace the appeal to lower-level microstructure with an appeal to same-level counterfactuals. Thus, Schiffer's proposal is, in essence, that an event under a description F causally explains an event E just in case F caused E and F would not have caused E *had it not been an F.* In determining whether it was the striking of the match or the lowering of a yellow object which caused the lighting, we are thus invited to consider two counterfactual cases. In the first, there is an event which is a lowering of a yellow object but not a striking. Here *(ceteris paribus)* there is no lighting. In the second, there is an event which is indeed a striking, but the object is not a yellow one. Here *(ceteris paribus)* we still get a lighting. Hence, the folk property of being a striking is causally efficacious but the co-instantiated folk property of being yellow is not (since in those possible worlds in which the color is varied but all else remains the same, the match lights, whereas in those worlds in which there is no striking but all else remains the same the match does not light). How might such a strategy apply in detail in the special case of mentalistic explanations?

The way to proceed is to unpack the claim that a particular belief was responsible for a given action by adverting to counterfactual cases in precisely the manner described above. Suppose my action is that of buying a beer. We can say that it was my belief that the beer was cool and not, say, my belief that dogs have fur that caused me to buy the beer, since in those close[11] possible worlds in which I still believe that dogs have fur but I lack the belief about the beer I don't buy the beer. This counterfact alone seems sufficient to warrant folk psychology in highlighting the beer belief rather than the dog belief in the explanation of that action. Such highlighting is justified entirely without recourse to facts concerning the inner representational system deployed. It is a purely macro-level justification achieved using the vocabulary and the kinds of events visible to folk psychology itself.

Here, then, we have our response to the worry of total causal holism. Stich's insistence (1991b, p. 180) that in cases of superpositional connectionist storage "there are no enduring, semantically characterizable states of the system that are causally active in certain processes and causally inert in others" does not undermine the folk practice, since the folk may be counterfactually justified in highlighting a specific belief even if no discrete inner analogue is to be found. (For another version of this response, see Jackson and Pettit (forthcoming).)

Of course, Ramsey, Stich, and Garon may reply that the counterfactually warranted highlighting of an individual belief falls short of establishing it as a genuine cause. To concede this is not, however, to seriously damage the folk framework. As long as it remains proper to highlight (e.g.) my belief that the movie began at 9 P.M. in an explanation of my lateness, the framework is (or so it seems to me) up and running. An additional argument, to the effect that all *good* explanation must be straightforwardly *causal* explanation, would be needed to amplify this concession into a fatal objection to the folk understanding of mind. Even a brief reflection on the varied panoply of human explanatory projects should convince us that no such general claim can be sustained.

What, though, of the special cases involving pairs of equipotent beliefs? Recall the setup. The agent believes that P (and P suffices to cause action A). She also believes that Q (and Q suffices to cause action A). Yet the folk allow that in the actual world the agent may do A and have (as long-term stored knowledge) both beliefs while in the actual causal chain leading to A only *one* of the two beliefs (say, the belief that P) was active. In such a case, Stich (1991a, p. 233) claims, it will not always be possible to unpick the explanatory links counterfactually, since in the close possible world in which the agent lacks the P belief she might still do A (since the previously inert Q belief might then become active and rush in to do the job). How is the macrostrategy to allow for such cases?

The first thing to do is recast the equipotency claim in terms of explanations rather than causes. Thus the issue becomes: Can the counterfactual approach allow the explanatory highlighting of just one of a pair of equipotent beliefs which are also mutually protective insofar as the absence of one is always shielded by the presence of the other? The answer is that it cannot; but this is because Stich has arbitrarily restricted our access to the counterfactuals. The essential question, if we are to decide whether something is a case of overdetermination (both beliefs were explanatorily relevant and each was sufficient) or a case of one belief's being the explanatorily relevant one, is just this: If one belief were absent *and all else were equal* would the action occur? That is, if the agent did not believe P, and if her Q belief played only the same explanatory role as it did in the actual world, would the action occur? If it would, and if the same is true if we delete the Q belief and hold the explanatory role of P constant, then the action was overdetermined. If not, then P alone must be held responsible. By stipulatively blocking our access to these counterfactuals, Stich does stymie the macrostrategist. But the stipulation is *ad hoc*, and should be rejected.

To sum up: We have now rejected both of the super-Fodorian dogmas displayed in the introductory section. We have rejected the picture of grasp of a concept as necessarily involving the occurrence of a unitary and recurring inner state, and we have rejected the picture[12] of complexes of such inner states as the causal determinants (billiard-ball style) of the actions we explain using propositional-attitude talk. Neither rejection looks set to sound the death knell of folk psychology.

Dennett and the Missing Innards

By treating concept ascription as ascription of cognitive skills (and not unitary states), and by treating propositional-attitude explanation as a way of picking out patterns in actual and counterfactual behavior (rather than as necessarily picking out discrete, causally active inner items which participate in the push and shove of creation), we put considerable distance between the folk framework and issues concerning the innards of organisms. In so doing we follow a tradition (Ryle 1949; Dennett 1981a, 1987) which is often cast as unacceptably susceptible to some clear (so they say) counterexamples. What, for instance, of the Giant Lookup Table, a being whose actual and counterfactual behavior is exquisitely honed to display the patterns characteristic of grasping concepts and acting on the basis of beliefs but whose inner computational life (consisting of an astoundingly large collection of preset responses to specific inputs and input sequences) seems curiously inappropriate for a True Believer? What of the Quantum Fluke Being, who gets all the behaviors right yet does so by a series of increasingly unlikely but never entirely impossible accidents? Its innards may be disorganised mush; surely *it* can't count as a True Believer?

Such objections have been standardly raised against Dennett's apparent championing of the view that the believing kind is really an *observational kind*. Dennett 1988a—a précis of Dennett's 1987 book *The Intentional Stance*—provides an exceptionally lucid, concise, and challenging statement of a doctrine which we can call *pure ascriptivism* concerning mental states. The pure ascriptivist holds that being a genuine believer is, in a certain sense, essentially a matter of how others might find it profitable to treat you. It is not, as the mental realist believes, a matter of how you are in yourself, regardless of the ways in which any other being might find it useful to consider you. On this Dennett is absolutely forthright. Whatever is "voluminously predictable" by the technique of treating it as if it had beliefs and desires *does* have beliefs and desires. When we treat something as having beliefs and desires, we are said to be looking at it from the viewpoint provided by an *intentional stance*. Thus, in Dennett's own words (1988a, p. 496): "Any object—whatever its innards—that is reliably and voluminously predictable from the stance is in the fullest sense of the word a believer. *What it is* to be a true believer, to have beliefs and desires, is to be an intentional system." And what it is to take the intentional stance to a system is, Dennett goes on to say, to ascribe beliefs and desires to it in line with a *rationality assumption*. This amounts to an assumption of (relatively) *good design*. The system will believe the true and desire what is good for it, subject to a few design shortcuts, malfunctions, and so forth (ibid.).

So it's all clear and straightforward—a believer is any system reliably and voluminously predictable by the use of belief/desire ascriptions mediated by an assumption of (fairly) good design? Alas no. Dennett, despite the forthright statement quoted above, soon backtracks. First the lectern. The lectern may seem voluminously predictable by the ascription of a few simple beliefs and desires (the desire to stay put, and so on). But is it thereby a true believer for Dennett? Of course not. The attributions of beliefs and desires to it are said to be *ad hoc* and to provide no "predictive leverage" (ibid.). Perhaps we may agree. But worse concessions follow. In his "author's response," Dennett (1988a, pp. 542–543) allows that "if one gets confirmation of a much too simple mechanical explanation . . . this really does disconfirm the fancy intentional level account." This is surely straightforwardly incompatible with the bold claim that all there is to being a true believer is to be reliably and voluminously treatable as one. As was noted above, a cannily devised device (for example, a robot operating via a giant lookup table) may be reliably and voluminously so treated, even if the underlying mechanical story is of the "overly simple" variety. Moreover, the appeal to simplicity seems *ad hoc*. It does not strike me as obvious that "simple innards" are incompatible with being a true believer. Oversimple innards may, as a matter of fact, have all sorts of empirical effects (e.g., on flexibility of behavior, on possession of a conscious mental life) which might themselves constitute grounds for withdrawing the intentional description. But it is surely not—how could it be?—simplicity *per se* which constitutes the problem.

Dennett's eventual response to the barrage of lookup tables, Zombies (see Lycan's commentary on pp. 518–519 of Dennett 1988a), and Martian Marionettes (Peacocke 1983) is revealing. He finally insists that it is a mistake to view him as a "peripheral behaviorist." Instead, he seems to want *internal* behavior to be part of the class of behaviors to be taken into account in deciding whether something really is an intentional system. "Everything the neuroscientist can look at is also," he says, "behavior by this criterion." (Dennett 1988a, p. 543)

Here then is the trouble. Dennett wants his ascriptivism to preserve belief talk from the discrediting effects of any discoveries concerning the "innards" of a system. It shouldn't *matter*, for the ascriptivist, whether we have a language of thought, a connectionist mush, or cream cheese in our heads. And yet, like (most of) the rest of us, Dennett is stuck with the niggling intuition that what's in there *does* matter somehow. Inner findings could, as he puts it, "disconfirm" fancy intentional accounts. But there is no logical space here for the pure ascriptivist to occupy. And the reason, as I shall now argue, is that Dennett's ascriptivism is very subtly misdirected. Instead of being an ascriptivist about *believers* ("all there is to being a true believer," and so on), he should be something more like an ascriptivist about *beliefs* (as picked out by propositional-attitude talk) and a realist about believers. That is, he should openly endorse further constraints on the *class of beings* for whom mentalistic interpretation is appropriate. Such constraints, I shall now argue, can plausibly be constructed along at least two dimensions, one concerning the issue of normativity and the other concerning that of consciousness.

The Defeasibility of the Folk Ascriptions

It is plausible to require that any being who can be said to grasp a concept C must be capable of judging that she has made a mistake in some previous application of C. More precise, we may reasonably demand the following:

> (Requirement of Normative Depth)
> The inner workings of an intentional system must be of a kind compatible with the description of that system as capable of making mistakes which involve the failure to respect those commitments in episodes of on-line processing.

This turns out to be an interesting requirement in that it is weak enough to allow for a wide variety of acceptable inner structures (certain kinds of connectionist and/or artificial-life architectures, as well as classical ones) yet strong enough to rule out the great "evil de-mons" of contemporary discussion, such as the Giant Lookup Table.

The above requirement is designed to highlight one key feature of our mental life: our ability to judge our own performance as either living up to our antecedent commitments or failing to live up to them. We can illustrate this point by adapting an example from Martin Davies. Consider the concept 'grandfather'. As a master of that concept, I command both a stereotypic picture (an old grey-haired gent who likes a little gin, perhaps) and a constitutive rule (any father of a parent). It is central to my grasping the concept that I realize that the constitutive rule is in the driving seat. If Jack Nicholson is the father of a parent, then he *ought* to fall under the concept 'grandfather', accidental characteristics notwithstanding. This is where the issue of judging our own performance comes in. I may, in daily commerce, easily fail to apply the concept 'grandfather' to nonstereotypic cases. In such cases it must be possible for me to step back and say "I can see, given my own canonical commitments, that I *ought* to have judged thus and so." This ability to recognize our own guiding cognitive commitments and to judge our own judgings as correct or mistaken is, I suspect, central to the idea of moral agency. And it may be that part of the motivation for a concern with the proper membership of the class of believers is a moral one, viz. that only those beings are properly assessable for their deeds and judgments.

The second strand concerns consciousness. It seems to me conceptually impossible for a being to count as grasping a concept and yet be incapable of ever having any conscious experience involving it. That is, part of what we *mean* when we say that someone grasps the concept 'dog' is that, on occasion, the person has conscious mental experiences which involve that very concept.

To endorse these requirements of normativity and of consciousness is, however, to begin to see how certain scientific discoveries just might upset the applecart of folk psychology. Notice that a Giant Lookup Table issues its various judgments and behaviors in full informational mutual isolation from one another. That is, the response today to a question like "Are you sure you spotted all the grandfathers in yesterday's quiz?" is in no way traceable to any internal process which retrieves a memory of the previous judgment and assesses it against the backdrop of the system's general knowledge and commitments. This being so, the discovery that a putative thinker was relying on a lookup table when it issued forms of words like "Sorry, I made a mistake; of *course* so and so is a grandfather" may cause us to doubt our previous ascription to that being of grasp of the concept.

We doubt the ascription not because we have failed to find a neat inner state corresponding to the concept, but because we can no longer accept that the system is able to judge its own performances at all. The total lack of any internal mechanism by which traces of earlier outputs can be stored and later reassessed undermines the surface image of the being as able to judge that it has misapplied the concept. The Giant Lookup Table thus falls foul of the normativity requirement. *Pacé* Dennett (1991c), we surely do not have anything like a good scientific theory of what makes *conscious qualitative* experience possible. But perhaps one day we will. (There's optimism for you!) When we do, it may become apparent that certain devices, despite exhibiting intricate and successful problem solving, are simply empirically debarred from the ranks of such conscious beings. If some class of device nonetheless exhibited patterns of "behavior" which would ordinarily warrant our crediting it with some body of beliefs, we might be forced to retract such ascriptions once we learn that the being can have no conscious mental life whatsoever. (Or we might be so convinced, by its behavior, that it does, that we have to retract our scientific theory of consciousness: there is a tricky dialectic here which I do not propose to pursue.)

If I am right, the very idea of a True Believer thus builds in two demands[13] (consciousness and the ability to issue genuine judgments about its own past performance) which scientific investigations might reveal not to be met in specific cases. And there may be other such demands. Thus, our macrostrategy in no way commits us to the absolute scientific irrefutability of folk ascriptions. Instead, it merely denies one *style* of imagined refutation: that which depends on the demonstration that the folk solids (concepts and propositions) cannot be directly rediscovered by means of the resources of our favorite scientific story about the inner workings of the brain. The folk might be wrong, but it will take more than the success of a broadly connectionist vision of cognition to prove it.

A Net to Cherish

Imagine a sophisticated computational device (a broadly connectionist associative engine) which moves and learns in a world of simple objects and other such devices. It speaks a simple language, and it happens to possess the kind of internal architecture which (according to some future theory of consciousness) is responsible for various kinds of qualitative experience. It also stores traces of some of its outputs, and it can judge its own performances as good or bad in the way we demanded. We find it natural, let us suppose, to speak of the device as doing X because it believed that Y, desired that Q, and so on. The folk framework gives us a neat and easy way of describing the device's rather complex dispositions to act and judge and of summarizing (via concept ascription) its state of knowledge. Suppose we then learn that the device's successful negotiation of the domain involves reliance on distributed, superpositional representations whose relation to the posits (concepts and propositions) of the folk theory is both shifting and obscure. Should we then withdraw our ascriptions of concept grasp and our proposition-citing explanations of its actions? Not for a moment! Instead, we need only recognize the folk story for what it is: a neat and efficient way of describing a space of likely actions and of fixing a rough body of knowledge. If folk psychology succeeds in this goal, then it succeeds in its task. The suspicion that the folk mentalistic ontology is not going to carve the inner cognitive economy at its computational joints is perfectly compatible with the view that the folk theory is a source of good explanations of thought and action. Only the brutal elegance of the language-of-thought story could ever have made us think otherwise.

Chapter 11

Associative Engines—The Next Generation

A Multi-Dimensional Space

The space of problems and issues addressed in the preceding chapters has multiple dimensions. Once, in an age of innocence and tranquility, I thought the task confronting us was to plot a philosophically sound and empirically plausible position in a simple two-space whose axes were defined by answers to the following questions:

> (1) Is there a text-like, recombinative inner code? (This is an empirical question.)
> (2) Is folk psychology a source of good (true) explanations of behavior? (The philosophical question here is: Is a negative answer to question 2 *determined* by a negative answer to question 1?)

The view expressed in Clark 1989a,b and elsewhere was that the answer to question 2 was *not* determined by the fate of question 1. Hence, there was a neat opening in the two-space of possible options. That space and some of its characteristic denizens are represented in figure 11.1.

The trouble is, the space is not so simple after all. At the very least, it now seems we are dealing with a three-space whose extra dimension (which has been a major concern of the present treatment) is *developmental*. That extra dimension is characterized by the following question:

> Is there a text-like inner code which represents the starting point of cognitive development, and should we conceive of representational change in terms of operations involving such a code?

The space of options now increases dramatically. For example, even if there were cause to regard some mature human cognition as involving the deployment of a text-like recombinative code, it might nonetheless be the case that such a code had distinctively connectionist developmental roots. Further questions immediately suggest

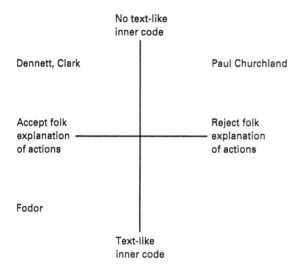

Figure 11.1
The (too-) simple two-space. Note the opening at the bottom right corner—a possible position which remains (to the best of my knowledge) unoccupied!

themselves. What shape might innate knowledge take if not the shape of a classical language of thought? How might we conceive of representational change if not in terms of a process of hypothesis formation and testing defined using the recombinative resources of a primitive symbol system? These were among the new issues I set out to explore. A partial summary of the main conclusions follows.

Macrocognition

Despite the advent of some new arguments supposed to establish the inference from connectionism (no text-like inner code) to eliminativism (folk explanations of actions to be rejected), I found no reason to abandon the spirit of the response floated in Clark 1989a. The folk solids (concepts and propositions as they figure in daily mentalistic talk and explanation) are not *compelled* to turn up as scientifically respectable objects in an inner logico-manipulative processing economy if folk explanations are to be capable of counting as true. The new arguments by Super-Fodorian[1] realists such as Davies (1991) and Ramsey, Stich, and Garon (1991) fail to establish either of the dogmas I considered and rejected in chapter 10. The first dogma is that beliefs and other propositional attitudes must be revealed by some reductive method as scientifically respectable and causally potent inner states if folk explanations are to be held acceptable; the second was that concept talk aims to pick out unitary inner states. Once these two dogmas are jettisoned, the alleged inferences from connectionism to eliminativism fail.

My position concerning folk psychology is slightly more radical in this monograph than in Clark 1989a. Gone is the overriding commitment to finding scientific analogues (albeit at some high level of description) to the folk solids so as to allow their reductive identification with straightforwardly causally potent inner states. Explanatory goodness need not be tied to such straightforward causal potency[2]. Instead we may adopt a macrostrategy (see chapter 10) in which explanatory goodness[3] is defeasibly (see below) established by gross behavioral patterns (actual and counterfactual). The ascription of conceptualized contents, we saw, requires large-scale flexibility in the use of bodies of stored knowledge. But it does not, at least on any philosophical grounds, require recurrent and classically manipulable inner data items corresponding to the folksy constituents. This position (which owes more than a little to Gilbert Ryle) falls short of out-and-out behaviorism in its being coupled with a desire to tell rich and illuminating stories involving a variety of inner representational states and in its explicit acknowledgment of the falsifiability of folk accounts by general discoveries concerning underlying cognitive architectures.[4] Such falsification would not follow from the mere discovery that a being does not utilize a language of thought, but it could follow from demonstrations that the being fails to meet plausible internal constraints on the ascription of normative judgments or on the possession of some form of self-consciousness (see chapter 10).

Bracketing Full Systematicity

Understanding the conceptual commitments of folk psychology is just one facet of the project of understanding the nature of mind. The naturalistically inclined philosopher wants to know in what human cognition might actually consist. To that end, I have described some key features of the most psychologically interesting subclass of connectionist models, including superpositional storage of distributed representations, context-sensitive retrieval, and the capacity to model representational change without importing a symbol system as representational bedrock (see chapters 1 and 7–9). I also showed how a substantial and novel account of knowledge of categories could be given by exploiting the capacity of such networks to extract central-tendency information from a body of training data, and I was able to relate some particular features of such encodings to psychological research concerning knowledge of concepts and categories (see chapter

5). But there was a definite limit to the good news. Several features of human cognition proved resistant to my basic treatment. In particular, I highlighted the difficulties of modeling structure-transforming generalizations in which knowledge is rapidly reorganized to deal with a new problem which is structurally related to one the organism has already solved (see chapter 4) and I highlighted the well-known problem of accounting for the full systematicity of conscious human thought.

To be sure, some progress was made. Several methods of achieving the flexible redeployment of stored knowledge were reported in chapters 6–9. Such progress is essential if connectionism is ever to illuminate genuinely conceptualized thought (as opposed to mere knowledge of categories), since the distinctive feature of such thought involves the flexible and multi-track use of stored bodies of information (see chapters 4 and 5). Moreover, great progress has been made with the problem of achieving structure-sensitive processing through the use of connectionist resources (chapters 6 and 7). All that said, it is time for a confession.

Nothing in my treatment is sufficient to fully exorcise the ghost of full Fodorian systematicity. I have chipped away at the problem by noting that systematicity *need not* be traced directly to the classical structure of an underlying architecture. It *might* be the product of some kind of acquired knowledge instead (see chapter 7). But a "might" is not a proof, and the full puzzle remains undischarged. Moreover, the demonstrations of structure-sensitive processing likewise fall short of accounting for the full interanimation of all our potential thoughts. There *is* some mystery here, and it is not yet solved. Three observations however, should help to cushion the blow.

First, the phenomenon of systematicity is best defined relative to the space of *potential conscious contents*. The restricted "systematicities" found in (e.g.) goldfish cognition (see Fodor and Pylyshyn 1988) pose no deep problem for a connectionist approach. The problem is raised to its full stature by the seeming unboundedness of the space of systematically interanimated human cognitive contents in combination with the fact that (thus restricted) the problem overlaps with another mystery easily as deep as systematicity itself—viz., how conscious content is possible at all. The fact that the most potent worry concerning systematicity is tied to such an area of genuine mystery as consciousness is a consolation. No one has much of a clue about consciousness yet. Perhaps when we do, systematicity won't seem so hard to explain.

Second, it is likewise (and simultaneously) plausible (Dennett 1991a) that full systematicity is the peculiar province of the users of a syntactically structured public language. If systematicity falls out of the use of structured language, the question of the preconditions for the robust emergence of systematic thought reduces to the question of the preconditions for the robust emergence of linguistic (especially syntactic) knowledge. And minimal nativist conditions (see chapter 9 and below) for the emergence of knowledge of syntax will typically fall far short of positing anything like a language of thought.

Third, we saw in chapter 5 that the classical solution to the systematicity problem itself gives rise to apparently intractable obstacles in the efficient real-time deployment of the knowledge base.

For all these reasons, I believe that the way forward is simply to bracket the problem of full systematicity (while continuing to investigate ways of promoting structure-sensitive processing)—in short, to forge ahead and pursue the connectionist paradigm for all it is worth. But what *is* it worth?

Macrocompositionality versus Microcompositionality

One profound benefit of the connectionist models we have considered lies in their ability to illuminate what may be dubbed the problem of microcompositionality. We saw how the connectionist's use of superpositional distributed representations allows her to model the data-driven development of a deeply interwoven system of nonarbitrary representations. By this I mean that the representations of semantically related items or states of affairs tend to cluster in the same region of a high-dimensional representational space (see especially chapters 2 and 5). This is because the representations involved have rich internal structure, and semantically similar items share significant amounts of this internal microstructure. In developing learning and encoding techniques which lead to the automatic discovery of such organized and interpenetrating representational systems, connectionist research is wonderfully well placed to illuminate the nature of our knowledge of categories and, to a lesser extent, of concepts (see chapter 5). Deep facts concerning the fluidity and the context sensitivity of our acquired knowledge are explained very naturally within such a microcompositional paradigm.

It remains true, as was noted above, that these very same properties of fluidity and context sensitivity cause problems when it comes to accounting for *macrocompositional* phenomena such as those highlighted in the systematicity argument. Macrocompositional phenomena (systematicity at the level of propositional knowledge) are most easily explained by positing unitary and invariant macro-level inner representational items (roughly, one such item per concept) and recombinative rules defined over such items. Thus, the path from micro- to macrocompositionality remains unclear. But that should not deter us unduly. The big picture is symmetrical; the macrocompositional approach founders on the properties exemplified with ease by microcompositional models and vice versa. Time will tell.

Minimal Nativism and Representational Change

Another exciting prospect—the focus of the present treatment—is to use connectionist approaches to illuminate developmental issues concerning the nature and the roots of representational change. The hope is to see how the increasingly flexible and context-variable deployment of knowledge can be brought about by applying gradualistic (e.g. gradient-descent) processes of learning to distributed encodings. In seeking to understand representational change in these terms, we are forced to pay increased attention to the role of the environmental input and the trajectory of learning (see chapters 7 and 8). But at the same time we are driven to recognize the importance of various kinds of innate prestructuring and to develop a new conception of in what innate knowledge might *consist*—a conception as appropriate to the connectionist approach as the "innate symbol system" idea was to the classical approach. Such a conception was seen to be highly compatible with a methodological commitment to a Minimal Nativism (see chapter 9 and Karmiloff-Smith 1992a,b) in which evolution bequeaths only small initial biases which, in the context of the actual training data the environment provides, lead to the robust development of specific cognitive competencies. This connectionist view departs fundamentally from the classical Fodorian picture, in which representational change (modulo accidental or purely maturational factors) can only consist in the selective recombination and redeployment of preexisting representational primitives. Minimal initial biases need not constitute such primitives, and subsequent changes need not be conceived of on the model of rationalistic, inferential processes.

A potential benefit of this Minimal Nativist orientation lies in its capacity to invoke forms of innate "knowledge" which are both evolutionarily and neurobiologically plausible. For example, significant and powerful biases might be introduced by restricting certain connection weights to be inhibitory, or to be excitatory, only.[5] Much connectionist work allows the sign (+ or −) of a weight to switch during learning. But this is not a feature of most natural neural systems, and it could easily be controlled in a network model as a means of biasing the learning. Other forms of minimal nativist bias were discussed in chapter 9.

Thus, increased attention to neural plausibility will surely be a hallmark of the next generation of associative engines. The heterogeneity of neural structures (and perhaps learning rules too) will have to be reflected and exploited, as I hinted in my discussion of the Jacobs-Jordan-Barto net in chapter 6. Other hallmarks of the next generation look set to include increased attention to the development of multiple problem-solving capacities in single systems, the integration of connectionist and artificial-life approaches[6] (see chapter 9), and increased roles for robotics and "situated" investigations.

What, finally, of the Syntactic Image? *Does* mature human cognition exploit, at least at times, a classically structured text-like symbol system? No one knows. What connectionism offers is, at least, a new way of thinking about basic cognitive processes of learning and representational change, and a new angle on the nature of innate knowledge. If mature cognition does involve a classical symbol system, we are beginning to discern its roots. If it does not, we may be glimpsing our cognitive essence.

What seems increasingly clear is that the language of thought is, at best, the symbolic problem-solving tip of a large and developmentally extended iceberg. Beneath the symbolic waters, and reaching back across our individual developmental histories, lie the larger, less well-defined shapes of our basic cognitive processes. To understand these is to address the fundamentals of cognition.

Notes

Chapter 1

1. This terminology is introduced in Cussins 1990.
2. I thank Tim van Gelder for impressing upon me the importance of the vehicle/content distinction and the special need to bear it in mind in discussing these issues.
3. In developing this contrast I have been much inspired by David Kirsh's (1991) discussion of explicit representation. I discuss this at some length in chapter 6.
4. Modulo any *purely* maturational changes—that is, changes which occur as a result of the genetic program just so long as appropriate nourishment etc. is provided, or any purely accidental changes such as might be caused by a bang on the head. Fodor's claim is that the only model of genuine *learning* we have available is that of hypothesis generation (using some fixed set of resources) and testing.

Chapter 2

1. I do not mean to imply that any of the individual properties treated are *only* possessed by connectionist networks. Rather, the USP will consist in the naturalness and centrality of a whole *feature complex*, given a connectionist approach.
2. For introductions see Rumelhart, McClelland, and PDP Research Group 1986; Rumelhart, McClelland, and PDP Research Group 1986; and (with a more philosophical slant) Clark 1989a and/or Churchland 1989.
3. That is, state A overlaps with B, and B overlaps with C, but A and C need not have any members in common. The classic example, due to Wittgenstein, is the class of *games*, which have no necessary and sufficient core of properties but which hang together much as the members of a family do (one has another's nose, another shares the jutting chin, another the eyes, and so on). For much more on this, see chapter 5.
4. They were Jeff Elman, Elizabeth Bates, Michael Dyer, and Chris Thornton.
5. This reference was drawn to my attention by Ross Gayler.
6. Especially useful here were comments by Chris Thornton and Ross Gayler.
7. A less obvious option is to preset the system to care more about inputs from certain sensory channels in learning to solve certain problems. This kind of pre-structuring is discussed in Plunkett and Sinha 1991, in Karmiloff-Smith 1992b, and in chapters 8 and 9 below.
8. Some crucial weightings may, of course, be immune to such revision. See Rumelhart and McClelland 1986a, p. 142.
9. Many readers will be aware of the long debate concerning the original past-tense model proposed in Rumelhart and McClelland 1986b. That model was heavily

criticized in Pinker and Prince 1988. The model treated in the present text (and described more fully in chapter 8 below) is a different version developed as a response to that critique. See Plunkett and Sinha 1991, p. 22–33.

10. I came upon this characterization of the difference in Cussins 1990, and subsequently in a personal communication from Jeff Elman and then in Plunkett et al. 1992.

Chapter 3

1. I owe this story to Andrew Barto. It is also reported in Christiansen and Chater 1992.
2. The fact that the "symbol" does not exist as in object *in* the system (but only as an external theorist's abstraction across various more fine-grained, context-reflecting, and distributed states) has a variety of quite profound consequences, both good and ill, which will occupy us greatly in subsequent chapters.
3. There are some wrinkles on this (see Sanger 1989, p. 116), but they do not affect this discussion.
4. Churchland generally refers to "partitions on the activation-vector space" where I speak of cluster analytic descriptions, but the two locutions are effectively synonymous. The partions are the boundaries which separate the clustered groups of activation patterns. A given set of partitions thus defines a given set of clusters, and vice versa.
5. More technical, PCA involves the linear rotation of a data distribution with a view to selecting the dimensions (coordinates) which account for the greatest variance in the data. For a fuller account see Devijver and Kittler 1982.
6. Sentences d–g are from p. 107 of Elman 1991b.

Chapter 4

1. This was presented to me as a true story. It does not matter, for the purposes of this illustration, whether or not such a net actually exists.

Chapter 5

1. 'Weight' is here used to mean 'numeric values indicating the importance of the attributed in defining the concept'. It is *not* used in the connectionist sense, though there are important similarities between the models (as we shall see).
2. The clapometer was a showpiece of 1960s talent shows. It gauged the audience's approval by measuring the strength of the acoustic signal produced by their clapping.
3. For full details of the four cases that follow, see pp. 104–107 of Barsalou 1987.
4. Interestingly, the network also exhibited a period of rapid growth in comprehension as well as in production, though the comprehension spurt occurred at a different point during learning. See Plunkett and Sinha 1991, pp. 46–48, for discussion.
5. The basic reason is that the net requires a critical mass of data points before it can learn to "attend" crucially to certain input parameters. The process of learning here involves extraction of the first principal component (that is, isolation of the source of greatest variance in the data).
6. For a fuller account of these, see pp. 212–218 of Churchland 1989.
7. For example, "[The child proceeds] from the atheoretical and probabilistic tabulation of large clusters of typical features to an understanding of a smaller num-

ber of central relations and properties supported by those relations—a situation in which a kind of qualitative change is possible" (Keil 1989, p. 264). Keil is careful, however, to recognize the extent to which the earlier understandings may in fact be not so much atheoretical as proto-theoretical—i.e., as involving a different theory than ours. This is the idea pursued in the current section.

8. The following question arises, of course: In what sense could such a different theory be counted as a theory of (precisely) weight or density? This issue is deep and important, not least because the very same issue arises in relation to the progress of scientific theories and the changing sense of terms such as 'atom'. For our purposes, however, the point is just that the child is plausibly seen as having some theory or other, so the labeling of the content need not concern us.

9. Such a system is detailed on pp. 20–23 of McClelland, Rumelhart, and Hinton 1986.

10. See p. 202 of Samet and Flanagan 1989 for further discussion.

Chapter 6

1. The Syntactic Image, thus unpacked, yields the position which Oaksford and Chater (1991, p. 3) call "logicism," in which "mental representations correspond to well-formed formulae and manipulations over them correspond to sound logical inferences." The logic in question need not be a familiar monotonic one, however.

2. Or perhaps "which are currently tokened in a way which bestows upon them a certain kind of functional role." Such a proviso allows for tokened contents which are counted as inexplicit because of their (present) causal inertia.

3. See, e.g., Dennett 1982, p. 216.

4. In fact, the network aims to achieve less than this. It inverts word order, but it is not required to produce verb-tense or subject-verb agreement. Thus, it should turn the input 'John love Michael' into the output 'Michael is love by John'.

5. For any given size of RAAM net there will be a limit on the depth and the complexity of tree it can encode, but for any finite depth there will be a RAAM capable of learning it. See Blank, Meeden, and Marshall 1991, p. 11.

Chapter 7

1. This sense of 'representational trajectory' is a thoroughly *developmental* one. It is, thus, different from the sense (common in the literature) in which 'representational trajectory' refers to the temporal flow of activation states which occur during a given episode of on-line processing.

2. Some would argue that the unlearning problem is an *artifact* of the backpropagation learning algorithm—a learning strategy which is widely accepted as itself psychologically unrealistic (not least because of its neurophysiological implausibility). Paul Churchland (forthcoming) writes: "There is no pretense that back propagation might be the specific procedure by which biological brains adjust their synaptic weights. It is a flawed candidate for several reasons. First, a real brain rarely possesses an exact error measure for each new performance, as the back-propagation procedure requires. Second, a real brain displays no central administrator to transform such a measure into a proprietary adjustment for each of its many billions of synapses. And third, it has no distribution system to effect such adjustments even if it could compute them. Back-propagation is just a very useful instance of a much more general class of 'gradient descent' procedures for exploring a network's weight-configuration space. It has been of decisive impor-

tance in furthering research into the capacities of neural networks. But the brain itself exploits some other technique within the enveloping class of gradient descent procedures."

While accepting that problems due solely to the use of backpropagation are thus, to an extent, merely pseudo-problems, I would still contend that the unlearning problem is of more general relevance—and hence more damaging. For it is a problem which seems concomitant with any use of superpositional storage techniques. And it is these techniques which (as we saw in chapter 2) give rise *also* to several attractive properties of connectionist approaches such as generalization and central-tendency extraction. One useful approach which allows us to maintain these benefits while helping avoid unlearning is the use of modules, described in chapter 6.

Chapter 8

1. See Lehnert 1987a,b and several recent studies reported in Hendler 1989.
2. Some models do not fall clearly into either of these two camps. For example, BoltCONS (Touretsky 1989) is a full-fledged connectionist symbol processor insofar as it can generate and act upon complex symbol structures. It thus attempts to tackle the issue (Fodor and Pylyshyn 1988) of compositionality, allowing the iterated recombination of symbolic structures into complex expressions. It has the ability to refer to its own data structures without recapitulating a full representation of their content (what Newell (1980) called "distal access"). Yet it is not just an implementation of a classical system, for it avails itself of powerful connectionist search techniques (including free content-addressable memory, partial pattern matching, and the efficient exploitation of multiple cues). It does not, however, use distributed subsymbolic representations, although such an extension is deemed "easily imaginable."
3. The use of a pattern associator with only two layers (as against the now more familiar three-layer devices, which include a layer of hidden units) is a further, and easily remediable, source of some of the limitations of the original model. See Plunkett and Marchman 1991.
4. In fact, the model was a four-layer device which included two peripheral layers whose task was to transform certain phonetic representations of the verbs (the so-called wickel phone representations) into a different kind of (distributed, context-reflecting) phonetic representations (the so-called wickelfeature representations). This nicety, which has been the focus of some critical attention (see Pinker and Prince 1988), need not detain us here.
5. In fact, after reaching a vocabulary size of about 27 verbs—see Plunkett and Marchman 1991, p. 18.
6. The idea here is to model, to some degree, the fact that early vocabulary growth is much less rapid than later growth.
7. Either factor might, in specific cases, be downplayed by a corresponding "turning up" of the other. Likewise, incremental learning (as discussed above) can be seen as a way of inducing a specific succession of SVMs *without* the need for gross architectural prestructuring. Similarly, the presence of certain kinds of architectural prestructuring may obviate the need for incremental training by effectively causing a machine to create its own incremental training regime (see chapter 9 below).
8. I was introduced to this simulation (which is due originally to Jeff Elman of UCSD) by Kim Plunkett as part of a practical exercise at the 1992 McDonell-Pew

Summer School on Connectionist Developmental Modeling held at the University of Oxford. Thanks to Kim Plunkett and others at the Summer School for stimulating discussions about the explanation of the network's behavior.

9. In fact, this is a problem for which the initial random weight assignment can be crucial. "Bad" initial weights prevent successful learning in any acceptable time frame. As a result, it was necessary to run the simulation several times before a promising result was achieved.

10. Special thanks to Kim Plunkett for helping me to see this as the most probable explanation of the network's behavior.

11. These speculations are, at the time of writing, the subject of an ongoing research project supported by a grant from the MRC/SERC HCI initiative.

Chapter 9

1. The term "associative engine" is used very broadly here. The systems I have been treating depart from classical psychological associationist ideas in several ways. First, they do not use "ideas" as basic elements. Connectionism is much, much finer-grained in its approach than that. Second, the computational functions involved can be rather complex nonlinear ones which compress and dilate a representational space. The term "associative" is used to stress the importance of pattern detection and pattern completion in the new paradigm and the role of the statistics of the training data in determining what knowledge is acquired and when. Connectionism has been described (Bechtel and Abrahamsen 1991, p. 103) as "associationism with an intelligent face." It is this intelligent face which I have in mind in depicting us as nature's associative engines.

2. Special thanks are due to Tim Smithers for raising this issue after I presented some of these ideas to the Artificial Intelligence Seminar at Edinburgh University.

3. For reasons rehearsed elsewhere, I believe there to be some dangers in the use of virtual worlds (simulations) rather than real situations and real robot organisms. But the economies of the simulation strategy are equally clear. For a discussion, see Clark 1987.

4. See the papers in the section "Evolution of Behavior" in Meyer and Wilson 1991.

5. FIve copies of each of the 20 were made, thus generating 100 individuals per generation. Each individual was allowed to live until it had performed 5,000 actions (outputs). But only those 20 which, in that time, had ingested the most food were allowed to reproduce. The copies of successful organisms were mutated by taking four weights at random from each subnet and adding a random value between $+1.0$ and -1.0 to each.

6. Beginning at about 20 generations—see Nolfi and Parisi 1991, p. 8.

7. The evolutionary process had the chance to select a teaching net specially geared to inducing successful learning in a standard net with a specific inherited set of initial weights.

8. To quote Nolfi and Parisi (1991, p. 11), the new net is "functionally symmetrical . . . both subnetworks generate output which is used . . . to change the weights of the other subnetwork. Teaching is bidirectional."

9. The position I describe in this section was developed largely as a result of interactions with Kim Plunkett and other members of the July 1992 McDonnell-Pew Summer School in Developmental Connectionist Modeling. Thanks to all concerned. In addition, Karmiloff-Smith's (1992b) treatment of skeletal domain-specific predispositions in connectionist learning helped to further convince me of the importance of connectionisms potential contribution to reconceiving innate knowledge.

Chapter 10

1. This does not rule out the use of localist representations *in addition* to the distributed ones. But purely localist approaches will lack some of the central features of the models treated in this book (e.g., the kinds of semantic-metric, free-generalization and interference effects described in chapter 2 and elsewhere) and hence fall outside my (admittedly partisan) definition.

2. Propositional-attitude talk ascribes mental states by relating a thinker to a proposition (a complex of folk-psychological solids) in terms of a particular attitude (such as belief, hope, longing, fear, or desire). Thus, we pinpoint Pepa's mental state by saying, e.g., "Pepa hopes that the game is not fixed." And this involves relating Pepa, via an attitude of hope, to a particular proposition: that the game is not fixed.

3. Stich has, however, recently rejected much of the substance of the view expressed in the paper. His new view is that there simply are no substantive questions of the form "Does the word such and such *refer?*" and hence the eliminative claim is rather empty. I shall not discuss the new view here. The interested reader should consult Stich's paper "Do True Believers Exist?" (*Proceedings of the Aristotelian Society*, Suppl. 65 (1991), pp. 229–244).

4. This is really quite intuitive. The network must learn a single set of weights capable of driving all of the required behavior. One option, if there are enough hidden units, is to learn a kind of lookup table with unique sets of weights implicated in each piece of behavior. In general, however, it is better to restrict the number of hidden units, hence forcing the network to use overlapping processing routes. The overlap means that the learned weights must be carefully orchestrated in a way dictated by the global behavior required. The result is that a net storing 17 propositions exhibits small but widely distributed weight differences to one storing 16, or 18, or 19, and so on.

5. That is, it is *not* required that, being master of the concepts 'green' and 'prime', you be capable of grasping the thought that all prime numbers are green.

6. Obviously, this would not be so in the case of a *localist* network. In such a network a single link between a 'bachelor' node and an 'unmarried' node might provide exactly the causal common factor Davies requires. Only those systems in which representation is distributed, dimension shifted, and context sensitive threaten to fail to provide for a causal common factor.

7. There is, in fact, a further wrinkle on Davies' position: His argument, in detail, turns out to focus not so much on our actual (daily, on-line) inferential transitions as on our inferential commitments. If we suppose that our considered reflections concerning how we *ought* to infer involve an inner representational system distinct from that implicated in daily on-line reasoning, then Davies' requirement is just that the inputs to the more reflective system should meet the demands of conceptual modularity. See Davies 1990b for a further discussion.

8. I owe a large vote of thanks to Tim van Gelder, David Ruben, Frank Jackson, and Philip Pettit for helping me to arrive at the view expressed in this section. It represents a departure from my previous insistence that mental talk must be seen as fully causal explanatory in just the same way as is say, talk of billiard balls, impacts, and subsequent trajectories. (See also Ryle 1949, p. 306.)

9. Actually, there would still be a hitch concerning the need to find *long-term* states corresponding to the belief rather than transient activation patterns. I argue elsewhere (Clark 1990b) that the insistence on finding long-term states is a red herring; however, I shall not rehearse this argument here, as the more radical response about to be developed makes it redundant.

10. In fact, this work became known to me only after I had given a talk (at the 1991

Joint Session—see Clark 1991a) detailing some of the ideas developed here. But it seems to me that Ruben's work prepares the ground very nicely for the position I subsequently adopt.

11. Here 'close' had better mean something like 'relevantly similar'. What we need is a world in which, according to the usual attributive tactics of folk psychology, the agent has (to whatever extent possible) all the beliefs, desires, hopes, fears, etc. that she has in the actual world, but lacks the specific one being highlighted by the intentional explanation. (Of course, some beliefs and desires depend on others, so in general it won't be possible to coherently imagine a world in which a single item is deleted. As the example shows, this fact does not affect our case. Indeed, in that respect connectionist models of the inner economy may fit the folk-psychological story better than fully discrete classical models—see O'Brien 1991.)

12. More accurate, we have rejected the claim that the presence of discrete causally potent inner items corresponding to the propositions in propositional-attitude ascriptions is a *philosophically necessary* condition of the truth of folk explanations (such as 'Pepa went to the fridge because she believed the beer was in the icebox'). It remains empirically possible that such inner items exist, although, for reasons rehearsed in the text, I am increasingly doubtful that they do.

13. It is also clearly possible that the two strands may come apart. Thus, a being may exhibit promising 'behaviors', meet the requirement of consciousness, yet fail to satisfy normativity. (Imagine if our best scientific theory of consciousness credited Giant Lookup Tables with rich qualitative experiences!) In such a case, I suspect the question "Is that being a True Believer?" will simply have no answer.

Chapter 11

1. To avoid misunderstanding, note that Fodor himself *does* seem committed to the view that the acceptability of folk psychology is tied to the truth of the Representational Theory of Mind. What it is not (constitutively) tied to is the truth of the Language of Thought Hypothesis as a way of implementing RTM. My own view is thus more radical than Fodor's, as I hold that the acceptability of folk psychology is tied only to much more minimal constraints than RTM (see chapter 10 above). However, since connectionism is, as it happens, a version of a Representational Theory of Mind (see Fodor and Pylyshyn 1988), this potential divide is seldom foregrounded. Thanks to Ron Chrisley for helping to clarify these issues.

2. Tim van Gelder, Frank Jackson, and Philip Pettit have all been instrumental in convincing me of this.

3. Someone might, of course, go further and attempt to reconceive the idea of *causality* in purely *explanatory* terms. All good explanation would then be causal. I chose not to pursue such issues here but see Davies 1992 for a good discussion.

4. Special thanks to Frank Jackson and Philip Pettit for forcing me to take a stance on the defeasibility issue.

5. Thanks to David van Essen for pointing out this potential source of bias.

6. There exist hints of unholy opposition here. Some artificial-life researchers castigate connectionism as overly representationalist. The methodological strategy of trying to see how far you can go with simple, environmentally situated systems is surely laudable (see Clark 1989a, chapter 4), but the ideological opposition to all representationalist approaches is unconvincing and counterproductive. The kinds of highly flexible systems we ultimately need to understand will, I am happy to bet, positively *require* some kind of representationalist analysis, even if it is of a distinctively nonclassical kind (see chapter 3 above).

Bibliography

Allard, F., and Starkes, J. (1991) "Motor skill experts in sports, dance, and other domains." In *Towards a General Theory of Expertise,* ed. K. Ericsson and J. Smith. Cambridge University Press.

Anderson, J. R. (1983) *The Architecture of Cognition.* Harvard University Press.

Anderson, J. R. (1987) "Skill acquisition: compilation of weak-method problem solutions." *Psychological Review* 94, pp. 192–210.

Armstrong, S. L., Gleitman, L. R., and Gleitman, H. (1983) "On what some concepts might not be." *Cognition* 13, pp. 263–308.

Baillargeon, R. R. (1987) "Young infants reasoning about the physical and spatial properties of a hidden object." *Cognitive Development* 2, pp. 170–200.

Barsalou, L. (1983) "Ad hoc categories." *Memory and Cognition* 11, pp. 211–227.

Barsalou, L. (1985) "Ideals, central tendency, and frequency of instantiation." *Journal of Experimental Psychology: Learning, Memory, and Cognition* 11, pp. 629–654.

Barsalou, L. (1987) "The instability of graded structure: Implications for the nature of concepts." In *Concepts and Conceptual Development.* Cambridge University Press.

Bates, E., Bretherton, I., and Snyder, L. (1988) *From First Words to Grammar: Individual Difference and Dissociable Mechanisms.* Cambridge University Press.

Bates, E., and Elman, J. (1992) Connectionism and the Study of Change. Technical report 9202, Center for Research in Language, University of California, San Diego.

Bechtel, W., and Abrahamsen, A. (1991) *Connectionism and the Mind.* Blackwell.

Bever, T. ed. (1982) *Regressions in Mental Development: Basic Phenomena and Theories.* Erlbaum.

Blank, D., Meeden, L., and Marshall, J. (1991) Exploring the Symbolic/Subsymbolic Continuum: A Case Study of RAAM. Technical report 332, Computer Science Department, Indiana University.

Block, N. (1990) "The computer model of mind." In *Thinking: An Invitation to Cognitive Science,* ed. D. Osherson and E. Smith. MIT Press.

Brooks, L. (1978) "Non-analytic concept formation and memory for instances." In *Cognition and Categorization.* Erlbaum.

Brooks, R. (1987) Planning Is Just a Way of Avoiding Figuring Out What to Do Next. Working paper 103, Artificial Intelligence Laboratory, MIT.

Brooks, R. (1991) "Intelligence without reason." In *Proceedings of the IJCAI,* Sydney.

Brown, A., Bransford, J., Ferrera, R., and Campione, J. (1983) "Learning, remembering, and understanding." In *Handbook of Child Psychology,* volume 3, ed. P. Mussen.

Bruner, J. (1970) "The growth and structure of skill." In *Mechanisms and Motor Skill Development,* ed. K. J. Connolly. Academic Press.

Butler, K. (1991) "Towards a connectionist cognitive architecture." *Mind and Language* 6, no. 3, pp. 252–272.

Bybee, J., and Slobin, D. (1982) "Rules and schemas in the development and use of the English past tense." *Language* 58, pp. 265–289.

Carey, S. (1985) *Conceptual Change in Childhood*. MIT Press.

Carey, S. (1990) "Cognitive development." In *Thinking: An Invitation to Cognitive Science*, ed. D. Osherson and E. Smith. MIT Press.

Chalmers, D. J., French, R. M., and Hofstadter, D. R. (1991) High-Level Perception, Representation, and Analogy: A Critique of Artificial Intelligence Methodology. CRCC technical report 49, Indiana University, Bloomington.

Chalmers, J. (1990) "Syntactic transformations on distributed representations." *Connection Science* 2, pp. 53–62.

Chater, N., and Oaksford, M. (in preparation) The Rough Ground: Implications of the Falsity of Commonsense Theories for Cognitive Science.

Chomsky, N. (1957) *Syntactic Structures*. Mouton.

Chomsky, N. (1986) *Knowledge of Language: Its Nature, Origin, and Use*. Praeger.

Christiansen, M., and Chater, N. (1992) "Connectionism, learning and meaning." *Connection Science* 4, no. 3–4, pp. 227–252.

Churchland, P. M. (1989) *The Neurocomputational Perspective*. MIT Press.

Churchland, P. M. (forthcoming) "Learning and conceptual change: The view from the neurons." In *Essays in Honour of Alan Turing*, volume 2: *Concepts, Connectionism and Folk Psychology*, ed. A. Clark and P. Millican. Oxford University Press.

Churchland, P. S., and Sejnowski, T. J. (1992) *The Computational Brain*. MIT Press.

Clark, A. (1987) "Being there: Why implementation matters to cognitive science." *Artificial Intelligence Review* 1, pp. 231–244.

Clark, A. (1989a) *Microcognition: Philosophy, Cognitive Science, and Parallel Distributed Processing*. MIT Press.

Clark, A. (1989b) "Beyond eliminativism." *Mind and Language* 4, no. 4, pp. 251–279.

Clark, A. (1990a) "Belief, opinion and the conscious rule interpreter." *Philosophical Psychology* 3, no. 1, pp. 139–154.

Clark, A. (1990b) "Connectionist minds." *Proceedings of the Aristotelian Society* 90, pp. 83–102.

Clark, A. (1991a) "Radical ascent." *Proceedings of the Aristotelian Society* suppl. 65, pp. 211–227.

Clark, A. (1991b) "In defence of explicit rules." In *Philosophy and Connectionist Theory*, ed. W. Ramsey, S. Stich, and D. Rumelhart. Erlbaum.

Clark, A., and Karmiloff-Smith, A. (in press) "The cognizer's innards: A psychological and philosophical perspective on the development of thought." *Mind and Language*.

Clark, E. (1983) "Meaning and concepts." In *Manual of Child Psychology*, volume 3, ed. J. H. Flavell and E. Markman. Wiley.

Cummins, R. (1989) *Meaning and Mental Representation*. MIT Press.

Cussins, A. (1990) "The connectionist construction of concepts." In *The Philosophy of Artificial Intelligence*, ed. M. Boden. Oxford University Press.

Davies, D. (1992) "Perspectives on intentional realism." *Mind and Language* 7, no. 3, pp. 264–285.

Davies, M. (1990a) "Thinking persons and cognitive science." *AI and Society*, special issue on connectionism.

Davies, M. (1990b) "Knowledge of rules in connectionist networks." *Intellectica* 9–10, pp. 81–126.

Davies, M. (1991) "Concepts, connectionism and the language of thought." In *Philosophy and Connectionist Theory*, ed. W. Ramsey, S. Stich, and D. Rumelhart. Erlbaum.

Dejong, G., and Mooney, R. (1986) "Explanation-based learning: An alternative view." *Machine Learning* 1, pp. 145–176.

Dennett, D. (1980a) *Brainstorms Philosophical Essays on Mind and Psychology*. MIT Press.

Dennett, D. (1980b) "A cure for the common code?" In *Brainstorms: Philosophical Essays on Mind and Psychology*. MIT Press.

Dennett, D. (1982) "Styles of mental representation." *Proceedings of the Aristotelian Society* 83, pp. 213–226.

Dennett, D. (1987) *The Intentional Stance*. MIT Press.

Dennett, D. (1988) Précis of *The Intentional Stance* and author's response. *Behavioral and Brain Sciences* 2, pp. 495–546.

Dennett, D. (1988) Review of J. Fodor, *Psychosemantics*. *Journal of Philosophy* 85, no. 7, pp. 384–389.

Dennett, D. (1991a) "Real patterns." *Journal of Philosophy* 89, pp. 27–51.

Dennett, D. (1991b) "Mother Nature versus the Walking Encyclopedia." In *Philosophy and Connectionist Theory*, ed. W. Ramsey, S. Stich, and D. Rumelhart. Erlbaum.

Dennett, D. (1991c) *Consciousness Explained*. Little, Brown.

Devijver, P., and Kittler, J. (1982) *Pattern Recognition: A Statistical Approach*. Prentice-Hall.

Dörner, D., and Schölkopf, J. (1991) "Controlling complex systems: or, Expertise as 'grandmother's know-how'" In *Towards a General Theory of Expertise*, ed. K. Ericsson and J. Smith. Cambridge University Press.

Dreyfus, H., and Dreyfus, S. (1986) *Mind over Machine: The Power of Human Intuition and Expertise in the Era of the Computer*. Free Press.

Dyer, M. (1990) "Distributed symbol formation and processing in connectionist networks." *Journal of Experimental and Theoretical Artificial Intelligence* 2, pp. 215–239.

Ellis, A., and Young A. (1988) *Human Cognitive Neuropsychology*. Erlbaum.

Elman, J. (1991a) Incremental Learning, or The Importance of Starting Small. Technical report 9101, Center for Research in Language, University of California, San Diego.

Elman, J. (1991b) "Distributed representations, simple recurrent networks and grammatical structure." *Machine Learning* 7, pp. 195–225.

Elman, J. (1991c) "Representation and structure in connectionist models." In *Cognitive Models of Speech Processing*, ed. G. Altmann. MIT Press.

Evans, G. (1982) *The Varieties of Reference*. Oxford University Press.

Fodor, J. (1975) *The Language of Thought*. Crowell.

Fodor, J. (1981) *RePresentations: Philosophical Essays on the Foundations of Cognitive Science*. MIT Press.

Fodor, J. (1983) *The Modularity of Mind: An Essay on Faculty Psychology*. MIT Press.

Fodor, J. (1987) *Psychosemantics: The Problem of Meaning in the Philosophy of Mind*. MIT Press.

Fodor, J. (1991) "Replies." In *Meaning in Mind: Fodor and His Critics*, ed. B. Loewer and G. Rey. Blackwell.

Fodor J. (forthcoming) "How things look from here." In *The Oxford Companion to the Mind*, ed. S. Guttenplan.

Fodor, J., and Pylyshyn, Z. (1988) "Connectionism and cognitive architecture: A critical analysis." *Cognition* 28, pp. 3–71.

French, R. M. (1991) Using Semi-Distributed Representations to Overcome Catastrophic Forgetting in Connectionist Networks. CRCC technical report 51, University of Indiana, Bloomington. Also in *Connection Science* 4 (1992), no. 3/4, pp. 365–378.

Garner, W. (1974) *The Processing of Information and Structure*. Erlbaum.

Geach, P. (1957) *Mental Acts: Their Content and Their Objects*. Routledge and Kegan Paul.

Goodman, N. (1965) *Fact, Fiction, and Forecast*. Bobbs-Merrill.

Halford, G. (1989) "Cognitive processing capacity and learning ability: An integration of Two Areas." *Learning and Individual Differences* 1, no. 1, pp. 125–153.

Hampton, J. (1991) "Combination of prototype concepts." In *The Psychology of Word Meanings*, ed. P. Schwanenflugel. Erlbaum.

Hampton, J. (1992) "Prototype models of concept representation." In *Categories and Concepts: Theoretical Views and Inductive Data Analysis*, ed. I. Van Mechelen, J. A. Hampton, R. Michalski, and P. Theuns. Academic Press.

Harnad, S. (1990) "The symbol grounding problem." *Physica D* 42, pp. 335–346

Hatano, G., and Inagaki, K. (1986) "Two courses of expertise." In *Child Development and Education in Japan*, ed. H. Stevenson et al. Freeman.

Haugeland, J., ed. (1981) *Mind Design: Philosophy, Psychology, and Artificial Intelligence*. MIT Press.

Hayes, P. (1979) "The naive physics manifesto." In *Expert Systems in the Micro-Electronic age*, ed. D. Michie. Edinburgh University Press.

Hayes, P. (1985) "The second naive physics manifesto." In *Formal Theories of the Commonsense World*, ed. J. Jobbs and R. Moore. Ablex.

Hendler, J., ed. (1989) Special issue on hybrid systems. *Connection Science* 1, no. 3.

Hinton, G. (1988) "Representing part-whole hierarchies in connectionist networks." In Proceedings of the 10th Annual Conference of the Cognitive Science Society, Montreal.

Hinton, G. (1989) "Connectionist learning procedures." *Artificial Intelligence* 40, pp. 185–234.

Hinton, G., and Shallice, T. (1989) Lesioning a Connectionist Network: Investigations of Acquired Dyslexia. Technical report CRG-TR-89-3, University of Toronto.

Holyoak, K. (1991) "Symbolic connectionism: Toward third generation theories of expertise." In *Towards a General Theory of Expertise: Prospects and Limits*, ed. K. Ericsson and J. Smith. Cambridge University Press.

Humphreys, G., and M. Riddoch (1987) *To See but Not to See: A Case Study of Visual Agnosia*. Erlbaum.

Jackson, F., and Pettit, P. (1988) "Functionalism and broad content." *Mind* 97, no. 387, pp. 381–400.

Jackson, F., and Pettit, P. (forthcoming) "Causation in the philosophy of mind." In *Proceedings of the 1990 Turing Colloquium*, ed. P. Millican and A. Clark. Oxford University Press.

Jacob, F. (1977) "Evolution and tinkering." *Science* 196, pp. 1161–1166.

Jacobs, R., Jordan, M., and Barto, A. (1991) "Task decomposition through competition in a modular connectionist architecture: The what and where visual tasks." *Cognitive Science* 15, pp. 219–250.

Johnson, M., and Morton, J. (1991) *Biology and Cognitive Development: The Case of Face Recognition*. Blackwell.

Jordan, M. (1986) Serial Order: A Parallel Distributed Processing Approach." Report 8604, Institute for Cognitive Science, University of California, San Diego.

Karmiloff-Smith, A. (1979) *A Functional Approach to Child Language*. Cambridge University Press.

Karmiloff-Smith, A. (1986) "From metaprocess to conscious access: evidence from children's metalinguistic and repair data." *Cognition* 23, pp. 95–147.

Karmiloff-Smith, A. (1987) A Developmental Perspective on Human Consciousness. Invited address, British Psychological Society Annual Conference, Sussex.

Karmiloff-Smith, A. (1990) "Constraints on representational change: Evidence from children's drawing." *Cognition* 34, pp. 57–83.

Karmiloff-Smith, A. (1992a) *Beyond Modularity: A Developmental Perspective on Cognitive Science.* MIT Press.

Karmiloff-Smith, A. (1992b) "Nature, nurture and PDP: Preposterous Development Postulates?" *Connection Science* 4, no. 3–4, pp. 253–270.

Keil, F. (1987) "Conceptual development and category structure." In *Concepts and Conceptual Development,* ed. U. Neisser. Cambridge University Press.

Keil, F. (1989) *Concepts, Kinds, and Cognitive Development.* MIT Press.

Kemler, D., and Smith, L. (1978) "Is there a developmental trend from integrality to separability in perception? *Journal of Experimental Child Psychology* 26, pp. 498–507.

Kemler, D. (1983) "Holistic and analytic modes in perceptual and cognitive development." In *Perception, Cognition, and Development: Interactional Analyses,* ed. T. Tighe and B. Shepp. Erlbaum.

Kirsh, D. (1991) "When is information explicitly represented?" In *Information, Thought, and Content,* ed. P. Hanson. UBC Press.

Kohonen, T. (1984) *Self-Organization and Associative Memory.* Springer-Verlag.

Lakoff, G. (1986) *Women, Fire, and Dangerous things: What Categories Tell Us about the Nature of Thought.* University of Chicago Press.

Lakoff, G. (1987) "Cognitive models and prototype theory." In *Concepts and Conceptual Development,* ed. U. Neisser. Cambridge University Press.

le Cun, Y., et al. (1989) "Back propagation applied to handwritten Zip Code recognition." *Neural Computation* 1, no. 4., pp. 541–551.

Legendre, G., Miyata, Y., and Smolensky, P. (1990a) Harmonic Grammar: A Formal Multi-Level Connectionist Theory of Linguistic Well-Formedness: Theoretical Foundations." Technical report CU-CS-465-90, Department of Computer Science, University of Colorado, Boulder. (A companion report detailing an application is CU-CS-464-90.)

Legendre, G., Miyata, Y., and Smolensky, P. (1990b) Harmonic Grammar: A Formal Multi-Level Connectionist Theory of Linguistic Well-Formedness: An Application. Technical report CU-CS-464-90, University of Colorado, Boulder.

Lehnert, W. G. (1987a) "Case-based problem solving with a large knowledge base of learned cases." In *Proccedings of the Sixth National Conference on Artificial Intelligence,* Seattle.

Lehnert, W. G. (1987b) "Word pronunciation as a problem in case-based reasoning." In Proceedings of the Ninth Annual Conference of the Cognitive Science Society, Seattle.

Leslie, A. (1984) "Infant perception of a manual pickup event." *British Journal of Development Psychology* 2, pp. 19–32.

Malcolm, C., Smithers, T., and Hallam, J. (1989) An Emerging Paradigm in Robot Architecture. Research paper 447, Department of Artificial Intelligence, Edinburgh University.

Marchman, V. (1988) "Rules and regularities in the acquisition of the English past tense." In Newsletter 2, Center for Research in Language, University of California, San Diego.

Marchman, V. (1992) Language Learning in Children and Neural Networks: Plasticity, Capacity, and the Critical Period. Technical report 9201, Center for Research in Language, University of California, San Diego.

Marcus, G., Ullman, M., Pinker, S., Hollander, M., Rosen, T., and Xu, F. (1990) Overregularization. Occasional Paper 41, Center for Cognitive Science, MIT.

Markman, E. (1987) "How children constrain the possible meanings of words." In

Concepts and Conceptual Development, ed. U. Neisser. Cambridge University Press.

Marr, D. (1977) "Artificial intelligence: A personal view." In *Mind Design*, ed. J. Haugeland. MIT Press, 1981.

McCarthy, J. (1968). "Programs with common sense." In *Semantic Information Processing*, ed. M. Minsky. MIT Press.

McClelland, J. (1989) "Parallel distributed processing—Implications for cognition and development." In *Parallel Distributed Processing—Implications for Psychology and Neurobiology*, ed. R. Morris. Clarendon.

McClelland, J., and Kawamoto, A. (1986) "Mechanisms of sentence processing: Assigning roles to constituents." In *Parallel Distributed Processing: Explorations in the Microstructure of Cognition*, volume 2, ed. J. McClelland et al. MIT Press.

McClelland, J., and D. Rumelhart (1986) "A distributed model of human learning and memory." In *Parallel Distributed Processing: Explorations in the Microstructure of Cognition*, volume 2, ed. J. McClelland et al. MIT Press.

McClelland, J., D. Rumelhart and, G. Hinton (1986) "The appeal of Parallel Distributed Processing." In *Parallel Distributed Processing: Explorations in the Microstructure of Cognition*, volume 2, ed. J. McClelland et al. MIT Press.

McClelland, J., D. Rumelhart, and PDP Research Group, eds. (1986) *Parallel Distributed Processing: Explorations in the Microstructure of Cognition*, volume 2: *Psychological and Biological Models*. MIT Press.

Medin, D. L., and Schaffer, M. M. (1978) "A context theory of classification learning." *Psychological Review* 35, pp. 207–238.

Medin, D. L., and W. Wattenmaker (1987) "Category cohesiveness, theories, and cognitive archaeology." In *Concepts and Conceptual Development*, ed. U. Neisser. Cambridge University Press.

Menzies, P. (1988) "Against causal reductionism." *Mind* 97, pp. 551–574.

Mervis, C. (1987) "Child-basic object categories and early lexical development." In *Concepts and Conceptual Development*, ed. U. Neisser. Cambridge University Press.

Meyer, J., and Wilson, S. (1991) *From Animals to Animats*. MIT Press.

Miller, G., and Chomsky, N. (1963) "Finitary models of language users." In *Handbook of Mathematical Psychology*, volume 2, ed. R. D. Luce et al. Wiley.

Mozer, M., and Smolensky, P. (1989) "Using relevance to reduce network size automatically." *Connection Science* 1, no. 1, pp. 3–17.

Murphy, G. L., and Medin, D. L. (1985) "The role of theories in conceptual coherence." *Psychological Review* 92, pp. 289–316.

Newell, A. (1980) "Physical symbol systems." *Cognitive Science* 4, pp. 135–183.

Newell, A. (1982) "The knowledge level." *Artificial Intelligence* 18, pp. 87–127.

Newell, A., and Simon, H. (1972) *Human Problem Solving*. Prentice-Hall.

Nolfi, S., and Parisi, D. (1991) Auto-Teaching: Networks that Develop Their Own Teaching Input. Technical report PCIA91-03, Institute of Psychology, CNR, Rome.

Norris, D. (1990) "How to build a connectionist idiot (savant)." *Cognition* 35, pp. 277–291.

Norris, D. (1991) "The constraints on connectionism." *The Psychologist* 4, no. 7, pp. 293–296.

Oaksford, M., and Chater, N. (1991) "Against logicist cognitive science." *Mind and Language* 6, no. 1, pp. 1–38.

O'Brien, G. (1991) "Is connectionism commonsense?" *Philosophical Psychology* 4, no. 2, pp. 165–178.

Osherson, D. N., and Smith, E. E. (1981) "On the adequacy of prototype theory as a theory of concepts." *Cognition* 9, pp. 35–58.

Patterson, K., Seidenberg, M., and McClelland, J. (1989) "Connections and disconnections: Acquired dyslexia in a connectionist model of reading aloud." In *Parallel Distributed Processing: Implications for Psychology and Neurobiology,* ed. R. Morris. Oxford: Oxford University Press.

Peacocke, C. (1983) *Sense and Content: Experience, Thought, and Their Relations.* Clarendon.

Peacocke, C. (1986) "Explanation in computational psychology: Language perception and level 1.5." *Mind and Language* 1, no. 2, pp. 101–123.

Peacocke, C. (forthcoming) "The relation between philosophical and psychological theories of concepts." In *Proceedings of the 1991 Turing Colloquium,* ed. A. Clark and P. Millican. Oxford University Press.

Piaget, J. (1955) *The Child's Construction of Reality.* Routledge and Kegan Paul.

Pinker, S., and Prince (1988) "On language and connectionism: Analysis of a parallel distributed processing." *Cognition* 28:, pp. 73–193.

Plunkett, K., and Marchman, V. (1989) Pattern Association in a back-Propagation Network: Implications for Language Acquisition. Technical report 8902, Center for Research in Language, University of California, San Diego.

Plunkett, K., and C. Sinha (1991) "Connectionism and developmental theory." *Psykologisk Skriftserie Aarhus* 16, no. 1, pp. 1–77. Also published in *British Journal of Developmental Psychology* 10 (1992), pp. 209–254.

Plunkett, K., and Marchman, V. (1991) "U-shaped learning and frequency effects in a multi-layered perception: implications for child language acquisition." *Cognition* 38, pp. 1–60.

Plunkett, K., Marchman, V., and Knudsen, S. L. (1990). "From rote learning to system building: Acquiring verb morphology in children and connectionist nets." In *Proceedings of the 1990 Connectionist Models Summer School,* ed. D. Towersky et al. Morgan Kaufmann.

Plunkett, K., Sinha, C., Möller, M., and Strandsby, O. (1992) "Symbol grounding on the emergence of symbols? Vocabulary growth in children and a connectionist net." *Connection Science* 4, no. 3–4, pp. 293–312.

Pollack, J. (1988) "Recursive auto-associative memory: devising compositional distributed." In *Proceedings of the 10th Annual Conference of the Cognitive Science Society.* Computing Research Laboratory, New Mexico State University.

Quillian, M. (1968) "Semantic memory." In *Semantic Information Processing,* ed. M. Minsky. MIT Press.

Ramsey, W., and Stich, S. (1991) "Connectionism and three levels of nativism." In *Philosophy and Connectionist Theory,* ed. W. Ramsey et al. Erlbaum.

Ramsey, W., Stich, S., and Garon, J. (1991) "Connectionism, eliminativism, and the future of folk psychology." In *Philosophy and Connectionist Theory,* ed. W. Ramsey et al. Erlbaum.

Ridley, M. (1985) *The Problems of Evolution.* Oxford University Press.

Robins, A. (1989) "The distributed representation of type and category." *Connection Science* 1, no. 4, pp. 345–366.

Rosch, E. H. (1973) "On the internal structure of perceptual and semantic categories." In *Cognitive Development and the Acquisition of Language,* ed. T. E. Moore. Academic Press.

Rosch, E. H. (1975) "Cognitive representations of semantic categories." *Journal of Experimental Psychology: General* 104, pp. 192–233.

Rosch, E. H. (1978) "Principles of categorization." In *Cognition and Categorization,* ed. E. Rosch and B. B. Lloyd. Erlbaum.

Rosch, E. H., and Mervis, C. B. (1975) "Family resemblances: Studies in the internal structure of categories." *Cognitive Psychology* 7, pp. 573–605.

Rosenberg, C., and Sejnowski, J. (1987) "Parallel networks that learn to pronounce English text." *Complex Systems* 1, pp. 145–168.

Roth, E. M., and Shoben, E. J. (1983) "The effect of context on the structure of categories." *Cognitive Psychology* 15, pp. 346–378.

Ruben, D. (unpublished) Folk Physics and Explanatory Relevance.

Rumelhart, D., and McClelland, J. (1986a) "PDP Models and general issues in cognitive science." In *Parallel Distributed Processing: Explorations in the Microstructure of Cognition*, volume 1, ed. D. Rumelhart et al. MIT Press.

Rumelhart, D., and McClelland, J. (1986b) "On learning the past tenses of English verbs." In *Parallel Distributed Processing: Explorations in the Microstructure of Cognition*, volume 2, ed. J. McClelland et al. MIT Press.

Rumelhart, D., Smolensky, P., McClelland, J., and Hinton, G. (1986) "Schemata and sequential thought processes in PDP models." In *Parallel Distributed Processing: Explorations in the Microstructure of Cognition*, volume 2, ed., J. McClelland et al. MIT Press.

Rutkowska, J. (1991) "Looking for 'constraints' in infants' perceptual cognitive development." *Mind and Language* 6, no. 3, pp. 215–238.

Rutkowska, J. (1992) "Action, connectionism and enaction: developmental perspective." In *Connectionism in Context*, ed. A. Clark and R. Lutz. Springer-Verlag.

Ryle, G. (1949) *The Concept of Mind*. Hutchinson.

Samet, J., and Flanagan, O. (1989) "Innate representations." In *Representation*, ed. S. Silver. Kluwer.

Sanger, D. (1989) "Contribution analysis: A technique for assigning responsibilities to hidden units in connectionist networks." *Connection Science* 1, no. 2, pp. 115–139.

Schiffer, S. (1991) "Ceteris paribus laws." *Mind* 100, pp. 1–16.

Schyns, P. (1991) "A modular neural network model of concept acquisition." *Cognitive Science* 15, pp. 461–508.

Seidenberg, M. (1989) "Visual word recognition and pronunciation: A computational model and its implications." In *Lexical Representation and Process*, ed. W. Marslen-Wilson. MIT Press.

Sejnowski, T., and Rosenberg, C. (1986) NETtalk: A Parallel Network That Learns to Read Aloud. Technical report JHU/EEC-86/01, Johns Hopkins University.

Sejnowski, T., and Rosenberg, C. (1987a), "Parallel networks that learn to pronounce English text." *Complex Systems* 1, pp. 145–168.

Sejnowski, T., and Rosenberg, C. (1987b) "Connectionist models of learning." In *Perspectives in Memory Research and Training*, ed. M. S. Gazzaniga. MIT Press.

Shallice, T. (1988) *From Neuropsychology to Mental Structure*. Cambridge University Press.

Shavlik, J., and G. Towell (1989) "An approach to combining explanation-based and neural learning algorithms." *Connection Science* 1, no. 3, pp. 231–254.

Shiffrin, R., and Schneider, W. (1977) "Controlled and automatic information processing. II. Perceptual learning, automatic attending and a general theory." *Psychological Review* 84, pp. 127–190.

Smith, E. E., and Medin, D. L. (1981) *Categories and Concepts*. Harvard University Press.

Smith, L. (1981) "Importance of the overall similarity of objects for adults and children's classifications." *Journal of Experimental Psychology: Human Perception and Performance* 7, pp. 811–824.

Smith, L., Carey, S., and Wiser, M. (1985) "On differentiation: A case study of the development of the concepts of size, weight and density." *Cognition* 21, pp. 177–237.

Smithers, T. (1991) "Taking eliminativism seriously: A methodology for autonomous systems research." In Proceedings of European Conference on Artificial Life, Paris.

Smolensky, P. (1986a) "Information processing in dynamical systems: Foundations of harmony theory." In *Parallel Distributed Processing: Explorations in the Microstructure of Cognition*, volume 1, ed. D. Rumelhart et al. MIT Press.

Smolensky, P. (1986b) "Neural and conceptual interpretation of PDP models." In *Parallel Distributed Processing: Explorations in the Microstructure of Cognition*, volume 2, ed. J. McClelland et al. MIT Press.

Smolensky, P. (1988) "On the proper treatment of connectionism." *Behavioral and Brain Sciences* 11, pp. 1–74.

Smolensky, P. (1991) "Connectionism, constituency and the language of thought." In *Jerry Fodor and His Critics*, ed. B. Lower and G. Rey. Blackwell.

Spelke, E. (1991) "Physical knowledge in infancy: Reflections on Piaget's theory." In *Epigenesis of the Mind: Essays in Biology and Knowledge*, ed. S. Cary and R. Gelman. Erlbaum.

Steels, L. (1991) "Towards a theory of emergent functionality." In *From Animals to Animats*, ed. J. Meyer and S. Wilson. MIT Press.

Stich, S. (1983) *From Folk Psychology to Cognitive Science: The Case Against Belief*. MIT Press.

Stich, S. (1991a) "Do true believers exist?" *Proceedings of the Aristotelian Society*, suppl. 65, pp. 229–244.

Stich, S. (1991b) "Causal holism and commonsense psychology: A reply to O'Brien." *Philosophical Psychology* 4, no. 2, pp. 179–182.

Strawson, P. (1959) *Individuals*. Methuen.

Thagard, P. (1990) "Concepts and conceptual change." *Synthese* 82, pp. 255–274.

Thornton, C. (1989) "Learning mechanisms which construct neighbourhood representations." *Connection Science* 1, no. 1, pp. 69–86.

Thornton, C. (1991a) "Why connectionist learning algorithms need to be more creative." Paper presented to Creativity Conference, City?

Thornton, C. (1991b) "Stirring shakes." *AISB Quarterly* pp. 16–24.

Touretsky, D., and Hinton, G. (1985) "Symbols among the neurons: Details of a connectionist inference architecture." In Proceedings of 9th IJCAI, Los Angeles.

Touretsky, D. (1989) BoltzCONS: Dynamic Symbol Structures in a Connectionist Network. Computer science research paper CMU-CS-89-182, Carnegie Mellon University.

van Gelder, T. (1990) "Compositionality: A connectionist variation on a classical theme." *Cognitive Science* 14, pp. 355–384.

van Gelder, T. (1991) "What is the 'D' in 'PDP'? A survey of the concept of distribution." In *Philosophy and Connectionist Theory*, ed. R. W. Ramsey et al. Erlbaum.

Varela, F. (1989) *Connaître—les Sciences Cognitives: Tendances et Perspectives*. Editions du Seuil.

Warrington, C., and McCarthy, R. (1987) "Categories of knowledge: Further fractionations and an attempted integration." *Brain* 110, pp. 1273–1296.

Index